AF560319

RIGHTS OF THE ACCUSED UNDER INDIAN LAWS

RIGHTS OF THE ACCUSED UNDER INDIAN LAWS

RAMAN SHARMA

REGAL PUBLICATIONS
New Delhi

RIGHTS OF THE ACCUSED UNDER INDIAN LAWS

ISBN 978-81-8484-541-9

Typeset by
RAHUL COMPOSERS
New Highway Apartments, Lakshmi Niwas
760, Pocket-D, Lok Nayak Puram, New Delhi - 110 041

Printed in India at
MAYUR ENTERPRISES
WZ Plot No. 3, Gujjar Market, Tihar Village, New Delhi - 110 018

Published by
REGAL PUBLICATIONS
F-159, Rajouri Garden, New Delhi - 110 027
Phone : 45546396, 25435369
E-mail : regalbookspub@yahoo.com, regaldeepbooks@yahoo.com

Dedicated to

my Grandparents

PANDIT JAGAN NATH

SMT. GEETA DEVI

My dearest nephews

TARU AND ARU

Contents

Preface

It is better that several guilty persons should escape punishment than one innocent should suffer. The Laws of India; Constitutional, evidentiary and procedural have made elaborate provisions for safeguarding the rights of accused with a view to protect his dignity as a human being and giving him the benefits of just, fair and impartial justice. The objective of this book is to dissect and give a holistic analysis of the various aspects of the rights of the accused in the context of Indian legal system. This book analyses various provisions related to the rights of accused under Cr.P.C, Constitutional rights, Indian Evidence Act, and Prisoners rights. The scope of this book has been to throw light on the safeguards of accused under Indian legal system. This book includes the role of judiciary in protecting the rights of the accused. This book is mainly based on the cardinal principle of criminal law that everyone is presumed to be innocent unless his guilt is proved beyond reasonable doubt. The present book is concerned with various provisions which entitle an accused of certain rights during the course of any investigation, enquiry or trial of an offence with which he is charged. It is hoped that this book will be useful for providing justice to the accused in India.

RAMAN SHARMA

Acknowledgements

It is my moral duty to acknowledge the genuine help and support, which I have received from others during the completion of this book.

First of all, I consider it to be a privilege to have done work under the scholarly supervision and esteem guidance of Dr. Bhajan Kaur, Professor, Department of Laws, Panjab University, Chandigarh. I express my deepest and profound gratitude to her who despite of her manifold academic and administrative responsibilities happily gave her valuable time, whenever I approached her in connection with this book.

I am highly indebted to my family members especially my father Sub. Maj. Roop Chand, my mother Bimla Devi and my dear friend Daya who have always been my pillars of strength, for their patience, blessings and suffering silently in the hope that this book will see the light of the day.

RAMAN SHARMA

Table of Cases

A Convict Prisoner in the Central Prison, Thiravantthapuran *v.* State of Kerala, 1993 Cri LJ 3242.
A.C. Razia *v.* Government of Kerala, AIR 2003 SC 2222.
A.K. Gopalan *v.* State of Madras, AIR 1950 SC 27.
A.K. Roy *v.* Union of India, AIR 1982 SC 710.
A.R. Antulay *v.* R.S. Nayak, AIR 1992 SC 1701.
Abdul Latif *v.* B.K. Jha, AIR 1987 SC 725.
Abhay Singh *v.* State of U.P., 2009 Cri LJ 2189.
Abraham Verghese *v.* State of Kerala, AIR 1965 Ker 175, 176.
Abtar Singh *v.* State of Punjab, 2002 Cri LJ 4330 at 4333 (SC).
Afrar Khan *v.* State of Karnataka, 1992 Cri LJ 1976 (Kant).
Aftab Ahmad *v.* State of U.P., 1990 Cri LJ 1636 (All).
Aftab Ahmed Ansari *v.* State of Uttaranchal, AIR 2010 SC 773.
Afzal *v.* State of Haryana, AIR 1996 SC 2326.
Aghnoo Nagesia *v.* State of Bihar, AIR 1966 SC 119.
Amant Kumar *v.* State of U.P., 1997 Cri LJ 1797.
Amanta Singh *v.* State, 1972 Cri LJ 1327 (Cal).
Amin *v.* State, AIR 1958 All 293, 302.
Amina Bewa *v.* Dukhmani Dasi, 1957 Cri LJ 669.
Amrit Singh *v.* State of Punjab, AIR 1956 All 341.
Amritalal *v.* Suratha Lal, AIR 1942 Cal 552.
Ananth Kumar *v.* State of A.P., 1977 Cri LJ 1797 (A.P.).
Anil Rai *v.* State of Bihar, AIR 2001 SC 3173.
Anwar Hussain *v.* State of Orissa, 1995 Cri LJ 863 (Ori).
Arvinder Singh Bagga *v.* State of U.P., AIR 1995 SC 117.
Ashok Kumar *v.* State of Rajasthan, 1995 Cri LJ 1231 (Raj).
Attorney General of India *v.* Lachma Devi, AIR 1986 SC 467.
Avinash Madhukar Mukhedken *v.* State of Maharashtra, 1983 Cri LJ 1883 (Bom).

B. Singh *v.* State of Orissa, 1990 Cri LJ 397 (Ori).
Babu Singh *v.* State of U.P., AIR 1978 SC 527.
Babubhai Patel *v.* State of Gujarat, 1982 Cri LJ 284 (Guj).
Bachand Jain *v.* State of M.P., AIR 1977 SC 366.
Balai De, (1907) 35 Cal 361.
Baliram *v.* Emperor, ILR 1945 Nag 151.
Balraj Singh *v.* Delhi Administration, 29 (1989) DLT 106.
Banassi Lal *v.* Neelam, AIR 1969 Del 304.
Basheer *v.* State of Kerala, AIR 2004 SC 2757.
Behary, 71 WR Cr 3.
Bhagwan R. Shinde *v.* State of Gujarat, (1999) 4 SCC 421.
Bheru Singh *v.* State of Rajasthan, (1994) 2 SCC 467.
Bhikari *v.* State, AIR 1966 SC 1.
Bhikhabhai Devshi *v.* State of Gujarat, AIR 1957 Guj 136.
Bhim Singh *v.* State of J & K, AIR 1986 SC 494.
Bhirug *v.* State of U.P., 2002 Cri LJ 271 (All).
Bhonder *v.* Emperor, AIR 1931 Cal 601.
Bidyanath P. Shrivastva *v.* State of Bihar, AIR 1968 SC 1393.
Bigan Singh, (1927) 6 Pat 691.
Bijoy, AIR 1958 Cal 121.
Birbhadra *v.* Distt. Magistrate Ajamgarh, AIR 1953 All 384.
Bishnu Parsad Sinha *v.* State of Assam, AIR 2007 SC 848.
Brijendra Nath Kalay *v.* State, 1994 Cri LJ 1194 (Cal).

Caralie Mullin *v.* Union of Territory of Delhi, AIR 1981 SC 746.
CBI *v.* Anupam J. Kulkarni, AIR 1992 SC 1768.
Chandra Shekhara Rao *v.* Kamla Kumari, 1995 Cri LJ 3508.
Charles Shobraj *v.* Supdnt. Central Jail, Tihar, AIR 1978 SC 514.
Chattar Singh *v.* State of Haryana, AIR 2009 SC 378.
Chief Inspector of Mines *v.* K.C. Thapar, AIR 1961 SC 838.
Chiranjit Lal *v.* Union of India, AIR 1951 SC 41.
Citizen for Democracy Through President *v.* State of Assam, AIR 1996 SC 211.
Citizen for Democracy *v.* State of Assam, AIR 1996 SC 2193.
Comman Cause, A Registered Society *v.* Union of India, AIR 1996 SC 1619.
Confd. Of Ex Servicemen Asso. *v.* Union of India, (2006) 8 SCC 399.

D. Anuradha *v.* Joint Secretary, (2006) 5 SCC 142.
D.B.M. Patnaik *v.* State of Andhra Pradesh, AIR 1974 SC 2092.
D.G. and I.G. of Police *v.* Prem Sagar, (1999)5 SCC 700.

D.J. Vaghela *v.* Kantibhai Jethbai, 1995 Cri LJ 974 (Guj).
D.K. Basu *v.* State of W.B., AIR 1974 SC 2082.
D.K. Basu *v.* State of W.B., AIR 1997 SC 610.
Daghu *v.* State of Maharashtra, AIR 1977 SC 1579.
Dakhi Singh *v.* State, AIR 1955 All 379.
Dalbir Singh *v.* State of U.P., AIR 2009 SC 1674.
Darpan Kumar Sharma *v.* State of T.N., AIR 2003 SC 971.
Dastagir *v.* State of Madras, AIR 1960 SC 756.
Daya Singh *v.* Union of India, AIR 1991 SC 1548.
Dayal Singh *v.* State of Rajasthan, AIR 2004 SC 2608.
Deb Sadhan Roy *v.* State of W.B., AIR 1972 SC 1924.
Debi Sah, AIR 1943 Punj 359.
Dev Ji Vallabhbhai *v.* Administrator, Goa, Daman *v.* Diu, AIR 1952 SC 1029.
Dhananjay Sharma *v.* State of Haryana, AIR 1995 SC 1795.
Dharambir *v.* State of U.P., (1979) 3 SCC 645.
Dharma *v.* Rabindra Nath, 1978 Cri LJ 864 (Ori).
Dinesh Dalmia *v.* State, 2006 (3) Cri LJ 2401.
Director of Enforcement *v.* Deepak Mahajan, AIR 1994 SC 1775.
DLF Power Limited *v.* Central Coal Fields, Ltd., (2009) 6 SCC 258.
Durga Singh *v.* M.D. Isa, (1969) 1 Cri LJ 827.
Duryadhan Mahanta *v.* S. Mahanta, 1992 Cri LJ 2231 (Ori).

Earl Pratt *v.* Att. Gen. of Jamaica, (1994) 2 AC 1.
Emperor *v.* Balai Ghose, AIR 1930 Cal 141.
Emperor *v.* Vimlabai Deshpande, AIR 1946 PC 123.

Francis Coralie Mullin *v.* Union Territory of Delhi, AIR 1981 SC 746.

Gangadharan *v.* Chellakpan, 1985 Cri LJ 1517.
Gitika Baglchi *v.* Shabhabrata Bagechi, AIR 1996 Cal 246.
Golaknath *v.* State of Punjab, AIR 1967 SC 1643.
Goolab Rasul, (1903) 5 Bom LR 597.
Gopal Naidu, (1922) 46 Mad 605: AIR 1923 Mad 528.
Gopal *v.* State of M.P., (1999) Cri LJ 1438 (M.P.).
Govind Prasad *v.* State of W.B., 1975 Cri LJ 1249 (Cal).
Gulam Haider *v.* State of Maharashtra, 1980 Cri LJ 145.
Gundap Bhimanna *v.* State of Hyderabad, (1935) SC 462.
Gunpati *v.* Nafisul Has Antian, AIR 1954 SC 636.
Gurbachan Singh *v.* State of Punjab, AIR 1957 SC 623.

Gurbaksh Singh Sibbla *v.* State of Punjab, AIR 1980 SC 1632.

Haji Ali Shar *v.* State of Rajasthan, 1976 Cri LJ 1658 (Raj).
Hansraj, AIR 1956 SC 641.
Hari Krishan *v.* State of Maharashtra, AIR 1962 SC 911.
Hari Om Prasad *v.* State of Bihar, 1999 Cri LJ 4400 (Pat),
Hariharanand *v.* Jailor, AIR 1954 All 601.
Harjiwan Laxman Patel *v.* State of Gujarat, 1981 Guj LR 264.
Hirendra *V.* Thakur *v.* State of Maharashtra, AIR 1994 SC 2623.
Hussainara Khatoon *v.* Home Secretary, AIR 1978 SC 1369.

I.R. Coelho *v.* State of T.N., AIR 2007 SC 861.
Icchu Devi *v.* Union of India, AIR 1980 SC 1983.
Iman Div *v.* Emperor, AIR 1934 Lah 76.
In Re, Nagendra Nath Chakravarti, AIR 1924 Cal 476.
In Secretary HSEB *v.* Suresh, AIR 1999 SC 1160.
Indira Nehru Gandhi *v.* Raj Narain, AIR 1975 SC 2999.

J. Abdul Hakeem *v.* State of T.N., AIR 2008 SC 3677.
Jagdish Chander Bhatia *v.* State, 1983 Cri LJ NOC 235 (Del).
Jagjit Kaur *v.* State of Haryana, (1997) 1 RCR 252 (P&H).
Jagta *v.* State of Haryana, AIR 1974 SC 1545.
Jang Bahadur Singh *v.* State of Haryana, 2001(1) RCR (Criminal) 233 (P&H).
Jaswant Rai *v.* State of Bombay, AIR 1986 SC 575.
Jibach Shah *v.* State, AIR 1965 Pat. 331.
Joginder Kumar *v.* State of U.P., AIR 1994 SC 1349.
Joginder Singh *v.* State of Punjab, 1988 (2) RCR 548.
Jose Poothrikkagil *v.* Union of India, 2009 (1) KJL 381.

K.V. Muhammad *v.* Chakkappayyan Kannan, AIR 1943 Mad 218.
Kadra Pahadiya *v.* State of Bihar, AIR 1981 SC 939.
Kadra Pahadiya *v.* State of Bihar, AIR 1982 SC 1167.
Kalawati *v.* State of M.P., AIR 1953 SC 131.
Kaluttumottil Razak *v.* State of Kerala, (2000) 4 SCC 465.
Kanaiya Lal *v.* Indumati, AIR 1958 SC 444.
Kartar Singh *v.* State, AIR 1956 Punjab 122.
Kasavanand Bharti *v.* State of Kerala, AIR 1973 SC 1461.
Kavita *v.* State of Maharashtra, AIR 1981 SC 1641.
Kedar Nath *v.* State of W.B., AIR 1953 SC 404.
Kehar Singh *v.* Union of India, AIR 1989 SC 653.

Kharak Singh *v.* State of U.P., AIR 1963 SC 1295.
Khatri (II) *v.* State of Assam, 1981 Cri LJ 424 (Gau).
Khatri *v.* State of Bihar, AIR 1981 SC 928.
Khushwant Singh *v.* Maneka Gandhi, AIR 2002 Del 58.
Kiki Bejonji *v.* State of Bombay, AIR 1961 SC 967.
Kishor Singh Ravinder Dev *v.* State of Rajasthan, AIR 1981 SC 625.
Kishori Mohan *v.* State of W.B., AIR 1972 SC 1749.
Kochummichic R. Chettian *v.* State of Kerala, 1977 Cri LJ 1872.
Kokul Tatwa *v.* Emperor, AIR 1926 Pat 23.
Krishna Lal *v.* State of Haryana, AIR 1980 SC 1252.
Kubic Barinsz *v.* Union of India, AIR 1990 SC 605.
Kuthu Goola *v.* State of Assam, 1981 Cri LJ 424.

Lahira Habibulla H. Sheikh *v.* State of Gujarat, AIR 2004 SC 314.
Lal Kamlendra P. Singh *v.* State of U.P., (2009) 4 SCC 437.
Lallubhai Jogibhai *v.* Union of India, AIR 1981 SC 728.

M. Hasan *v.* Government of A.P., AIR 1998 AP 35.
M.G. Badakkanavar *v.* State of Karnataka, AIR 2001 SC 260.
M.H. Haskot *v.* State of Maharashtra, AIR 1978 SC 1548.
M.K. Ghosh *v.* State of West Bengal, 1990 Cri LJ 26.
M.N. Shreedharan *v.* State of Kerala, 1981 Cri LJ 119.
M.P. Sharma *v.* Satish Chandra, AIR 1954 SC 300.
Mada Deo *v.* State, 1990 Cri LJ 858 (All).
Madhab Roy *v.* State of W.B., AIR 1975 SC 255.
Madhav *v.* Hariwardhan Rao, AIR 1978 SC 1548.
Madhulimye *v.* State of Bihar, AIR 1969 SC 1014.
Maneka Gandhi *v.* Union of India, AIR 1978 SC 597.
Mannallal, AIR 1967 Cal 478.
Manoj *v.* State of M.P., (1999) 3 SCC 715.
Manrab Ali *v.* Irsan, AIR 2003 SC 707.
Mantoo Majumdar *v.* State of Bihar, AIR 1980 SC 846.
Maru Ram *v.* Union of India, AIR 1980 SC 247.
Matru *v.* State of U.P., (1971) 2 SCC 76.
Mh. Ali *v.* Ram Swarup, AIR 1954 SC 300.
Miss Veena Sethi *v.* State of Bihar, AIR 1983 SC 339.
Mohammad Gia Suddin *v.* State of A.P., AIR 1977 SC 1926.
Mohammed Ajmal Mahammad Amir Kasab @ Abu Majahid *v.* State of Maharashtra, 2012 AD (SC) 249.
Mohan Lal Sharma *v.* State of U.P., (1989) 2 SCC 314.
Mohd. Azad *v.* State of W.B., AIR 2009 SC 1037.

Shantisar Builders *v.* Narayanan K. Tobame, AIR 1990 SC 630.
Sharifbai *v.* Abdul Rajak, AIR 1961 Bom 62.
Sheo Balak Dusadh *v.* Emperor, AIR 1948 All 103.
Sheo Shankar, 26 Cri LJ 62.
Shiv Bahadur Singh *v.* State of Vindhya Pradesh, AIR 1963 SC 394.
Shiv Mohan Singh *v.* State of Rajasthan, 1992 Cri LJ 1335 (Raj).
Shvaji *v.* State of Maharashtra, AIR 1973 SC 2622.
Sidharth Vashisht *v.* State of NCT of Dehli, AIR 2010 SC 2352.
Sita Ram *v.* State, (1966) Supp SCR 265.
Smt. Poonam Lata *v.* Wadhawan & Others, AIR 1987 SC 1382.
Sodhi Transport Corporation *v.* State of U.P., AIR 1986 SC 1092.
Soni D. Babubhai *v.* State of Gujarat, AIR 1991 SC 2173.
State (NCT of Delhi) *v.* Navjot Sandhu, (2005) 11 SCC 600.
State of A.P. *v.* N. Venugopal, AIR 1964 SC 33.
State of Bihar *v.* Kapil Singh, AIR 1969 SC 53.
State of Bombay *v.* Kathi Kaluoghad, AIR 1961 SC 1806.
State of Gujarat *v.* H.C. Gujarat, (1987) 7 SCC 392.
State of Gujarat *v.* Natwar H. Thakur, 2005 Cri LJ 2957.
State of Maharashtra *v.* Bharat Chagan Lal, AIR 2002 SC 409.
State of Maharashtra *v.* Champalal, AIR 1981 SC 1675.
State of Maharashtra *v.* Christian Community W.C. of India, AIR 2004 SC 7.
State of Maharashtra *v.* K.K.S. Ramswamy, AIR 1977 SC 2097.
State of Punjab *v.* Baldev Singh, AIR 1999 SC 2378.
State of Rajasthan *v.* Balchand, 1978 Cri LJ 195.
State of U.P. *v.* Ram Chandra, AIR 1955 All 438.
State of U.P. *v.* Krishna Gopal, AIR 1987 SC 2184.
State of W.B. *v.* Subodh Gopal Bose, AIR 1954 SC 92.
State *v.* Ravikant Sharma, 2005 (2) SCC 347.
State *v.* Tanman, AIR 1960 SC 210.
Subhaya Gauder *v.* Bhookala, AIR 1959 Mad 396.
Sukh Dev *v.* State of Arunachal Pradesh, AIR 1986 SC 911.
Sumna *v.* State, AIR 1967 Ori 4.
Sunder Singh *v.* State of Bihar, 1990 Cri LJ 1904 (Pat).
Sunil Batra *v.* Delhi Adm., AIR 1980 SC 1579.
Sunil Batra *v.* State of Karnataka, AIR 1978 SC 1675.
Sunt Bir *v.* State of Bihar, AIR 1962 SC 1410.

T.N. *v.* Senthil Kumar, AIR 1999 SC 971.
T.R. Ganesan, AIR 1951 Mad 246.
Talab Haji Hussain *v.* State, AIR 1958 SC 376.

Tarapada De *v.* State of W.B., AIR 1951 SC 174.
Thaneilvictor *v.* State, 1991 Cri LJ 2416 (Mad).
Triveni *v.* State of Gujarat, AIR 1989 SC 1335.
Tukaram G. Geokar *v.* R.K. Shukla, AIR 1968 SC 1050.

Udayabhan Shuki *v.* State of U.P., 1999 Cri LJ 274 (All).
Ujjal *v.* State of W.B., AIR 1972 SC 1446.
Union of India *v.* Ashok K. Mitra, AIR 1993 SC 1976.
Union of India *v.* Sukuman Pyne, AIR 1966 SC 1206.

V.C. Shukla *v.* State (CBI), 1980 Supp SCC 92.
Vakil Prasad Singh *v.* State of Bihar, (2009) 3 SCC 358.
Vakil Singh *v.* State of J & K, AIR 1974 SC 2337.
Varkey Joseph *v.* State of Kerala, AIR 1993 SC 1812.
Vassiliadesh *v.* Vassiladea, AIR 1945 PC 38.
Vatheeswaran *v.* State of T.N., AIR 1983 SC 361.
Veera Ibrahim *v.* State of Maharashtra, AIR 1976 SC 1167.
Venkataranianappa *v.* State of Karnataka, 1992 Cri LJ 2268.

Wookmington *v.* Director of Public Prosecutions, (1935) AC 462.

Yusufalli *v.* State of Maharashtra, AIR 1968 SC 147.

1

Introduction

RIGHTS OF ACCUSED: A HISTORICAL PERSPECTIVE

(a) Rights of Accused in Ancient India

A king who punishes those who do not deserve to be condemned and fails to punish those who deserve punishment, becomes infamous and is ultimately doomed to hell.[1] Ancient Hindu jurists suggested that by committing a crime, the Criminal comes to owe a debt towards the society and this debt can be discharged when he suffers punishment at the hands of society. Thus, Manu, the ancient law giver observed: Men who are guilty of crimes and who have been punished by the king, go to heaven becoming pure like those who performed meritorious deeds[2] Manusmriti made provisions for payment of compensation to the victim of bodily injury to the extent required for treatment and also for loss of property.[3]

The Manusmriti is the Hindu Code of Ancient India, which dealt with the relationships between social and ethnic groups, between men and women, the organization of the workings of Karma, and all aspects of the law. It also deals with Crime, Justice and punishment. The Criminal Justice System in ancient India was found to be based on the Varna system and the Manusmriti defined Crime and punishment for each Varna in a hierarchical mode. The jurisprudence of Ancient India, which was essentially Hindu-ruled, was shaped by the concept of 'Dharma', or rules of right conduct, as outlined in the various manuals explaining the Vedic scriptures such as 'Puranas' and 'Smritis'. The King had no independent authority but derived his powers from 'Dharma' which he was expected to uphold. The Maurya Dynasty, which has extended to substantial parts of the central and eastern regions during the 4th century, B.C., had a rigorous penal system which prescribed mutilation as well as death penalty for even trivial offences. About the 2nd or 3rd century A.D., Manu, an important Hindu Jurist, drew up the Dharamsastra Code, which was called as Manusmiriti. The Code recognized assault and other bodily injuries and property offences such as theft and robbery. Manusmriti dealt with various aspects.

ADMINISTRATION OF JUSTICE

From the Vedic period onward, the perennial attitude of Indian Culture has been justice and righteousness. Justice, in the Indian context, is a human expression of a wider universal principle of nature and if men were entirely true to nature, his actions would be spontaneously just. Men in three major guises experience Justice, in the sense of a distributive equity, as moral justice, social justice, and legal justice. Each of these forms of justice is viewed as a particularization of the general principle of the universe seen as a total organism. From the broadest to narrowest conception, then, ancient Indian views on justice are inextricably bound up with a sense of economy. The State performed its duty of protection of society and the individual through Coercive enforcement of the standards of justice. Through practical law- enforcement, the State must actually seek to controvert the ignorance of those men in society who remain unaware or unconvinced of the very purposes for which they themselves, the State, and society exist. Accordingly, the traditional Indian King has been invested with danda, "the scepter", a symbol of the power and authority of the State, which rules, inexorably by law and punishment. Manu, insists in his discussion of the role of the king that if he does not ".... inflict punishment on those worthy to be punished, the stronger would roast the weaker like fish on a spit...." "Having fully considered the time and place (of the offence), the strength and knowledge (of the offender), let him justly inflict that punishment on men who act unjustly". The exercise of the coercive power of danda with regard to law-enforcement is considered just in highest sense, since particularistic legal codes are considered to be concrete and detailed embodiments of the more abstract and exalted principles of justice which are fundamental to the cosmos. The administration of legal justice and infliction of punishment was performed on the basis of Varna System. Manusmriti considers that is only natural to take Varna account in the administration of legal justice. Manu indicates that the king, acting as judge should consider "the strength and knowledge are estimated as functions of his Varna. Legal Consideration of Varna rank has two main outcomes, one having to do with responsibility, the other with privilege, and one concerning the perpetrators of crime and the other its victims. Crimes against persons were adjudicated with reference to the Class-status of the victim and the perpetrator. The penalties for a crime were increasingly serving the higher the Varna of the victim and lower the Varna of the perpetrator. One of the chief duties of the king was the maintenance and protection of the Varna system through his power of *danda* (the scepter). In order to extract the truth and to arrive at fair justice, Manusmriti has specified the part of the judge's function to probe the heart of the accused and the witness by studying their posture, mind and changes in voice and eyes. Manu felt that the internal working of the mind could be perceived through the aspects, the motions, the gait, the gestures, the speech, and the changes in the eye and of the face. Hence, it can be asserted that Manusmriti is the first code of law to take account of judicial psychology. Regarding the punishment, Manu strongly believed that the 'danda' (the scepter), a symbol of the power and authority was created by God and only fear alone would make the human beings to swerve not from their duties. Manu sturdily has advocated the theory of deterrence as the purpose of punishment and the infliction of punishment should be according to the principles of natural justice. Manu felt that only punishment can control all the human beings on the earth and gave utmost importance to punishment. Manu supported retributive justice. Manu is against unjust punishment, it will destroy reputation among men, and fame (after death), and will cause even in the next world the loss of heaven.[4]

Kautilya's Arthasastra is not only a treatise on economic rights but it also elaborately make mention of civil and political rights. Kautilya envisaged a welfare State where, "the king shall provide the orphan, the dying, the infirm, the affected and the helpless with maintenance, he shall also provide subsistence to mothers as well as the children whom they give birth.[5] Arthasastra provides, "All urgent matters shall be heard at once and shall not be put off, for matter when postponed, become difficult or even impossible to settle,[6] and "any person who keeps an innocent man in confinement shall be punished with the first amercement".[7]

From the perusal of Arthasastra the following rights of accused person can be listed out:

(i) When a person keeps or causes to keep a person or a minor in illegal confinement, he shall be punished with fine of 1000 panas.

(ii) When a person accused of theft proves in his defence the complainant's amenity or hatred toward himself, he shall be acquitted.

(iii) When the superintendent of jails put any person in lock-up without declaring the grounds of provocation (Samkruddha–Kamana Khyaya), he shall be fined 24 panas; when he subjects any person to unjust torture, 48 panas, where he transfers a prisoner to another place, or deprives a prisoner of food and water, 96 panas; when he troubles or receive bribes from a prisoners, he shall be punished with the middle most amercement; when he beats a prisoner to death, he shall be fined 1000 panas.

(iv) Kautilya say, "Any one who keeps an accused cleansed of guilt in confinement, shall be punished with first amercement".

(v) There existed system of commutation of sentences Kautilya's as "on ruler's birthday or on full moon days such prisoners as are very young, old diseased or disabled shall be released".[8]

Kautilya has not even spared the king from the punishment. He provides, "if an innocent person is punished, Magistrate and judges are punished for wrong judgment; even the ruler must impose on himself a fine thirty times that amount, and offer it, to Varna (Chastiser of Kings) and thereafter distributes it among Brahmins so that the sin of wrongful punishment may thereby be wiped out.[9] Arthasastra provide for basic necessities to be made available in a prison house and steps to be taken to ensure safety and security of inmates. It laid down that, separate wards for males and females with hall, pits, wells, bathroom and places of worship of respective deities shall be construed, providing sanitary arrangements, protection against fire and poisonous and other dangerous creatures.[10] Those whose guilt was found probable were subjected to torture and torture was to be given on alternative days and only once in a day. No pregnant women or one who has not passed month after delivery shall be put to torture.[11] In general, the criminal law made it incumbent upon the king to punish those who deserved to be punished. The primary concern of criminal law was thus to punish the offenders rather than paying any compensation to the victims.

The reason for this was probably that mere payment of compensation was not regarded as sufficient, to meet the ends of justice. Moreover, the ancient jurists also recognised the fact that the urge for vengeance which develops in the crime could be satisfied only through imposition of punishment.[12]

(b) Rights of Accused in Medieval India

The invasions by Muslims started with the expedition of India by Mohd. Bin Qasim in 712 A.D. but real penetration was made by Kutubuddin Aibek in 1206 A.D. Muslim Rule along with Muslim legal system continued in India till 1857.[13] With the assumption of sovereign power by the Muslim Rulers, the Muslim system of government came to be established in several parts of India.[14] Muslim law was mainly contained in Quran, Haddies, and Sunnahas & Kiyas. Islamic jurists says that State belonged to God and thus the violation of any right created by the State, that is a public right was treated as an offence against the God. Various crimes mentioned by these jurists fell under two heads namely, the public offences and the private offences. The public offences were to include, first, the offences against God, e.g. adultery, apostasy, theft, etc., and secondly, offences against the ruler, e.g. Rebellion, misrule and moral turpitude or the part of chieftains.[15] Various punishments imposable for the crimes were divided into four categories viz., Kisa, Hadd, Tazeer and Diya. Kisa meant retaliatory punishment, i.e. tooth for tooth and eye for eye. Hadd meant specific penalties for specific offences, which could be varied at the discretion of the Magistrate. Tazeer meant discretionary punishment dependent on discretion of judge. Under this head even punishment coming under other head like Diya or Dyut, meant for blood money, could be imposed.[16] Diya used to award in certain cases of unintentional injuries to the victim himself or the next of his kith or kin, on a fixed scale. Dyut the kith or kin of the victim used to forgo his claim of revenge against the offender. While fixing the precise amount of blood money the judges were to take into account the factor like nature of the injury, loss sustained and culpability of the act causing it. Under the Islamic law compensation could be paid by the wrongdoer to the victim when so demanded by the victim or his heirs as an alternative to killing even in a case of homicide. Thus, it can be said that in medieval period also the victim compensation continued to exist, although in a form different from that in the classical period of Hindu jurisprudence, unlike the position under ancient Hindu law. The payment of compensation or diya during medieval period could entitle the offender to escape punishment. Moreover, in majority of the cases diya used to be awarded on a fixed scale, rather than in accordance with the peculiar facts and circumstances of the cases.[17] It is truism that under Muslim law, there was no specific provision regulating the Constitution and organisation of the State.[18] The Muslim concept of administration of Justice is based on the tenets and injunctions of Holy Quran. The Quran may, thus be described as the Supreme Legislative Code of Islam which laid down basic rules of justice.[19] Every Muslim ruler was required to rule in conformity with the tenets of their sacred law, the Quran which laid down the broad principles governing the social life of Muslims.[20] There was no separation of criminal and civil Court and Kazis used to administer justice. Muslim law was never the national law of the land. Sher Shah Suri brought in tremendous change and separated civil and criminal Courts. During his regime Chief Munishif was to look after civil matters and Siqdar used to deal with criminal matters. "Under the Islamic jurisprudence justice is regarded as part and parcel of the Divine nature. Another point on which emphasis is laid is that the administration of justice must be without a tinge of bias or partiability".[21] G.S. Rankin who translated A.L. Badayuni while referring to criminal justice system during Mohammed Tuglaq's period (pre Mughal period) say "The Sultan used to keep four muftis to whom he allotted quarters in the precincts of his own palace. So that when anyone was arrested upon any charge, he might in the first place argue with Muftis about his due punishment. He used to say, be careful that you do not fail in the slightest degree by defect in speaking that which you consider right, because of anyone should be put to death wrongfully the blood of that man will be open your head. Then if after long discussion they convicted (the prisoner) even though it was mid-night he would pass order for his execution".[22] In Mughal period, quick disposal as a right of accused during Muslim rule in India was well recognised. The institution of lawyers was found, and an accused of an offence, if he so desired, had a right to be represented through a lawyer. Expert knowledge of law was required both for practice of law and for acting as Quzi.[23] The authorities of that time referred the institution of lawyers as Vakils, every person, having resources could engage vakil. Zamindars, Manusabdars, faujdars and Kotwals used to be represented by vakils in their case, before King (Emperor). During Mughal rule, the Indian Legal system is recorded to have an institution of bail with the system of releasing an arrested person on his furnishing a surety, the use of this system finds reference in the seventeenth century travelogue of Italian Traveller Manucci who himself was resorted to his freedom by bail from imprisonment for a false charge of theft. He was granted a bail by the then ruler of Punjab but kotwal released him only after he furnished a surety.[24] The responsibility of administration Muslim personal law was vested in the officer designated as Quiz, his duty was to decide cases falling within jurisdiction after considering the facts and circumstances and the law applicable as an enunciated by the official law officers called Muftis. Thus, the Court where in existence but the aim of justice was to provide effective machinery for protection of the interest of rulers. The justice was made less intricate during the regime of Aurangzeb and the corruption in judiciary was made an offence for the first time in whole Muslim rule in India and if delay in justice resulted in loss to a party, the aggrieved party could be compensated by the judge himself. Aurangzeb made it a rule that no one was to be detained in jail except an authority of a Qazi. He has further directed that no warrant of arrest should be issued unless there was prima facie case against the person in question. After arrest, he should be produced before a law Court within the shortest possible time and his case quickly decide. He also framed rules regarding release of persons on bail.[25] The right of an accused to be released on bail did exist during Mughal rule in India. The judgment used to be pronounced by the Presiding officer in open court. The right to speedy trial of criminal cases developed during the period of Mohd. Tughlaq and Akbar the great. The entire State machinery had nothing to do with the welfare of the masses but was meant to perpetrate the existence of the Empire. Further, under the Muslim Law, non-Muslims did not enjoy all the rights and privileges which the Muslim did. However, the fundamental concepts underlying Muslim law, like the Hindu law was the authority of the king, who was subordinate to that of law. It is imperative to mention here that the Muslim rulers did not interfere with the law of the Hindus and the Hindus continued to be governed by their own laws in personal matters.[26] The right to benefit of doubt was not unknown to the Muslim jurisprudence in the administration of criminal justice. The benefit of doubt was known as the doctrine of Shuba (doubt) which entitled an accused to be acquitted. The Magna Carta was enacted in 1215 in England, which was contemporary to the Muslim period. Magna Carta, a corner stone of human rights was the first charter which codified human rights. It provides . . . No freeman shall be taken, imprisoned, dieselized, outlawed, banished, or in any way destroyed, nor will we proceed against or prosecute him, except by the lawful judgment of his peers and by the law of the land.[27]

(c) Right of Accused during British Period

When East India Company was established by Britishers in India, they brought with them the common law of England which remained restricted to British subjects in the company's factory. These factory establishments thus became the nurseries of English law in India, which in course of time brought about tremendous influence over the laws and the system of administration of justice in the whole sub continent?[28] Gradually, Britishers grabbed administration all over India and created Mayor's Courts in presidency town in 1726. Mayors Courts were abolished in presidency towns and jury system was introduced. Thus, the trial by jury of serious offences started for the first time in 1672 at Bombay. Jury trial was accorded statutory recognition by the Code of Criminal Procedure in all trials before High Courts in relation to felonies committed within the limits of the presidency towns but outsides the presidency towns the trials before Sessions Courts were either by jury or judge but left to the particular government. The jury trial continued till its abolition was recommended by the 1955 Law Commission of India.[29] The second half of 19th century is called statutory period when statutes like Indian Penal Code, 1860; Criminal Procedure Code, 1861 (later Criminal Procedure Code, 1898), Police Act, 1861 and the Indian Evidence Act, 1872 were enacted besides other laws pertaining to contract and other civil matters. Lord Macaulay was architect behind these laws. While commenting about possibility of improvement in Mohammedan Criminal Law, Lord Macaulay observed that it is so defective that it can be reformed only by being entirely taken to pieces and reconstructed. In England, after the abolition of the Courts of star Chambers, the principles was recognised that the accused shall not be put on oath and no evidence shall be sought from him. This right was conceded to the accused by the end of the regime of King Charles II of England.[30]

The British while justifying their colonial rule in India claimed. Indians lacked civilised system of self rule and their presence in this country gave India a sense of justice and rule of law. The British supplanted ancient Indian law and introduced in its place their own system of law. One has to understand that this was not a simple change of laws but was the imposition of a totally alien philosophy, understanding of human nature, belief system and way of life and concept of polity. India became a nation under the British who arrived in the early 17th century as traders of the East India Company. The company slowly acquired territory across the sub continent, strictly for commercial operations in the beginning, but gradually assumed considerable powers of governance. Considering the Muslim Criminal Law to be irrational and draconian, the company brought about several reforms through a series of regulations which modified or expanded the definitions of some offences, introduced new offences and altered penalties to make them more logical and reasonable. An Indian Penal Code defining crimes and prescribing appropriate punishments was adopted in 1860 following the painstaking work of the first law commission, particularly its Chairman Lord Macaulay, drawing inspiration from the English criminal law; the Indian Penal Code has stood the test of time. As a sequel to the Indian Penal Code, a code of Criminal Procedure was enacted in 1861 and established the rules to be followed in all stages of investigation, trial and sentencing. This code was replaced and a new code came into effect in 1974. These two codes, along with parts of the Indian Evidence Act of 1872, form the essence of India's criminal law.

Thus, British rule in India introduced a more or less unified legal system in the continent, which may be considered a major step in the globalisation of laws. The quarter of a century following the takeover by the Crown the governing of India from East India Company in 1858 was the major period of codification of law and consolidation of the Court system in India.[31]

The privilege was fully recognised only in the year 1700. The transplantation of English law in India imported this practice to Indian soil also. Gradual changes came into existence.[32] India followed the British pattern in this regard. Thus, Section 3 of Act 15 of 1852 recognised that the accused, in a criminal proceeding, was not a competent and compellable witness for or against him. This provision was repealed by the Evidence Act, 1872. In the meantime, Sections 204 and 203 of Criminal Procedure Code, 1861 provided, respectively, that no oath was to be administered to the accused and it was in the discretion of the Magistrate to examine him. Section 250 of Criminal Procedure Code, 1872 made compulsory a general questioning of the accused after witnesses for the prosecution had been examined and Section 345 provided that no oath or affirmation was to be administered to the accused. These provisions were continued in the later Criminal Procedure Code and were incorporated into Section 342 of Criminal Procedure Code of 1898 (now Section 313 of the Criminal Procedure Code, 1973). Thus, the Indian law as regards self incrimination continued to be the same as the English common law as regard the accused and production of documents, but was modified as regards witnesses by compelling them to answer incriminating questions and giving them immunity from prosecution based on their answers.[33] The Code of Criminal Procedure, 1898 and the Indian Evidence Act, 1872 laid down many procedural rights during criminal trial and prominent among them are; the rights to presumption of innocence of accused. (Section 102 and 105 of Indian Evidence Act, 1872); right against protected confession accepting guilt of accused (Section 25 of Indian Evidence Act, 1872); right to cross examine the prosecution witnesses (Sections 136-138 of Indian Evidence Act, 1872); and to also cross examine witness if he turns hostile (Section 154 of Indian Evidence Act, 1872); right to secrecy of communication with Council (Section 126 of Indian Evidence Act, 1872); right to get copies of documents and statements of prosecution witnesses for defence (Sections 173, 251A(1), Criminal Procedure Code, 1898); right to produce before the Magistrate (Section 60, 61, Criminal Procedure Code); right to counsel (Section 341(1) Criminal Procedure Code); right to be tried in open Court (Section 352, Criminal Procedure Code); right to production of evidence in presence of accused (Section 353, Criminal Procedure Code); right to discovery of statement (Sections 161, 162, 173, 207A(3) of Criminal Procedure Code); right against testimonial compulsion (Section 342 (2) 342(A) of Criminal Procedure Code); right against double jeopardy (Section 403 of Criminal Procedure Code); right to bail (Sections 496, 426, 497 of Criminal Procedure Code); Right of appeal (Section 371 (3) of Criminal Procedure Code); right to sanction for prosecution in case accused is public servant or judge (Sections 195, 196, 197, 197A); right to produce evidence for defence (Section 251A (8) to (10)); right to be tried by independent and impartial judge, Magistrate (Sections 556, 352, 191 of Criminal Procedure Code) and right to get copy of judgment (Sections 371 and

548 of Criminal Procedure Code, 1898). British institution of bail was statutorily transposed into Indian legal system by the passing of Criminal Procedure Code in 1861 followed by its re-enactment in 1872 and 1898 respectively. Its latest reflection is the improved version of the provisions relating to bail in the Criminal Procedure Code, 1973 which were preceded by the adoption of the Constitution in 1950 and some recommendations of Constitution in 1950 and some recommendations of the Law Commissions brought out in the 41st report in 1969.[34] The Indian Evidence Act, 1872 and the Criminal Procedure Code, 1973 enunciated number of procedural safeguards for the accused. These provisions are based on English common law and statute law. The provision of Criminal Procedure Code, 1898 continued even after independence and some of the rights have also been guaranteed in Constitution of India. The Criminal Procedure Code, 1898 was repealed in 1973 when new Code of Criminal Procedure, 1973 as enacted in which drastic changes were made.[35]

(d) Rights of Accused in Modern India

The Universal Declaration of Human Rights, 1948 which was adopted by United Nations, declared "whereas recognition of the inherent dignity and of the equal and inalienable rights of all members of the human family is the foundation of freedom, justice and peace in the world",[36] and it is essential if man is not to be compelled to have recourse as a last resort to rebellion against tyranny and oppression, that human rights should be protected by the rule of laws.[37] This declaration provided for the following specific rights for the accused person:

(i) No one shall be subjected to torture or to cruel, in human or degrading treatment or punishment.

(ii) No one shall be subjected to arbitrary arrest, detention or exile.

(iii) Everyone is entitled in full equality to a fair and public hearing by an independent and impartial tribunal in the determination of his rights and obligations and of any criminal charge against him.

(iv) Everyone charged with a penal offence has the right to be presumed innocent until proved guilty according to law in a public trial at which he has had all the guarantees necessary for his defence.

(v) No one shall be held guilty of any penal offence on account of any act or omission which did not constitute a

> penal offence under national or international law at the time when it was committed, no heavier penalty shall be imposed than the one that was applicable at the time the penal offence was committed.[38]

The substance of various human rights proclaimed and adopted by UNO in Universal Declaration of Human Rights, 1948 were incorporated in the Constitution of India by constituents Assembly. The reflection of all human rights provided in the declaration can be visibly noticed in Fundamental Rights and the Directive Principle of State Policy. Some of human rights are already available in the procedural laws like Criminal Procedure Code and Indian Evidence Act, 1872.[39]

Thus, it is crystal clear from the above discussion that basic human rights were in existence in the ancient times, medieval and British period of India. Hinduism had preached the good and happiness of all humanity and in fact of all living beings including animals and birds. With its development in Medieval European moral and political theory and these human rights and rights of accused person were in vogue in one or the other form. These were some legal rights available to accused person in ancient, medieval and during British India regime.[40]

Notes and References

1. P.N. Sen, *An Introduction to Hindu Jurisprudence,* 336 (1984).
2. S.N. Mishra, *Quoting from Manusmariti*, 111 (1983).
3. Manusmriti, Ch. 8.
4. Manusmriti, "The Criminal Justice tenets in the Ancient Indian Hindu Code", available at *www.erces.com/.../V03_05.htm.*
5. Gokulesh Sharma, *Human Rights and Social Justice*, 11 (1997).
6. *Kautilya Arthasashtra, Book* (i), Ch. 19.
7. R. Sharma Sastry, K.A., 250 (1967).
8. Kautilya Arthasashtra Book (i).
9. *Ibid.*
10. Kautilya Arthasashtra Book (ii), 5.56.
11. *Ibid.*
12. P.V. Kane, *History of Dharamshastra*, 387 (1974).
13. S.K. Puri, *Indian Legal and Constitutional History*, 22 (1st Edition).
14. Rama Jois, *Legal and C.H. of India*, 1 (1984).
15. M.P. Jain, *Outlines of Indian Legal History*, 324 (1981).
16. *Ibid.*
17. *Supra* note 4 at 20.
18. *Supra* note 13 at 4.
19. A.N. Chaturvedi, *Rights of Accused Under Indian Constitution*, 28 (1984).

20. *Supra* note 13 at 4.
21. *Ibid.*
22. G.S. Rankin (Translation), *Al ba dayuni, Bibliothica Indica Calcutta*, (1889). See *supra* note 18 at 30, 31.
23. *Ibid.*
24. "Right to Bail", ILI Publication, 45 (2000).
25. A.B. Pandey, *Society and Government in Medieval India*, 165 (1965).
26. Dunil Deshta, Kiran Deshta, *Fundamental Human Rights – the Right to Life and Personal Liberty,* 28 (2003).
27. Clause 39 Magna Carta, 1215; King John–1 signed the historical document of Magna Carta in 1215.
28. Clause 39, Magna Carta, 1215.
29. *Ibid.*, at 46.
30. *Halsbury's Laws of England,* Vol. 10 (3rd Edition), Pollock and Maitland's *History of English Law*, 507 (2nd Edition).
31. ASCII text file—Bureau of Justice Statistics, available at *www.bjs.gov/.../WFBCJIND.txt.*
32. G. Williams, *The Proof of Guilt,* 63-64 (1963).
33. H.M. Seervai, *Constitutional Law of India*, 500 (1983).
34. "Right to Bail", *ILI Publication*, 5 (2000).
35. *Ibid.*
36. Preamble, Universal Declaration of Human Rights, 1948.
37. *Ibid.*
38. *Ibid.*
39. P.L. Mehta and Neena Verma, *Human Rights under the Indian Constitution*, (1999).
40. M. Jagannadha Rao, "Human Rights: The Indian Scenario with International and Comparative Perspectives", *Cochin Law Review*, Vol. XVII.

2

Rights of the Accused under the Code of Criminal Procedure, 1973

The rights of accused have been a globally debated topic and various scholars, criminologist, Jurists have talked and debated it on the human rights basis. In India mostly this topic i.e. "rights of the accused" has caught eyes of various eminent people, mainly because of the added importance of such fairness to accused owing to the current stand of India in terms of corruption, police brutality, and political influences and under table settlements etc. the idea is that accused is the one who suffers the most.

The Indian Criminal legal system offers the accused person all the necessary guarantees that ensure his dignity and liberty during the criminal investigation made by either judicial police officers or public prosecution. The accused person even under the stage of accusation must be dealt with in the way that does not harm his dignity, he is still considered to be a part of the society whether his crime has been proved or not. Thus, the procedures and restrictions taken against him for the purpose of investigation must be in accordance with the spirit of law and justice. The investigation is described as "danger period", because it represents a very serious stage where the legal system restrains the liberties, freedom and the rights of the accused. The principle of the presumption of innocence is already guaranteed by the criminal justice system. The protection of the rights of the accused is in harmony with the criminal justice system and the principle of the social defence which embodies real values that aims at safe guarding State and the society against the phenomenon of the criminality. The spirit of justice requires a kind of balance between the benefits and rights of the accused and benefits and the security of the society during the criminal investigation.

Thus, the primary object of criminal procedure is to ensure a fair trial to every person accused of any crime.

IMPORTANCE OF FAIR INVESTIGATION AND TRIAL

One principle object of criminal law is to protect society by punishing the offenders. However, justice and fair play require that no one be punished without fair investigation and fair trial. A person might be under a thick cloud of suspicion of guilt, he might have been caught red handed, and yet he is not to be punished unless and until he is tried and adjudged to be guilty by a competent Court. It is a principle of criminal jurisprudence that the accused should not be unnecessarily jeopardised and the natural justice demands fairness in the trial and conviction. In the administration of justice it is of prime importance that justice should not only be done but must also appear to have been done. Further, it is one of the cardinal principles of criminal law that everyone is presumed to be innocent unless his guilt is proved beyond reasonable doubt.

(a) Meaning of Accused

As per concise law dictionary, "accused means a person against whom an allegation has been made that he has committed an offence, or who is charged with an offence".

Thus, in simple words an accused is one who is charged with a crime.

The term "accused", in criminal procedure code means a "person over whom a Magistrate or other "criminal" Court is exercising jurisdiction".[1]

The word 'accused' or 'accused person' is used only in a generic sense in Section 167 (1) and (2) denoting the 'person' whose liberty is actually restrained on his arrest by a competent authority on well founded information or formal accusation or indictment.[2]

Accused of an Offence

Where evidence oral or circumstantial points to the guilt of a person and he is taken in custody and interrogated on that basis, he becomes a person accused of an offence. The mere fact that his name was not mentioned as an accused in the first information report will not take him out of the category of persons accused of an offence.[3]

Accused of Any Offence

Only a person against whom a formal accusation relating to the commission of an offence has been levelled, which in the normal course may result in his prosecution, would fall within the ambit of the term "accused of any offence".[4]

Accused Person

The expression "accused person" connotes a person against whom evidence is sought to be led in a criminal proceeding and it does not predicate a condition of that person at the time of making the statement.[5]

As per Black Law dictionary, "accused" means a person who has been blamed for wrong doing, specifically a person who has been subjected to actual restraints on liberty through an arrest or a person against whom a formal indictment or information has been returned.[6]

As per Law Lexicon, accused person charged with crime, commonly called "the prisoners" if the crime is felony and the defendant if it be a misdemeanour.[7]

(b) Rights of the Accused under the Code of Criminal Procedure, 1973

The soul of criminal justice system is adversarial system which provides with a prospect for the parties to case, advance and present their arguments, gather and submit evidence, call and question witness and control the information presented conferring to the law and legal procedure.

"It is better that several guilty person should escape punishment than one innocent person should suffer".

In order to maintain order and peace in society the State and for that matter the police as its principal law enforcing agency have the undoubted duty to bring offenders to book. Even so, the law and procedure adopted by the State for achieving this social objective must be fair and just and to conform to civilised standards. In their battle against crime and delinquency, State and its officers cannot on any account for sake the decency of State behaviour and have recourse to extra legal methods for the sake of detention of crimes and even criminals. For how can they insist on good behaviour from others when their own behaviour is blameworthy, unjust and illegal? Thus, in a democratic society even the rights of the accused are sacrosanct, far though accused of an offence he does not become a non-person.[8]

As a matter of fact, the laws of India constitutional, evidentiary and procedural have made elaborate provisions for safeguarding the rights of accused with a view to protect his dignity as a human being and giving him benefits of a just, fair and impartial trial.[9]

However, in this chapter the present study is concerned with those provisions of the code which entitle an accused of certain rights during the course of any investigation, enquiry or trial an offence with which he is charged. For convenience, the rights which are available to the accused have been categorised under the following heads:

(I) RIGHTS OF THE ACCUSED BEFORE TRIAL

(a) Arrest of Person and Protection against Arbitrary or Illegal Arrest

The provisions in this regard are discussed as follows:

An accused has certain right during the course of any investigation, inquiry or trial of an offence with which he is charged should be protected against arbitrary or illegal arrest. It is very much clear that an arrest must always be based on probable cause. Probable cause to arrest exists when, at the time of the arrest, the officer is relying on reasonably prudent person to believe that the accused has committed or is committing a crime. An officer need not to obtain an arrest warrant for an accused except in non-cognizable offences, however, he must receive an arrest warrant provided that the accused provides his name and address. In non-cognizable cases in order to enter an accused's home to arrest the accused, police must generally have a warrant. Upon entry, the officer may search for the person to be arrested but no provision is made for a general search of the premises for evidence.[10]

(i) Arrest of Persons without Warrant

Arrest means apprehension of a person by legal authority resulting in deprivation of his liberty. The code contemplates two types of arrests:

(a) Arrest made in pursuance of a warrant issued by a Magistrate; and

(b) Arrest made without such warrant but made in accordance with some legal provision permitting such arrest.[11]

In case of arrests without warrant the decision to make arrest is no doubt made by persons other than magistrates and Courts i.e. by police officers, private citizens, etc. These persons may not have the judicious mind and detached outlook, and yet because of the exigencies of certain situations the code allows them to make the arrest decisions them without obtaining warrants of arrest from the magistrates. In a case where a serious crime has been perpetrated by a dangerous person and there is every chance of the person absconding unless immediately arrested, it would be certainly unwise to insist on the arrest being made only after obtaining a warrant from a Magistrate. Preventive action may sometimes be necessary in order to avert the danger of sudden outlook of crime and immediate arrest of the trouble maker may be an important step in such preventive action.[12]

Under Section 41 very wide powers are conferred on the police in order that they may act swiftly for the prevention or detection of cognizable offences without the formality and delay of having to go to a Magistrate for order of arrest. Courts should, therefore, be particularly vigilant to see that the powers are not in any way abused or lightly used for the satisfaction of private feelings or of designing complainants. Therefore, the arrest and detention of persons without warrant are not matters of caprice but are governed by rules and principles clearly lay down by law.[13] The duty of the police when they arrest without warrant is, no doubt, to be quick to seek the possibility of crime, but equally they ought to be anxious to avoid mistaking the innocent far the guilty. When a constable has taken into custody a person reasonably suspected of committing a crime, it is his duty to act reasonably. No definition is possible of what is reasonable complaint or reasonable suspicion as it depends as much as the special facts of each case.[14] Reasonable means a bona fide belief that an offence had been committed or is about to be committed.[15] Mere suspicion is not enough. The burden is on the police officer to satisfy the Court before which the arrest is challenged that he had reasonable grounds of suspicion.[16] To arrest person without justification is one of the most serious encroachments upon the liberty of a subject.[17]

Amendment

Criminal Procedure Code (Amendment) Act, 2008 (Clause (5)

An amendment is made regarding Section 41 relating to power of police to arrest without warrant. It amends clauses (a) and (b) of sub-clause (1) so as to provide that the powers of arrest conferred upon the police officer must be exercised after reasonable care and justification and that such arrest is necessary and required under the Section. Amendment is also made in sub-Section (2) of Section 41 so as to provide that subject to the provisions of Section 42 relating to arrest on refusal to give name and residence, no person shall be arrested in a non-cognizable offence except under a warrant or order of a Magistrate.[18]

Thus, it is very much clear that the arrest of person must be justified and in accordance with rules and principles clearly laid down by law.

(ii) Notice of Appearance before Police Officer

This provision under Section 41A has been recently added to the Criminal Procedure Code by Criminal Procedure Code (Amendment) Act, 2008 [Clause (6)], which provides that the police officer shall, in all cases where the arrest of a person is not required under the provisions of sub-Section (1) of Section 41, issue a notice directing the person against whom a reasonable complaint has been made, or credible information has been received, or a reasonable suspicion exists that he has committed a cognizable offence to appear before him.[19] It further states that where such a notice is issued to any person, it shall be the duty of that person to comply with the terms of the notice.[20] Where such person complies and continues with the notice, he shall not be arrested in respect of the offence referred to in the notice unless, for reasons to be recorded, the police officer is of the opinion that he ought to be arrested.[21] Where such person, at any time, fails to comply with the terms of the notice or is unwilling to identify himself, the police officer may, subject to such orders as may have been passed by a competent Court in this behalf, arrest him for the offence mentioned in the notice.[22]

(iii) Procedure of Arrest and Duties of Officer making Arrest

Section 41B lays down the procedure of arrest and duties of officer making arrest. It is pertinent to mention here that this provision has been added in the Criminal Procedure Code as a result of the pronouncement of the Supreme Court in *D.K. Basu v. State of West Bengal.*[23] The police officer carrying out the arrest and handling the interrogation of the arrestee should bear accurate, visible and clear identification and name tags with their designation. A memo of arrest shall be prepared by the police officer carrying out the arrest at the time of arrest and such memo shall be attested by at least one witness, who may be either a member of the family of the arrestee or a respectable person of the locality from where the arrest is made. It shall also be countersigned by the person arrested. The arrested person shall be informed, unless the memorandum is attested by the member of his family, that he has a right to have a relative or a friend named by him to be informed of his arrest.[24]

(iv) Control Room at Districts

Section 41C requires the State Government to establish a police control room in every district and at the State level, where the names and addresses of the persons arrested, nature of offences with which they are charged, and the name and designation of the police officers who made the arrest are to be displayed.[25]

(v) Right of Arrested Person to Meet an Advocate of his Choice during Interrogation

Section 41D[26] makes provisions for the right of the arrestee to meet an advocate of his choice during the interrogation, though not throughout interrogation.[27]

(vi) Arrest on Refusal to give Name and Residence

A step little short of arrest is the ascertainment of the name and residence of a person. Section 42 applies only to a person (1) who commits a non-cognizable offence in the presence of a police officer, or (2) who is accused of committing such offence before such officer, if he refuses to give name and address. If the name and address are as curtained or are otherwise known to the police officer, the person is to be released on his executing a bond to appear before a Magistrate.[28]

If the person does not give his name as residence, as gives a name and residence which the police officer believes to be false, he may be taken into custody pending the ascertainment. He can on no account be detained beyond twenty four hours, but should be placed before a Magistrate.[29]

(vii) *Arrest by Private Person and Procedure on such Arrest*

Section 43 is based on the principle that every citizen has the duty to help, keep the peace and so has the right to make over or cause to be made over to the authorities any offender who breaks the law. As per this Section, a private person is entitled to arrest or cause to be arrested any person (1) who in his views[30] commits a non-bailable and cognizable offence, or (2) who is a proclaimed offender. He must without unnecessary delay make over such person to a police officer, or either take him or cause him to be taken to the nearest police station. This right of arrest arises under the common law which applies to India.[31] No arrest can be made on mere suspicion or information.[32] Private Citizen cannot follow and arrest a person on the statement of another person, however unimpeachable, that the former committed a non-bailable and cognizable offence.[33]

(viii) *Arrest How Made*

Section 46 describes the mode in which arrests are to be made. Whether the arrest to be made is with a warrant or without a warrant, it is necessary that in making such an arrest the police officer or other person making the same actually touches or confines the body of the person to be arrested unless there be a submission to custody by word as action.[34] Section 46 envisages three modes of arrest: (a) submission to custody; (b) confining the body (c) touching the body physically. The word "arrest" when used in its ordinary and natural sense means the apprehension or restraint or the deprivation of one's personal liberty to go where he pleases. Unless there is submission to custody, by words or by conduct, arrest must be made by actual contact.[35] If such person forcibly resists the endeavour to arrest him, as attempt to evade the arrest, such police officer or other person may use all means necessary to effect the arrest. All means necessarily includes help from other persons and it also applies to arrest by private citizen.[36] However, this Section does not give a right to cause death of a person, who is not accused of an offence punishable with death or with imprisonment for life. Accordingly, police officer in attempting to re-arrest escaped thief has no right to shoot.[37]

Amendment relating to Section 46 (Inserted by Criminal Procedure Code (Amendment) Act, 2008

A proviso has been added to Section 46(1) so as to provide that where a woman is to be arrested, unless the circumstances otherwise require or unless the police officer is a female, the police officer shall not touch the person of the woman to arrest her. Similarly, yet another provision in the form of sub-Section (4) has been added to Section 46 to prohibit arrest of woman after sunset and before sunrise, and where such exceptional circumstances exist, the woman police officer shall, by making a written report, obtain the prior permission of the judicial Magistrate of the first class within whose local jurisdiction the offence is committed as the arrest is to be made.[38]

However, earlier the Supreme Court has held that while arresting a female person, all efforts should be made to keep lady constable present but in circumstances where the arresting officer is reasonably satisfied that such presence of a lady constable is not available as possible and/or the delay in arresting caused by securing the presence of a lady constable would impede the course of investigation, such arresting officer for reasons to be recorded either before the arrest or immediately after the arrest, be permitted to arrest a female person for lawful reasons at any time of the day or night depending on the circumstances of the case even without the presence of a lady constable.[39]

(ix) Search of Place Entered by Person Sought to be Arrested

Section 47 provides that the persons residing or being in charge of such place, where the person to be arrested has entered or is hiding, should afford all facilities to the police officer's for search of person to be arrested. As per Section 47, if any person acting under a warrant of arrest, as any police officer having authority to arrest, has reason to believe that the person to be arrested has entered into, or is within, any place, any person residing in, or being in charge of such place shall, on demand of such person acting as aforesaid or such police officer, allow him free ingress thereto, and afford all reasonable facilities for a search therein.[40] It further provides that if difficulties are placed before a police officer regarding the ingress to such place, force may be used to obtain ingress. But if such place is an apartment in the actual occupancy of a female (not being the person to be arrested) who, according to custom, does not appear in public, such person or police officer shall, before entering such apartment, give notice to such female that she is at liberty to withdraw and shall afford her every reasonable facility for withdrawing, and may than break open the apartment and enter it.[41]

(x) No Unnecessary Restraint

As per Section 49, the person arrested shall not be subjected to more restraint than is necessary to prevent his escape, i.e., reasonable force may be used for the purpose, if necessary, but before keeping a person under any form of restraint there must be an arrest. Restraint or detention without arrest is illegal.

(xi) Person Arrested to be Informed of Grounds of Arrest and of the Right of Bail

Section 50 says that every person arrested without a warrant shall be informed of the grounds of the arrest and if the arrest is made for an offence which is bailable, he shall also be informed of his right to be released on bail so that he may arrange for the sureties etc.[42] The provisions of this Section are in conformity with Article 22(1) of the Constitution which provides that an arrested person is entitled to know the grounds of his arrest. Contravention of this provision will amount to disregard of the procedure established by law.[43] It is expected that the grounds of arrest should be communicated to the arrested person in the language understood by him otherwise it would not amount to sufficient compliance, with the constitutional requirement under Article 22(1) and Section 50(1) of the Code of Criminal Procedure.[44]

The Allahabad High Court has observed in *Udayabhan Shuki v. State of U.P.*,[45] that the right to be informed of the grounds of arrest is a precious right of the arrested person as it enables him to move the proper Court for bail, or for a writ of habeas corpus, or to make expeditious arrangements for his defence. Arrest without compliance of this provision will be illegal and will make the officer or person making such illegal arrest liable to all such remedies as are available in case of an illegal arrest. Section 50 is mandatory if particular of offence are not communicated to an arrested person, his arrest and detention are illegal.

(xii) Obligation of Person making Arrest to Inform about the Arrest etc., to a Nominated Person

This provision has been added recently, in the form of Section 50A (inserted by Criminal Procedure Code (Amendment) Act, 2005) to require the police to give information about the arrest of the person as well as the place where he is being held to any one of his friends, relatives or such other persons who may be nominated by him for giving such information etc. A record of such information having been given by the police officer shall be maintained in the police station where the arrestee is lodged. The Section also requires the Magistrate to make sure that the provision of this Section has been followed by the police officer making the arrest.

(xiii) Search of Arrested Person

Section 51 deals with the provision which allows a police officer to make a personal search of arrested persons, but it comes into operation after arrest (with or without warrant) and not before. The search of an arrested person without communicating him the grounds of his arrest will be illegal.[46] The officer making a search should obtain independent and respectable witnesses.[47] But this provision under Section 51, as has been held, does not permit medical examination of the accused without his consent. Forcible examination of the body of an arrested person without his consent, through a doctor for procuring evidence against him is not permissible and amounts to assault.[48]

Examination of accused by doctor not for benefit of health but by way of second search is not permitted in law without his consent.[49] This Section does not require that the signature of the person searched shall be taken on the recovery memo but it does require giving a receipt in respect of articles seized from the arrested person as a measure of precaution. Sub- Section (2) requires that the person of a woman can be searched only by a female with strict regard to decency and this cannot be done in the presence of men. But, simply because there was some irregularity in making such search, that itself will not render the search evidence inadmissible.[50]

(xiv) Examination of Accused by Medical Practitioner at the Request of Police Officer

As per Section 53, where there are reasonable grounds for believing that an examination of the arrested person will afford evidence as to the commission of an offence, it shall be lawful for a registered medical practitioner, acting at the request of a police officer not below the rank of sub inspector and for any person acting in good faith in his aid and under his direction, to make such an examination of the person arrested as is reasonably necessary in order to ascertain the facts which may afford such evidence, and to use such force as is reasonably necessary for that purpose. If the person of a female is to be examined, the examination shall be made only under the supervision of a female registered medical practitioner.[51] Such examination is a part of investigation as defined in Section 2(4) subjecting an arrested person to medical examination under Section 53 is a proceeding and, therefore, forms part of an investigation.[52]

In *Neeraj Sharma v. State of U.P.*,[53] the High Court of Allahabad has ruled that taking of hair samples comes within the ambit of medical examination of the accused and a Magistrate or a Court trying the case has powers to direct such examination as sample of hair, blood, nails etc. where there is reasonable ground to believe that such examination will afford evidence as to commission of an offence. The Court further held that such an examination is not violative of the constitutional provision of Article 20(3) and that a person cannot be said to have been compelled "to be a witness" against himself if he is required to undergo medical examination under Section 53.[54]

(xv) Examination of Person Accused of Rape by Medical Practitioner

As per Section 53A[55] which provide for a detailed medical examination of a person accused of an offence of rape or an attempt to commit rape by the registered medical practitioner employed in a hospital run by Government or by a local authority and in the absence of such a practitioner within the radius of sixteen kilometres from the place where the offence has been committed by any other registered medical practitioner.

(xvi) Examination of Arrested Person by Medical Practitioner at the request of the Arrested Person

Section 54 provides that when a person who is arrested, whether on a charge or otherwise, alleges, at the time when he is produced before a Magistrate or at any time during the period of his detention in custody that the examination of his body will afford evidence which will disprove the commission by him of any offence or which will establish the commission by any other person of any offence against his body, the Magistrate shall, if requested by the arrested person so to do, direct the examination of the body of such person by a registered medical practitioner unless the Magistrate considers that the request is made for the purpose of vexation or delay or for defeating the end of justice.[56]

The aforesaid Section 54 has been amended[57] in favour of the accused, so as to make it obligatory on the part of the State to have the arrested person examined by a medical officer in the service of Central or State Governments and in case the medical officer is not available by a registered medical practitioner soon after the arrest is made. It also provided that where the arrested person is a female, the examination of the body shall be made only by or under the supervision of a female medical officer, and in case the female medical officer is not available, by a female registered medical practitioner. This amendment is also in consonance with the spirit of the judgment of the Supreme Court in *D.K. Basu v. State of West Bengal.*[58]

In *D.J. Vaghela v. Kantibhai Jethabhai*,[59] the Hon'ble Court states that the provision of Section 54 relates to examination of the body of the person who is arrested at his request, alleging that such medical examination will afford evidence which will disprove his involvement in the commission of the alleged offence or will establish his physical torture or maltreatment in police custody.

(xvii) ***Identification of Person Arrested***

Criminal Procedure Code (Amendment) Act, 2005 [Clause (ii)] insert a new Section 54A to empower the Court to direct specifically the holding of the identification of the arrested person at the request of the prosecution.

In *Matru v. State of U.P.*,[60] it was held by the Supreme Court that identification test do not constitute substantive evidence. They are primarily meant for the purpose of helping the investigation agency with an assurance that their progress with the investigation into the offence is proceeding on the right lines. The identification can be used only as corroborate of the statement in the Court.

(xviii) ***Procedure when Police Officer Deputes Subordinate to Arrest without Warrant***

The power to arrest under Section 55 has to be exercised in such cases where obtaining of a warrant from a Magistrate would involve inordinate delay which might defeat the arrest or would cause unnecessary delay in effecting the arrest.[61] This Section applies where any officer-in-charge of a police station requires an officer subordinate to him, to arrest without warrant any person, he must deliver to the officer required to make such arrest, an order in writing. In absence of an order in writing the arrest will be wholly illegal.[62]

(xix) ***Health and Safety of Arrested Person***

A new Section 55A,[63] inserted in the Criminal Procedure Code in the year 2009, make it obligatory on the part of the person having the custody of the accused to take reasonable care of the health and safety of the accused.

(xx) Person Arrested to be taken before Magistrate or Officer Incharge of Police Station and not to be Detained more than Twenty-four hours

The object of Section 56 is to protect the liberty of a person and not to allow his detention unless there is a valid legal sanction for it. Thus, it is very much clearly stated in Section 56 that a person arrested by the police officer without warrant should be brought before a Magistrate having jurisdiction in the case without unnecessary delay. As per Section 57, no police officer shall detain in custody a person arrested without warrant for a longer period than under all such period shall not, in the absence of a special order of a magistrate under Section 167, exceed twenty hours exclusive of the time necessary for the journey from the place of arrest to the Magistrate's Court.[64] The constitutional and legal requirements to produce an arrested person before a judicial Magistrate within 24 hours of the arrest must be scrupulously observed.[65] Section 57 is concerned solely with the question of the period of detention. It does not deal with the question of bail. The intention is that the accused shall be brought before the Magistrate competent to try or commit, with the least delay.[66] The provision laid down in Section 57 seems to be designed to ensure that within not more than 24 hours some Magistrate should have information as to the nature of the charge against the accused, however, incomplete the information may be.[67] Where a police officer fails to produce an arrested person before a Magistrate within 24 hours of the arrest, he shall be held guilty of the offence of wrongful detention.[68]

(xxi) Police to Report Apprehensions

Section 58 requires that officers-in-charge of police station must report to the District Magistrate and where the District Magistrate so directs, to the Sub-Divisional Magistrate, all cases of person who have been arrested without warrant in order to enable him to prevent illegalities in arrests by examining the arrest reports submitted to him. Thus, the purpose of this Section is to detect the fairness of arrest made by police.

(xxii) Arrest to be made Strictly According to the Code

Section 60A[69] provides that no arrest shall be made except in accordance with the provisions of this code or any other law for the time being in force providing for arrest.

(xxiii) Arrest to Prevent the Commission of Cognizable Offences

Section 151 empowers the police officer to arrest the person who is believed to have a design to commit a cognizable offence and keep him in custody up to a maximum period of 24 hours, unless authorised by another law for the time being in force. Arrest under Section 151 is possible only if the person concerned is believed to have a design to commit a cognizable offence.[70] Under Section 151 two prerequisites are necessary, (1) the police officer knew that the offender has a design to commit a cognizable offence, and (2) that the commission could not be otherwise prevented.[71]

(b) Rights of the Accused against Search of Premises by an Investigating Authority

(i) When Search Warrant may be Issued

A search warrant is a written order issued by a Competent Magistrate or a Court directing a police officer or other person to take search of any place either generally or for specified documents or things or for persons wrongfully detained. Since a search involves invasion of the sanctity and privacy of individuals, the Court or the Magistrate should exercise utmost care and caution while using their power to issue a search warrant.[72] The Magistrate is required to record reasons before issue of a search warrant. An illegal order of search and seizure shall vitiate the seizure of the articles.[73] This provision is available under Section 93, which is supplementary to Sections 91 and 92, the object being to make provisions effective by issue of a search warrant. While an arrest is a deprivation of personal liberty, a search is an invasion of the sanctity and privacy of a citizen's home. A power of search and seizure is an overriding power of the State for the protection of social security and that power is necessarily regulated by law. Article 20(3) of the Constitution is not defeated by the provision for searches.[74] The Supreme Court in *M.P. Sharma v. State*[75] observed that a search by itself is not a restriction on the right to hold and enjoy property as it is only a temporary interference with the right to hold in premises searched and the articles seized. Therefore, it cannot be said that it is violative of Article 19(1) (f) of the Constitution.

Before issuing research warrant, the Magistrate must give reasons. It should not be issued on mere asking.

(ii) Search of place suspected to contain stolen property, forged documents, etc.

The protection against illegal and arbitrary search by the police is provided under Section 94. Before issuing a search warrant under Section 94, the Magistrate must satisfy that there is some allegation or information which is sufficient to draw an inference that a particular place is used for deposit of the stolen property or forging the documents or manufacturing of counterfeit coins, false seals etc. He has also to record the grounds on this belief. The order must, therefore show that the Magistrate has applied his mind before ordering the search of the place.[76]

The Magistrate must give reason before issuing search warrant under Section 94 of the code and the failure to do so will render such order to be illegal.[77]

(iii) Search for persons wrongfully confined

Application of Section 97 provides that if there is reason to believe that any person is confined under such circumstances that the confinement amounts to an offence, search warrants may be issued with the direction to search the person so confined and the same should be made in accordance with the search warrants. The confinement should be such that before the issue of search warrant the Magistrate has "reason to believe" that it amounts to an offence.[78] When the circumstances afford no ground for the belief required by the Section, issue of warrant is illegal. Before issuing a search warrant under Section 97, the Magistrate has to apply his mind and must be satisfied that the confinement amounts to an offence.[79]

(iv) Persons in Charge of closed place to allow search

Procedure with regard to search of a closed place, in charge of a person, is contained in Section 100. The provisions of Section 100 are applicable to both kinds of searches, namely, search under a warrant issued or search conducted without a warrant. The object of the Section is threefold:

(a) The occupant of the place to be searched extends all reasonable facilities to the persons authorised to conduct a search;

(b) The police and other authorised to make search are given necessary powers for the effective conduct of the search; and

(c) Reliable evidence is obtained by making a search and possibilities of concoction, malpractice such as planting of articles or of fabrication of any false evidences is completely eliminated.[80]

If the person to be searched is a woman then, in order to protect her modesty, her search should be made by another woman with utmost decency. It is obligatory on the part of the police officer to call on and get two or more respectable inhabitants of the locality to be witnesses of the search. These witnesses must be called before the search is started. Before searching a person, the searching officer should allow his person to be searched to avoid any possibility of implanting any object.[81] So, search without any offer to search the searching officer is illegal.[82]

It further provides that the police officer or other person making the search shall prepare a list of articles and things seized in the course of the search and it shall be signed by the witnesses.

(v) Search by Police Officer

The provisions of Section 165 are mandatory are meant to authorise the police officer making an investigation to conduct a general search on the chance that something relevant to the commission of the offence may be found. But the police officer must record in writing the reasons for his making a search.[83] He must clearly record the grounds of his belief and specification of the thing for which search is to be made. Omission to mention these grounds would amount to gross violation of the provisions of this Section.[84] Section 165 empowers the police officer specified to make a search without warrant subject to certain safeguards. The pre-requisites for a search are that:

1. Search must be necessary for investigation.
2. The offence must be such as the police officer is authorised to investigate i.e. cognizable offence.
3. Reasonable grounds must exist for believing that the thing required will be found in a place.
4. Grounds of belief as to necessity of search must be previously recorded.

All the above conditions must be fulfilled. Searches have to be conducted strictly in accordance with the formalities and within the legal limits prescribed in the code.[85]

To prevent misuse of power and as a safeguard against needless harassment, the Section casts an obligation on the police officer to place on record the reasons for making a search without taking a warrant.[86]

(c) Rights of the Accused to be Produced without Delay before the Magistrate after Arrest

There are two Sections of the code which deals with this right of the accused, which are as follows:

(i) Person arrested to be taken before Magistrate or officer-in-charge of police station

This right is contained in Section 56 of the Code. Whether the arrest is made without warrant by a police officer, or whether the arrest is made under a warrant by any person, the person making the arrest must bring the arrested person before a Magistrate or officer in charge of police station without unnecessary delay. It is also provided that the arrested person should not be confined in any place other than a police station before he is taken to Magistrate.[87]

As per Section 56, a police officer making an arrest without warrant shall, without unnecessary delay and subject to the provisions herein contained as to bail, take or send the person arrested before a Magistrate having jurisdiction in the case, or before the officer in charge of a police station.[88]

As per Section 76, the police officer or other person executing a warrant of arrest shall produce the arrested person before the Court without unnecessary delay and this time limit should not exceed beyond 24 hours in any case excluding the time necessary for journey from the place of arrest to the Magistrate's Court.

(ii) Person arrested not to be detained more than twenty-four hours[89] (Section 57)

The right to be brought before a Magistrate within a period of not more than 24 hours of arrest has been created with a view. . .

(a) To prevent arrest and detention for the purpose of extracting confessions, or as a means of compelling people to give information;

(b) To prevent police stations being used as though they were prisons—a purpose for which they are unsuitable.

(c) To afford an early recourse of a judicial officer independent of the police on all questions of bail or discharge.[90]

The precautions laid down in Section 57 seem to be designed to secure that within not more than 24 hours some Magistrate shall have the knowledge of what is going on and some knowledge of the nature of the charge against the accused, however incomplete the information may be.[91]

This healthy provision enables the Magistrate to keep check over the police investigation and it is necessary that the magistrates should try to enforce this requirement and where it is found disobeyed, come heavily upon the police.[92]

(d) Right of accused to get the complaint filed against him for the alleged offence within the period of limitation

The object of the criminal procedure in putting a bar of limitation of prosecution is clearly to prevent the parties from filing cases after a long time as a result of which material evidence may disappear and also to prevent abuse of the process of the Court by failing vexatious and belated prosecutions long after the date of the offence. The object which the statute seeks to sub serve is clearly in consonance with the concept of fairness of trial as enshrined in Article 21 of the Constitution.[93] It is, therefore, of the utmost importance that any prosecution, whether by the State or a private complaint must abide by the letter of law or take the risk of prosecution falling on the ground of limitation.[94] Section 468 provides for bar to taking cognizance after lapse of the period of limitation.

Commencement of the period of limitation

While Section 468 prescribes the period of limitation, Section 469 prescribes when such period of limitation shall commence. The provision is simple enough. It shall commence on the date the offence is committed. But if the commission of the offence is not known to the person aggrieved or the police or the identity of the person is not known either to the person aggrieved or to the police the period of limitation will commence in the former case on the date the commission of the offence is known to the person aggrieved or the police, whichever event happens earlier, or in the latter case, from the date on which the identity of the person is known to the person aggrieved or the police, whichever is earlier. But in computing the period of limitation, the day on which the period of limitation commences, shall have excluded. Section 470 provides about exclusion of time in certain cases. It recognises certain well recognised rules of exclusion of time in computing the period of limitation namely,

(a) exclusion of time of proceedings bonafide in a Court without jurisdiction;
(b) exclusion of time in cases when there is an order of a Court for stay or injunction;
(c) period covered by notice and the time taken in obtaining sanction or consent statutorily required;
(d) Period of absence from India.

Section 471 takes about exclusion of date on which Court is closed. Where the period of limitation expires on a day when the Court is closed, the Court may take cognizance on the day on which the Courts reopen. Section 472 talks about continuing offence, it simply states that in the case of continuing offence, a fresh period of limitation shall begin to run at every moment of the time during which the offence continues. If an Act committed by an accused constitute an offence and if that Act continues from day to day, then from day to day a fresh offence is committed by the accused so long as the Act continues.[95] Section 473 provides about extension of period of limitation in certain cases. Section 473 vests discretion in the Courts to waive the bar of limitation for the institution of a criminal case, if:

(i) in the light of the facts and circumstances of the case, the delay is properly explained; or
(ii) It is considered so to do in the interest of justice.[96]

(e) Rights of Accused against Police from Extorting Confession by using Illegal Means

Following are the Sections which deal with this right of the accused:

(i) Police officer's power to require attendance of witnesses and statements to police not to be signed: Section 160/162

In course of crime investigation, the police may secure the attendance of persons who can supply necessary information regarding the commission of the offence. The investigating officer should issue written order addressed to the person whose presence is sought specifying date, time and place where he has to appear for interrogation. But a male under the age of fifteen years or a woman cannot be required to attend at any place other than the place where he or she resides. An order directing a woman to appear in police station is violative of Section 160(1) of the Code.[97] Any person required by the investigating police officer to attend in connection with the investigation of a cognizable offence is under a legal duty to comply with the order issued under Section 160(1). A person wilfully or intentionally omitting to attend is liable to be punished under Section 174, Indian Penal Code. But the police officer has no authority to use force to compel attendance of such person, nor can be arrest or detain such witness. So also, a Magistrate has no power to issue any process compelling a person to appear before a police officer.[98]

Amendment of Section 160[99]

In Section 160 of the code of Criminal Procedure, in sub Section (1), in the proviso, for the words "under the age of fifteen years or woman", the words "under the age of fifteen years or above the age of sixty-five years or a woman or a mentally or physically disabled person" shall be substituted.

(ii) ***Statements to police not to be signed***

Section 162 protects the person making statements during police investigation under duress of inducement. Under that the accused may not be prejudiced in any way by the improper use of such statements recorded loosely or inaccurately by the police; Section 162 lays down specifically the mode in and the purpose for which the statements may be used in evidence. The object is to protect the accused both against overzealous police officers and untruthful witnesses.[100]

Another object of the Section is to "encourage the free disclosure of the information or to protect the person making the statement from a supposed unreliability of police testimony as to alleged statement or both.[101] The words of Section 162 are wide enough to include a confession made to a police officer in the course of an investigation.[102]

(iii) ***Examination of witnesses by police [Section 161]***

Under Section 161, a police officer making an investigation can examine the person acquainted with the facts of the case, and reduce the statement made by such person into writing. There should not be a long delay on the part of the investigating authorities in recording statements. Section 161 does not authorise beating or confining a person with a view to induce him to make a statement.[103] Delay in examination does not necessarily make the evidence untrustworthy. Investigating officer should be asked specifically about the reason for the delay.[104] The accused person cannot be forced to answer questions.

Amendment of Section 161[105]

In Section 161 of the code, in sub Section (3) after the proviso, the following proviso shall be inserted, namely:

Provided further that the statement of a woman against whom an offence under Section 354, 354A, 354B, 354C, 354D, Section 376, Section 376A, 376B, 376C, 376D, 376E or Section 509 of the Indian Penal Code is alleged to have been committed or attempted shall be recorded by woman police officer or any woman officer.

The provision of Section 161 make it obligatory for a person who is examined by police in course of investigation, to answer all questions put to him truly other than questions the answers to which are likely to incriminate him or expose him to a criminal charge.

(iv) ***No inducement, threat or promise to extract a favourable statement to be offered [Section 163]***

This Section prohibits the police officer or investigating authorities from making or offering any inducement, threat or promise to extract a favourable statement from him. Nor shall he be pressurised or confined with a view to inducing him to make a statement. Use of such foul tactics to extract statements or confessions is violating of Section 24 of the Evidence Act and also contrary to the provisions of sub Section (4) of Section 164.

The Supreme Court in *State of A.P.* v. *Venugopal*,[106] observed that the provision of Section 163 do not authorise a police officer to beat, confine or detain a person with a view to induce him to make a statement. The statement extract by using such unfair means may hamper the due course of administration of justice.

(v) ***The mode of recording a confession and statements [Section 164 (Recording of confessions and statement]***

Section 164 empowers any metropolitan or judicial Magistrate whether or not he has jurisdiction in the case to record any confession or statement of a person made in the course of investigation by the police, or (when the investigation has been concluded) at any time afterwards but before the commencement of the inquiry or trial. It applies only to statements recorded in investigation and is limited to the period before the inquiry or trial.[107] The effect of this Section, when read with Sections 24, 26, 25 and 29 of the Indian Evidence Act, is that:

(a) A confession made by an accused person to a police officer is inadmissible in evidence.
(b) If a person in police custody desires to make a confession, he must do so in the presence of a Magistrate.
(c) A Magistrate shall not record it unless he is, upon inquiry, from the person making it, satisfied that it is voluntary.
(d) When the Magistrate records it, he shall record it in the manner provided.
(e) Only when so recorded the confession becomes relevant and admissible in evidence.

A statement recorded under Section 164 is not substantive evidence. It can be used either for contradiction or for corroboration.

Comes into play during investigation

Section 164 comes into play when in the course of an investigation an accused or any other person desiring to make any statement is brought to a Magistrate so that any confession or statement that he may be deposed to make of his free will is recorded.

Right to Consult Lawyer

Recording of confession being a proceeding under Section 303 an accused has a right to consult his lawyer, and hence the Magistrate before confession should explain to him this, as also to a poor, economically and socially backward accused that he has right to have free legal aid under Section 304.[108]

Amendment of Section 164[109]

In Section 164 of the code, after sub Section (5), the following sub Section shall be inserted, namely:

(5A)(a) in cases punishable under Section 354, Section 354A, 354B, 354C, 354D, sub Section (1) or sub Section (2) of Section 376, 376A, 376B, 376C, 376D, Section 376E or Section 509 of the Indian Penal Code, the judicial Magistrate shall record the statement of the person against whom such offence has been committed in the manner prescribed in sub Section (5), as soon as the commission of the offence is brought to the notice of the police:

Provided that if the person making the statement is temporarily or permanently mentally or physically disabled, the Magistrate shall take the assistance of an interpreter or a special educator in recording the statement:

Provided further that if the person making the statement is temporarily or permanently mentally or physically, disabled the statement made by the person, with the assistance of an interpreter or a special educator, shall be video graphed.

(b) A statement recorded under clause (a) of a person, who is temporarily or permanently mentally or physically disabled, shall be considered a statement in lieu of examination in chief, as specified in Section 137 of the Indian Evidence Act, 1872 such that the maker of the statement can be cross examined on such statement, without the need for recording the same at the time of trial".

Amendment, inserted by code of Criminal Procedure (Amendment) Act, 2009

A proviso has been inserted to sub Section (1) relating to recording of any confession/statement under this provision even though audio video electronic means in the presence of the advocate of the person accused of an offence.

(f) Inquiry by Magistrate into cause of death of person in police custody [Section 176]

This Section provides that when any person dies while in police custody, it is obligatory for the nearest Magistrate to hold an inquest personally. Thus, Section 176 relates to inquiry by a Magistrate empowered in cases of suspicious death. The Section proceeds on the basis that inquiry into a suspicious death should not demand merely upon the opinion of the police, but there should be a further check.[110]

It has been observed that an inquiry under Section 176, Criminal Procedure Code is contemplated independently by the Magistrate and not jointly with a police officer when the role of the police officers itself is a matter of inquiry.

Amendment to Section 176[111]

Sub Section (1A) has been inserted to provide that in the case of death or disappearance of a person or rape of a woman while in the custody of the police, there shall be a mandatory judicial inquiry and in case of death, examination of the dead body shall be conducted within twenty four hours of death.

(II) RIGHTS OF THE ACCUSED DURING TRIAL

(a) Rights of the Accused during Trial to be defended by a counsel of his choice and free legal aid

Adversary system as a means of securing fair trial would necessarily require not only competent and independent judges and magistrates, but also competent and able lawyers adequately representing the parties before the Court. Free legal aid to person of limited means is a service which the modern State, in particular a welfare State, owes to its citizens.[112] The provisions to deal with this right under the code are discussed as under:

(i) Right of person against whom proceedings are instituted to be defended

The precious right of the accused who commits a crime are of questionable value without representation by a competent lawyer experienced in criminal defence. Most individuals accused of crimes for which a jail sentence may be imposed are entitled to competent representation and those that cannot afford to hire private counsel may be entitled to be represented at no charge, representation should be secured in order to ensure that these precious constitutional rights are meaningfully afforded to a criminally accused person.[113]

Section 303 recognises the right of any person brought before the criminal Courts to answer any charge or accusation to be defended by a lawyer of his choice. The right of an arrested person to consult his lawyer begins from the moment of his arrest.[114] Recording of confession is a "proceeding" within Section 303. It is absolutely essential for all magistrates to explain to the accused, before proceeding to record confession, his fundamental right under Article 22(1) and 20(3) and provisions of Section 303 that he has a right to consult his lawyer.[115] Article 22 of the Constitution also confers on a person, who is arrested the right to consult and to be defended by a practitioner of his choice. Arrest and trial in jail in hot haste on the next day without an opportunity to defend or informing the accused of their right under Article 22 of the Constitution and Section 303 is in a sense a denial of fundamental rights.[116]

(ii) Legal aid to accused at State expense in certain cases

Section 304, enables the Sessions Court to assign a pleader for the defence of the accused at the expense of the State provided he is unrepresented and the Court is satisfied that he has no sufficient means to engage a pleader. Section 304 of the Code of Criminal

Procedure specifically embodies this right as a statutory right vested in an accused person. A representation by a lawyer at Government expense to an accused person has been provided for statutorily, appointment of such lawyer to defend such an accused and the facilities to be allowed to such lawyers by the Courts and the fees payable to such lawyer by the Government are to be framed by the High Court with the previous approval of the State Government. Section 304 in fact gives effect to the constitutional mandate contained in Articles 21 and 39A of the Constitution. It is obvious that the right to be defended is essentially connected with right to life, which every citizen enjoys as conferred by Article 21. Denial of an inadequately competent advocate to defend the accused when he is unable to defend himself is factually violation of Article 21 of the Constitution, which nobody can be allowed to do.[117]

In *Ashok Kumar v. State of Rajasthan*,[118] an accused having sufficient means cannot claim for free legal assistance of a lawyer at the expenses of the State, particularly when he has already engaged a defence counsel of his choice. The Court, before whom the accused appears, is under a duty to inform the accused that if he is unable to engage the services of a counsel on account of poverty or indigence, he is entitled to obtain free legal service aid.

The Supreme Court in *Sukh Dev v. State of Arunachal Pradesh*[119] has held that a conviction of the accused in a trial in which he was not provide legal aid would be set aside as being violative of Article 21 of the Constitution.

(b) Right to open trial

Section 327 provides that the place in which a trial held shall be deemed to be an open Court to which the public may have access subject to the orders of the trial Magistrate in a particular case that the public or a particular person shall not have access thereto.[120] Thus, the public should have access to the Court if it can conveniently accommodate them.

Amendment inserted by Code of Criminal Procedure (Amendment) Act, 2008

The provision of Section 327 has been amended to provide that in camera trial under sub Section (2) shall be conducted as far as practicable by a woman judge or Magistrate. A proviso is also added to sub Section (3) so as lift the ban on printing or publication of trial proceedings in relation to an offence of rape, subject to maintaining confidentiality as to identity of the parties.[121]

(c) Right of the accused regarding the examination of witnesses

(i) Evidence to be taken in presence of accused

Section 273 makes it obligatory that evidence for the prosecution and defence should be taken in the presence of the accused. A trial is vitiated by failure to examine the witnesses in the presence of the accused.[122] Mere cross examination in the presence of the accused is not sufficient.[123] However, where the accused person by his own misbehaviour causes his expulsion from the Court room, such an expulsion will not be inconsistent with the provisions of the Section 273 and in that case, evidence for prosecution and defence can be recorded without the presence of the accused.[124] However, the expelled accused can reclaim his right to be present at the trial on a bonafide promise of proper behaviour.[125] Section 273 clearly states that except as otherwise provided all evidence whether for the prosecution or the accused must be taken in the presence of the accused. This rule is imperative subject to the exceptions contained in Sections 205, 291, 292, 293, 299, 317 and 391.

The explanation of this Section makes it clear that the word accused used in this Section also includes a person against whom any proceedings for taking security for keeping peace and for good behaviour have been commence under chapter VIII of the code.[126] The term "presence", as used in this section, is not used in the sense of actual physical presence. So long as the accused and/or his pleader are present when evidence is recorded by video conferencing that evidence is being recorded in the "presence" of the accused and would, thus, fully meet the requirements of Section 273, Criminal Procedure Code.

(d) Rights of the accused to get relevant copies of statements of prosecution witnesses and other documents

The provisions which deal with this right of accused are discussed as under:

(i) Supply of copy of police report and other documents to the accused[127]

Section 207 provides that in any case where the proceeding has been instituted on a police report, the Magistrate shall without delay furnish to the accused, free of cost, a copy of each of the following:

1. The police report;
2. The first information report recorded under Section 154;
3. The statements recorded under sub Section (3) of Section 161 of all persons whom the prosecution proposes to examine as its witnesses, excluding there from any part in regard to which a request for such exclusion has been made by the police officer under sub-Section (6) of Section 173;
4. The confessions, and statements, if any recorded under Section 164;
5. Any other document or relevant extract thereof forwarded to the Magistrate with the police report under sub-Section (5) of Section 173.

Thus, this Section enjoins a duty upon the Magistrate to furnish to the accused relevant documents or extracts thereof where the proceeding has been instituted a police report so that the accused may know the charges brought against him and the material on the basis of which they are going to be substantiated by the prosecution.[128] Non-supply of the materials mentioned Section 207 by the Magistrate may be sufficient grounds for quashing the proceedings against the accused.[129] The expression "due process of law" in Article 21 of the Constitution is to be deemed to include fairness in trial. It places an implied obligation upon the prosecution to make fair disclosure. The concept would take in its ambit furnishing documents to the accused which the prosecution relies upon whether field in the Court or not. Non-furnishing of a copy of the ballistic report of one of the experts to the accused which the prosecution opted not rely upon was held as violating the right of the accused to disclosure.[130]

In a case of murder, the written report of the incident made to the police by the complainant was not produced without any explanation despite on an application for its production made by the accused. The Court held that it could be said that the prosecution had suppressed the document.[131] The object of supplying copies of statements of witnesses and other documents to the accused is to put him on notice of what he has to meet at the inquiry or trial.[132]

(ii) ***Supply of copies of statements and documents to accused in other cases triable by Court of Session***

Section 208 states that in respect of cases exclusively triable by a Court of Session and instituted on complaint or otherwise than on a police report, it casts a statutory duty like the one in Section 207 on the Magistrate to furnish the accused free of cost with copies of:

1. Statements of all person examined by the Magistrate;
2. Statements and confessions recorded under Section 161 or Section 164; and
3. Documents on which prosecution relies. Provision has also been made for inspection of documents as in Section 207, when the document is voluminous.

This is in order to enable the accused to get adequate information about the charge against him and to prepare for his defence. The Supreme Court has held that the provision requiring the Magistrate to furnish to the accused, free of cost, a copy of the documents specified in the Section is mandatory.[133]

(e) Rights of the accused to know the accusations against him in the form of charge

In all criminal trials under the code the accused is informed of the accusations against him in the form of "charge" which is formulated with great precision and clarity.

Provisions regarding this aforesaid right are given under:

(i) Contents of Charge

The right to have precise and specific accusation is contained in Section 211; Criminal Procedure Code 'charge' serves as a notice or information to the accused and contains accusations which the accused is called upon to face in his criminal trial.[134] Thus, the provisions relating to 'charge' are intended to provide that "the charge" shall give the accused full notice of the offence charged against him. The purpose of a charge is to tell an accused person as precisely and concisely as possible of the matter with which he is charged and must convey to him with sufficient clearness and certainty what the prosecution intends to prove against him and of which he will have to clear himself.[135]

It has been repeatedly, held that the framing of a proper charge is vital to a criminal trial and that this is a matter on which the judge should bestow the most careful attention.[136] An accused is entitled to know with the greatest precision and particularly of the acts said to have been committed and the Section of the penal law infringed; otherwise he would be seriously prejudiced in his defence.[137] In summons cases no formal charge need to be framed, but in warrant cases, if the Magistrate is of the opinion that a *prima facie* case has been made out, a charge must be framed. Mere mention of a Section under which a person is accused without mentioning the substance of the charge amounts to a serious breach of procedure. The charge shall be written in the language of the Court.

(ii) Particulars as to time, place and person

Section 212 states that an accused person is entitled to know with certainty and accuracy the exact nature of the charge brought against him. Unless he has his knowledge he would be seriously prejudiced in his defence. This Section requires that the charge should contain particular as to time and place of the alleged offence, and the person against whom the offence has been committed or the thing (if any) in respect of which it has been committed. Thus, under Section 212 even the particulars qua the time, place and person are to be given in the charge.[138]

(iii) When manner of committing offence must be stated

Section 213 further extends the right of the accused as provided under Sections 211 and 212. This Section clearly states that when the particulars mentioned in Sections 211 and 212 do not give the accused sufficient notice of the matter which he is charged, the Magistrate must give in the charge such particulars of the manner in which the alleged offence was committed, as will be sufficient for that purpose. Thus, the manner in which the offence was committed has to be detailed out as required by this Section but it is only when the particulars required by Sections 211 and 212 does not give the accused sufficient notice of the matter with which he is charged.[139]

(f) Rights of accused to enter on his defence and adduce evidence

The relevant provisions which deal with this right of accused are discussed as below:

(i) Right to apply for process for compelling the attendance of witnesses/entering upon defence

Section 233 provides that if the judge does not acquit the accused under Section 232 on the ground that there is no evidence, he shall call upon the accused to enter on his defence and adduce evidence and file with the record any written statement, if put in by the accused, if the accused desires to call any witness and apply for issue of process for compelling attendance of witnesses or production of any document or thing an adjournment has necessarily to be given for the purpose. The calling upon the accused to enter on his defence is essential and omission to do so is not a mere irregularity. It is a mere irregularity unless prejudice is caused.[140] To call an accused for the purpose of entering his defence is not a mere formality but is an essential part of criminal trial. The accused may apply for issue of process to compel attendance of witnesses or production of documents or things and the judge, unless he considers the application to be vexatious or made for the purpose of delay or defeating the ends of justice, shall issue such process.[141] The judge should record his reasons for refusal.

(ii) Reasonable opportunity to the accused to produce evidence/evidence for defence

The provisions of Section 243 granting right to the accused to produce witnesses in his defence, apply equally to cases instituted on police report or on private complaint. After the examination and cross examination of all prosecution witnesses, i.e., after the completion of the prosecution case the accused shall be called upon to enter upon his defence and any written statement put in shall be filed with the record. He may even call further for cross examination. The judge shall go on recording the evidence of prosecution witness till the prosecution closes its evidence. The accused in order to test the veracity of the testimony of a prosecution witness has the right to cross examination him.[142] Omission to call upon the accused to enter upon his defence would not vitiate the trial, provided that accused was not denied an opportunity of stating his defence and of examining witnesses.[143]

(iii) Compensation for accusation without reasonable cause

Section 250 deals with this right of the accused. This Section provides for payment of compensation to those accused against whom complaints of accusation were made without any reasonable ground. Before making an order of compensation under this Section, the Magistrate should afford an opportunity to the complainant to show cause and he should be heard in reply. The object of the sanction is to avoid frivolous accusations being filed before the Court in the name of complaint. The provisions of this Section apply to both, summons as well as warrant cases.[144]

Under this provision, conditions applicable for award of compensation for false accusation are:

(a) Case must be instituted upon complaint or upon information given to a police officer or to a Magistrate;
(b) It must be triable by a Magistrate;
(c) the Magistrate must be satisfied that there was no reasonable ground for making the accusation;
(d) Action must be taken simultaneously with the discharge or acquittal of the accused by calling upon the complaint forthwith to show cause why compensation should not be awarded.
(e) The acquittal or discharge order must show on the face of it that the prosecution case was clearly false and vexatious.[145]

(iv) Accused's right to produce witnesses in his defence when not convicted in trial of summons cases by Magistrate

Section 254 lays down the procedure to be followed where the accused has not admitted all the accusation made against him or where the Magistrate does not convict the accused under Sections 252 or 253 of the code, the Magistrate must proceed to hear the case and take evidence adduced by the parties and cannot accept a subsequent plea of guilty as there is no provision to question the accused a second time.

The Magistrate is bound to take all such evidence as may be produced by the prosecution. He is also bound to examine all witnesses produced by the accused. After examining the witnesses, the Magistrate is bound to make a memorandum of the substance of their evidence in the language of the Court.[146] Accused is not debarred from examining prosecution witness and may ask for issuing summons under Section 254 (2).

(g) Rights of the accused to cross-examine the prosecution witnesses

Following are the Sections which deal with the right to cross examine the prosecution witnesses.

(I) Evidence for Prosecution

Section 231 contains the procedure for recording of prosecution evidence. As per Section 230, if the accused refuses to plead, or does not plead, or claims to be tried or is not convicted under Section 229, the judge shall fix a date for the examination of witnesses. Under Section 231, the accused in order to test the veracity of the testimony of a prosecution witness has the right to cross examine him. Considerable latitude is given in cross examination and it need not be confined to the facts elicited in examination-in-chief or to strictly relevant facts.[147]

Cross examination must be within reasonable limits and when the privilege is abused, the judge has always discretion as to how far it may go or how long it may continue.[148] After prosecution witnesses are examined, cross examination by the accused and re examination (if any) shall follow immediately in the order stated in Section 138, Evidence Act. There is no right to reserve cross examination. Ordinarily examination and cross examination are to be a continuous process; but sub Section (2) vests the judge with discretion to permit for sufficient reason, either:

(i) The cross examination of any witness to be deferred until any other witness or witnesses have been examined, or
(ii) Recall any prosecution witness for further cross examination.

It has been held that it is demand of criminal jurisprudence that criminal trial must proceed day to day. Examination-in-chief if commenced on a particular day, trial judge has to ensure that his cross examination must conclude either on the same date or the next day if cross examination is lengthy or can continue on consecutive dates.[149]

(h) Rights of the accused to settle the matters through plea bargaining

"Plead guilty and bargain lesser sentence" is the shortest possible meaning of plea bargaining. In its most traditional and general sense, "plea bargaining" refers to pre trial negotiations between the defendant, usually conducted by the Counsel and the prosecution, during which the defendant agrees to plead guilty in exchange for certain concession by the prosecutor. "Plea bargaining" falls into two distinct categories depending upon the type of prosecutorial concession that is granted. The first category is "charge bargaining" which refers to a promise by the prosecutor to reduce or dismiss some of the charges brought against the defendant in exchange for a guilty plea. The second category, "sentence bargaining" refers to a promise by the prosecutor to recommend a specific sentence or to refrain from making any sentence recommendation in exchange for a guilty plea. Both methods affect the dispositional phase of the criminal proceedings by reducing defendant's ultimate sentence.[150] The concept of plea bargaining was introduced in India Criminal Justice System in the year 2005 by means of Criminal Law (Amendment) Act, 2005. By this amendment a new chapter XXIA has been introduced in the Code of Criminal Procedure.[151]

Based on the recommendation of the law commission, the new chapter on plea bargaining making plea bargaining in cases of offences punishable with imprisonment up to seven years has been included in Criminal Procedure Code and the same has come into effect from 05.07.2006. A consideration of chapter XXIA dealing with plea bargaining will show that certain procedure prescribed for plea bargaining under Section 265A to 265L of Criminal Procedure Code are to be complied to make it a valid plea bargaining.[152]

Moreover it does not apply to cases where the offence committed is a socio-economic offence or where the offence is committed against a woman or a child below the age of 14 years. Also once the Court passes an order in the case of 'plea bargaining' no appeal shall lie to any Court against that order. The Wikipedia Encyclopaedia defies it as to make an agreement in which the defendant pleads guilty to a lesser charge and the prosecutors in return drops more serious charges. The object of 'plea bargaining' is to reduce the risk of undesirable orders for the either side. Another reason for the introducing the concept of 'plea bargaining' is the fact that most of the criminal Courts are over burdened and hence unable to dispose of the cases on merits. Criminal trial can take day, weeks, months and sometimes years while guilty pleas can be arranged in minutes. In other words, a 'plea bargaining' is a deal offered by the prosecutor to induce the defendant to plead guilty. Therefore we can safely say that 'plea bargaining' is nothing but a contract between the prosecution and the defendant or accused and both the parties are bound by this contract. For most defendants the principal benefit of plea bargaining is receiving a lighter sentence that what might result from taking the case to trial and losing. Another benefit which the defendant gets is that they can save a huge amount of money which they might otherwise spend on advocates. It always takes more time and effort to bring a case to trial than to negotiate and handle a plea bargain.[153]

To reduce the delay in disposing criminal cases, the 154th report of the Law Commission first recommended the introduction of 'plea bargaining' as an alternative method to deal with huge arrears of criminal cases. This recommendation of the law committee finally found a support in Malimath Committee Report. In its report, the Malimath Committee recommended that a system of plea bargaining be introduced in the Indian Criminal Justice System to facilitate the earlier disposal of criminal cases and to reduce the burden of the Courts. The Supreme Court has also time and again blasted the concept of plea bargaining saying that negotiation in criminal cases is not permissible. More recently in *State of U.P. v. Chandrika,*[154] the Apex Court held that it is settled law that on the basis of plea bargaining Court cannot dispose of the criminal cases. The Court has to decide it on merits. If the accused confesses his guilt, appropriate sentence is required to be implemented. The Court further held that, mere acceptance or admission of sentence. Despite this huge hue and cry, the government found it acceptable and finally Section 265A to 265L have been added in the Criminal Procedure Code.[155]

While commenting on their aspect, the division bench of the Gujarat High Court observed in *State of Gujarat v. Natwar H. Thakor,*[156] that the very object of law is to provide easy, cheap and expeditious justice by resolution of disputes, including the trial of criminal cases and considering the present realistic profile of the pendency and delay in disposal in the administration of law and justice, fundamental reforms are inevitable. There should not be anything static. It can thus be said that it is really a measure and redressal and it shall add a new dimension in the realm of judicial reforms.

Application for the plea bargaining[157]

A person accused of an offence may file application for plea bargaining in the Court in which such offence is pending for trial. Such application shall contain a brief description of the case relating to which the application is filed including the offence to which the case relates and shall be accompanied by an affidavit sworn by the accused stating therein that he has voluntarily preferred, after understanding the nature and extent of punishment provided when the law for the offence.

Report of the mutually satisfactory disposition to be submitted before the Court[158]

Where in a meeting (for mutually satisfactory disposition) a satisfactory disposition of the case has been worked out, the Court shall prepare a report of such disposition which shall be signed by the presiding officer of the Court and all other persons who participated in the meeting and if no such disposition has been worked out, the Court shall record such observation and proceed further in accordance with the provisions of the code from the stage of filing of the application.

Disposal of the Case

Where a satisfactory disposition of the case has been worked out, the Court shall dispose of the case in the prescribed manner.

Judgment of the Court

The Court shall deliver its judgment in terms of Section 265E in the open Court and the name shall be signed by the presiding officer of the Court. The judgment delivered by the Court under Section 265G shall be final and no appeal (except the special leave petition under Article 136 and writ petition under Articles 226 and 227 of the Constitution) shall lie in any Court against such judgment.[159]

Non-application of the Chapter XXIA

It is also provided that nothing in this chapter shall apply to any juvenile or child as defined in sub-clause (k) of Section 2 of the Juvenile Justice (Care and Protection of children) Act, 2000

(i) Rights of the accused to be heard in the question of quantum of sentence

We can discuss this right of the accused in the light of following Sections:

(i) Judgment of acquittal or Conviction: Section 235

Section 235 provides that where the accused is convicted, except in case of admonition or release on probation of good conduct under Section 360. The judge must hear the accused in the question of the quantum of sentence.

Explaining the true construction of Section 235 of the code, the Supreme Court in *Santa Singh v. State of Punjab*,[160] held that the Court must in the first instance, deliver a judgment convicting or acquitting the accused. If the accused is acquitted no further question will arise. But if he is convicted, then the Court must hear him on the question of sentence to be imposed on him, and it is only after hearing him on this point, that the Court can proceed to pass the order of sentence against him.

The object of this Section is that, after a Court holds a person guilty, it must consider the question of sentencing in the light of various factors such as the prior criminal record of the offender, his age, employment, educational background, home life, sobriety and social adjustment, emotional and mental condition, and the prospects of his returning to normal path of conformity with the law. It was therefore considered that the accused as well as the prosecution should be given an opportunity to put forward their viewpoints on the question of the sentence. The provisions of this Section are mandatory.[161]

(ii) Acquittal or conviction in cases triable by Magistrate, Section 248

As per this Section in a warrant case both instituted on police report and private complaint the only order that can be passed after charge is either (a) acquittal, or (b) conviction. The provision of sub Section (2) is analogous to the provisions in Section 235 (2). It gives an opportunity to both parties to bring to the notice of the Court facts and circumstances for personalising the sentence from a reformative angle.[162] After the order of conviction is recorded it is obligatory for the Court to hear the culprit on the question of sentence unless it releases him on probation of good conduct or admonition under Section 360 or if the Magistrate finds under Section 325 that he cannot inflict sufficient punishment in the case and it requires him to submit the case to the Chief Judicial Magistrate.

As regards opportunity of hearing to accused on question of sentence, the Allahabad High Court in *Bhirug v. State of U.P.*,[163] held that where only counsel of the accused was asked to make an oral submission on the question of sentence and no opportunity of hearing was given to him, the procedure adopted by the trial Court was wholly against the spirit and object of provision contained in Section 248 (2) of the code as it will cause prejudice to the accused.

(i) Reasonable opportunity to Accused to give his explanation

Section 313 is intended to establish a direct dialogue between the Court and the accused so as to give him an opportunity to give his explanation. The purpose of examination of the accused by the Court under this Section is certainly not to cross examine him or trapping him to make an admission of facts which the prosecution has failed to establish against him, but to afford him an opportunity of explaining the circumstances that appear to be against him in the evidence.[164] For instance, if some articles are found and recovered from accused's house, which points at his involvement in the crime, the Court should examine and give him an opportunity to explain how those articles happened to be present in his house.[165] The object underlying in Section 313 is to draw accused's attention to every inculpatory material against him so as to enable him to explain it in his defence. This being a basic requirement of a fair trial, failure in this may gravely imperil the validity of the trial itself, if consequential miscarriage of justice or prejudice is proved.[166]

The accused is not bound to answer the questions and according to sub-Section (3) he shall not render himself liable to punishment if he refuses to answer the questions put to him by the Court or gives false answers. Nor is any oath to be administered to him. The reason being that under this Section, he is not being examined as a witness. However, his answers may be put in evidence for or against him, in inquiry or trial for some other offence. The Apex Court, in *Avtar Singh v. State of Punjab*,[167] has once again reiterated that the object of examination of accused under Section 313 is to afford an opportunity to him to explain the circumstances appearing in the evidence against him. Since the statement of the accused under Section 313 is not substantive evidence, a conviction cannot be based on such examination alone. The Supreme Court in *Bishnu Prasad Sinha v. State of Assam*[168] reiterated that statements of accused make under Section 313 of Criminal Procedure Code cannot be sole basis of conviction but the effect thereof may be considered in the light of other evidences brought on record.

Amendment inserted by the Code of Criminal Procedure Amendment Act, 2008 is made to the provisions of this Section, relating to power of the Court to examine the accused. The clause inserts a new sub-Section (5) to the said Section so as to eliminate delay in trial, by providing that the Court may take help of prosecutor and defence counsel in preparing relevant questions to be put to the accused.

(k) Accused person to be competent witness

Section 315 deals with the right to appear as defence witness, it provides that an accused person can be a competent witness for the defence and like any other witness he is entitled to give evidence on oath in disproof of the case brought against him by the prosecution. Where the accused voluntarily offers him to be examined as a defence witness, the prosecution is entitled to examine him and the evidence so obtained may be used against the co-accused. However, the Section precludes the Court from drawing any adverse inference from the non-examination of the accused as a defence witness.[169]

In number of cases it was held by Courts that if an accused along with others, voluntarily steps in the witness box as a defence witness, he is subject to cross examination by the prosecution counsel and the evidence brought out in such cross examination can be used against his co-accused.[170] Accused is not compelled to be a witness if he voluntarily gives evidence in his defence and Article 20(3) of Constitution is not violated.[171]

(III) RIGHTS OF THE ACCUSED AFTER TRIAL

(a) Rights of the accused to file appeal against the order of Conviction

This is one of the safeguard which is given to the accused under the code. It can be discussed under the following heads:

(i) Appeals from convictions

Appeal is the effective safeguard available to an accused in the administration of justice against possible error in judgment. Despite all precautions and detailed procedural law for ensuring a just and fair trial, the possibility of mistakes or errors in the judgments of the Courts cannot be ruled out and therefore, the parties aggrieved by the decision of the lower Court may move in appeal to the higher Court for scrutiny and reconsideration of the decision in the interest of justice. Highlighting the significance of the provision of appeal, the Supreme Court in *M.H. Haskot v. State of Maharashtra*,[172] observed, "it is integral to fair procedure, natural justice and normative universality save in special cases like the original tribunal being a high bench sitting on a collegiate basis, and subject to just exceptions, at least one right of appeal, as provided in the Criminal Procedure Code, manifests the values upheld in Article 21 of the Constitution of India". As per literal meaning an appeal is a complaint to a superior Court of an injustice done or error committed by an inferior one, whose judgment or decision the Court above is called upon to correct or reverse. Section 372 of the code provides that there can be no right of appeal against a judgment or decision of a lower Court unless a provision for appeal is specifically provided by the law itself. It is thus clear that there is no inherent right of appeal because an appeal is a creature of the statute. Section 374 provides three different forums for filing appeals by the accused against the order of conviction. They are as follows:

(i) If the trial is held by the High Court in exercise of its extraordinary original criminal jurisdiction, an appeal would lie to the Supreme Court and not to a large bench of judges of that High Court.

(ii) If the trial is held by the Session Judge or an Additional Sessions Judge, or by any other Court in which sentence of imprisonment for more than seven years has been passed, an appeal would lie to the High Court.

(iii) If the trial is held by a metropolitan Magistrate or assistant Session judge or Magistrate of the first or second class except in cases falling under Sections 325 and 360, an appeal will lie to the Court of Session.[173]

(ii) Appeal against conviction by High Court in certain cases: Section 379

Section 379 gives a right to an accused person to file an appeal to the Supreme Court against the reversal of an order of acquittal into conviction by the High Court in appeal provided sentence of death or imprisonment for life or an imprisonment for a term of ten years or more has been awarded by the High Court. In other cases of lesser punishment, appeal can be filed to the Supreme Court only if the High Court certifies that the case is fit one for such appeal.

(iii) Special Right of Appeal in certain cases

Section 380 provides that notwithstanding anything contained in this chapter (Appeals), when more persons than one are convicted in one trial, and an appellate judgment or order has been passed in respect of any of such persons, all or any of the persons convicted at such trial shall have a right of appeal. Thus, this Section gives a right of appeal to an accused person whose sentence is non appealable if any of his co-accused has been awarded a sentence which is appealable.

(iv) Suspension of sentence pending the appeal; release of applicant on bail: Section 389

Under this Section, the appellate Court can exercise power to grant bail to a convicted person pending his appeal. The Appellate Court can also order suspension of sentence of the convicted person who is in confinement. The High Court of Madhya Pradesh in *Gopal v. State of M.P.*[174] has emphatically stressed that an application for bail and suspension of sentence pending appeal is maintainable as an integral part of the appeal under Section 389 of the code. Under sub Section (2) the High Court has given concurrent jurisdiction in the matter. Existence of an appeal is a condition precedent for granting bail; hence application for condonation of delay should be disposed off before suspending sentence.[175]

Bail to a convicted person is not a matter of right irrespective whether the offence is bailable or non-bailable and should be allowed only when after reading the judgment and hearing the accused it is considered justified. Further, the record of reasons for granting bail is mandatory. Reasons need not be recorded for refusing bail.[176]

(i) Whether any person *prima facie* ground is disclosed for substantial doubt about the conviction; or
(ii) Whether the disposal of the appeal or revision is likely to take an unreasonable time.

Reiterating the need for granting bail or suspension of sentence under Section 389, the Supreme Court in *Bhagwan R. Shinde v. State of Gujarat*,[177] inter alia observed that so long as the Appellate Court is not in a position to hear the appeal of the accused expeditiously, ordinarily he should be released on bail unless there are cognet grounds for refusing bail. The reason being that the accused is ultimately found to be innocent, he would have not to remain in jail for unduly long time.

Amendment is inserted w.e.f. 23.06.2006 to sub Section (1) of Section 389 to the effect that:

(i) the Appellate Court will give notice to the prosecution before releasing a convicted person on bail, if he was convicted on an offence punishable with death, imprisonment for life or imprisonment for a term of not less than ten years; and
(ii) The prosecution should be permitted to move an application for cancellation of bail granted by the appellate Court.[178]

(b) Accused once convicted or acquitted not to be tried for same offence

Section 300 deals with this right, the Section embodies the common law principle contained in the doctrine of autrtfois acquit and autrefois convict which means that if a person is tried and acquitted or convicted of an offence he cannot be tried again for the same offence or on the same facts for any other offence. This doctrine is also incorporated in Article 20(2) of the Constitution. Thus, the rule is based on the principle that a person may not be put twice in jeopardy for the same offence.[179]

In order to bar the trial of a person already tried, it must be shown that:

(i) He had been tried by a competent Court for the same offence or one for which he might have charged or convicted on the same facts;
(ii) That he had been convicted or acquitted at the trial;
(iii) That such conviction or acquittal is in force.[180]

(IV) RIGHTS OF THE ACCUSED AND PROVISIONS AS TO BAIL

The object of arrest and detention of the accused person is primarily to secure his appearance at the time of trial and to ensure that in case he is found guilty he is available to receive the sentence. The releas on bail is crucial to the accused as the consequence of pre trial detention is given. If release on bail is denied to the accused, it would mean that though he is presumed to be innocent till the guilt is proved beyond reasonable doubt, he would be subjected to the psychological and physical deprivation of jail life. Bail has been defined in the law lexicon as security for the appearance of the accused person on giving which he is released pending trial or investigation.[181]

(i) Meaning and object of granting bail

'Bail' means the security taken from a person to appear on a fixed date before a Court. Bail is an agreement in which a person makes a written undertaking, to the Court. A person who is in custody, because he or she has been charged with an offence or is involved in pending criminal proceedings, may apply to be released on bail. There are two authorities that may grant bail is 'the police' and 'the Court'.

In concise oxford dictionary defines 'bail' as security for the appearance of prisoner on giving which the accused is released pending trial.

Bail is the most important legal service in the criminal legal system of India. The object of bail is to release a person who is in custody after giving security of his appearance before the Court. The nature of the offence determines whether the accused is entitled to bail or not. In some of the cases the accused is entitled to bail by the police and are called bailable offence in common parlances. The accused is given bail by the police in such cases after completing the formalities for bail bond and proper surety.[182]

In some cases the offence is categorised as non-bailable, accused can get bail from the designated Court itself. In some cases the accused approaches the Court for grant of anticipatory bail apprehending his arrest by the police. The Court after hearing the pleas of the accused through his counsel determines whether the accused is entitled to be granted anticipatory bail or not.[183]

(ii) Right to bail when investigation cannot be completed within prescribed time period (Rights available before trial)

Section 167 lays down the procedure to be adopted when the investigation against accused person cannot be completed within 24 hours of his arrest and there are grounds for believing that the accusation against him is well founded.

The provisions of this Section are attracted under the following conditions:

(a) When the accused is arrested without warrant and is detained by a police officer in his custody;
(b) It appears that more than 24 hours will be needed for his investigation.
(c) There are grounds to believe that the accusation or information against him is well founded.
(d) The officer in charge of the police station or the investigating officer not below the rank of a sub inspector forwards the accused for remand before a Magistrate.

Thus, a person arrested without a warrant cannot be detained by the police for more than 24 hours. If the police officer considers it necessary to detain such a person for a longer period for the purposes of investigation, he can do so only after obtaining a special order of a Magistrate under Section 167. The scheme of the Section is intended to protect the accused from an unscrupulous police officer. The object is to see that persons arrested by the police are brought before the Magistrate with the least possible delay so that the Magistrate could decide whether the persons produced should further be kept in police custody and also to allow them to make such representations as they may wish to make.[184] In *Uday Mohanlal Acharaya* v. *State of Maharashtra*,[185] it was held that the provision of Section 167 Criminal Procedure Code is supplementary to Section 57, in consonance with principle that accused is entitled to demand that justice is not delayed. Proviso to Section 167(2) stipulates that accused shall be released on bail on failure of prosecution to file the challan within the period specified, an indefensible right accrues to the accused to be released on bail. The Magistrate to whom an accused person is so forwarded may, whether he has or has no jurisdiction to try the case, from time to time, authorise the detention of the accused person in such a custody as such a Magistrate may think fit, for a term not exceeding 15 days on the whole; and if he has no jurisdiction to try the case or commit it for trial, and considers further detention unnecessary, he may order the accused to be forwarded to a Magistrate having such jurisdiction. Proviso to Section 167(2) empowers the Magistrate to authorise the detention of an accused, otherwise than in police custody beyond the period of 15 days if he is satisfied that adequate grounds exist for doing so. However, a Magistrate shall not authorise the detention of accused in custody for total period exceeding:

(i) 90 days, where investigation relates to offence punishable with death or imprisonment for life or imprisonment for a term not less than 10 years;
(ii) 60 days, where investigation relates to any other offence.

On the expiry of above said period, as the case may be, the accused person shall be released on bail.[186] The right accrued to the accused for being enlarged on bail under provision to Section 167(2) of Criminal Procedure Code is not an absolute right. It gives only absolute right to be granted bail if the charge sheet is not filed within the prescribed period but the detention nonetheless continues to be authorised. Thus, Section 167(2) is mandatory if the period specified therein has expired without charge sheet being filed and this make the ground for the accused that he must be released on bail. Merits of the case are irrelevant at that stage and right of the accused to be released on bail under this provision is absolute.[187] An order for release on bail under proviso (a) to Section 167(2) may appropriately be termed as an order on default. Indeed, it is a release on bail on the default of the prosecution in filing a charge sheet within the prescribed period. In fact, the Magistrate has no power to remand a person beyond the stipulated period of 90/60 days. He must pass an order of bail and communicate the same to the accused to furnish the requisite bail bonds. The accused cannot, therefore, claim any special right to remain on bail. If the investigation reveals that the accused has committed a serious offence and charge sheet is filed, the bail granted under proviso (a) to Section 167(2) could be cancelled.[188] If the judicial Magistrate is not available, the accused is produced before an executive Magistrate, such an executive magistrate may, for reasons to be recorded in writing authorise the detention of the accused person in such a custody as he may think fit for a term not exceeding seven days in the aggregate. Before the expiry of the said period, the executive Magistrate is required to transmit to the nearest judicial Magistrate the records of the case together with a copy of the entries in the case diary which was transmitted to him by the police. If the period of detention so authorised expires and no further detention of the accused person is authorised by a competent judicial Magistrate, the accused person shall be released on bail.[189]

In *State (Delhi Admn.) v. Dharam Pal*,[190] the nature of the custody can be altered from judicial custody to police custody and vice versa during the first period of 15 days mentioned in Section 167(2). After 15 days the accused can only be kept in judicial custody or any other custody as ordered by the Magistrate, but not the custody of the police. It has been specifically provide that no Magistrate shall authorise detention in any custody under Section 167 unless the accused is produced before him. The object of requiring the accused to be produced before the Magistrate is to enable the Magistrate to decide judicially whether remand is necessary and also to enable the accused to make any representation to the Magistrate to controvert the grounds on which the police officer has asked for remand.[191]

In *Madhu Mimaye, In re*,[192] it was stated that the Magistrate has to exercise his judicial mind while deciding whether or not the detention of the accused in any custody is necessary. The order of detention is not to be passed mechanically as a routine order on the request of the police for remand. The prescribed period of 90 days or of 60 days as mentioned in proviso (a) to Section 167(2) is to be computed from the date the Magistrate authorises detention of an accused person. But it has been ruled that the day of arrest of an accused or his surrender in Court may have to be excluded. If in any case triable by a magistrate as a summons case, the investigation is not concluded within a period of six months from the date on which the accused was arrested, the Magistrate shall make an order stopping further investigation of the offence unless the officer making the investigation satisfies the Magistrate that for special reasons and in the interest of justice the continuation of the investigation beyond the period of six months is necessary.[193] If the Magistrate orders the investigations to be stopped as mentioned above, but the Sessions Judge is satisfied, on the application made to him or otherwise, that further investigation into the offence ought to be made, he may vacate the order made by the Magistrate and direct further investigation to be made into the offence subject to such directions with regard to bail and other matters as he may specify.[194] The Supreme Court in *Hussainara Khatoon v. State of Bihar,*[195] has emphasised that it is the duty of the Magistrate to inform the accused that he has a right to be released on bail under proviso to Section 167(2) and also the State is under a constitutional obligation to provide free legal services to an indigent accused not only during trial but when he is remanded from time to time. It has been held by the Supreme Court that the object behind the enactment of Section 167 is to see that the detention of the accused should not be permitted in custody for any unreasonably longer period.[196]

Amendment to the proviso to sub Section (2) of Section 167

It has been amended in the year 2009 in order to make provision for the Magistrate to extend further detention in judicial custody of the accused also through the medium of electronic video linkage except for the first time where the production of the accused in person is required. The clause also inserts a further proviso to the said sub Section (2) to provide that in the case of a woman under 18 years of age, the detention shall be authorised to be in the custody of a remand home or recognised social institution.[197]

(iii) In what cases bail to be taken (Section 436) (Right available before trial)

Where a person who is not accused of a non-bailable offence is arrested or detained without warrant, and he is prepared to give bail, the police officer or the Court having custody of such person is required to release him on bail. The police officer or Court, instead of taking bail from such person may even release him on executing a bond without sureties. Right to seek bail in respect of bailable offences is a matter of right. The value of bond and the nature of surety is the only discretion vested in the Court. The proviso to the provision in Section 436 also make it clear that the officer in his opinion or the Court in its opinion in their discretion may release the person by taking only a personal bond without insisting surety for the appearance. The provision also makes it clear that grant of bail need not necessarily be by the Court only. The police officer has also the jurisdiction to release the person on bail with or without surety. Therefore, insistence of the personal bond and the surety are essentially a matter of discretion and within the jurisdiction of the Court under Section 436, Criminal Procedure Code.[198] The right to be released on bail in case of a bailable offence being a legal and constitutional right of the accused person, refusal of this right is a curtailment of the right of personal liberty guaranteed by Article 21 of the Constitution and therefore, such refusal must be in exceptional circumstances to meet the exigency of the case.[199] Where a person accused of a bailable offence has been released on bail has failed to comply with the conditions of the bail, the Court may refuse to release him on bail, when on a subsequent occasion in the same case he appears or is brought in custody before the Court.

(iv) Safeguards to undertrial prisoners against indiscriminate incarceration (Right available during trial)

Section 436A, where a person has during the period of investigation, inquiry or trial under this code of an offence under any law (not being an offence for which the punishment of death has been specified as one of the punishments under that law) undergone detention for a period extending up to one half of the maximum period of imprisonment specified for that offence under that law, he shall be released by the Court on his personal bond with or without sureties. There are huge numbers of under trial prisoners languishing in different jails in the State, undergoing detention for more than even the maximum period of sentence prescribed for the offence or offences alleged against them. Application of Section 436A of the code by the Criminal Courts will be one of the remedies for this evil. The Court may, however, order the continued detention for a period than one half in exceptional cases for reason to be recorded in writing.[200]

(v) Release of an accused on bail in a non-bailable case

When a person is detained for a non-bailable offence, he cannot deem to be released on bail as a matter of right. He can, however, request the Court to grant bail. The provisions in this case are governed by Section 437.

This Section gives the Court or a police officer power to release an accused on bail in a non-bailable case unless there appear reasonable grounds that the accused has been guilty of an offence punishable with death or with imprisonment for life. But

(a) A person under the age of sixteen years;
(b) A woman; or
(c) A sick or infirm person may be released on bail even if the offender is charged with an offence punishable with death or imprisonment for life.[201]

Where a person is charged with a non-bailable offence, but it appears in the course of the trial that he is not guilty of such offence, he can be immediately released on bail pending further inquiry. The same may be done after the conclusion of a trial and before judgment is pronounced, if the person is believed not to be guilty of a non-bailable offence. The Court should take into consideration various matters such as nature and seriousness of the offence, the character of evidence, circumstances which are peculiar to the accused, a reasonable possibility of the presence of the accused not being secured at the trial, reasonable apprehension of witnesses being tempered with, the interest of the public or the State and similar other considerations before granting the bail.[202]

The power of the Court is discretionary. It has to be exercised with great care and caution by balancing the individual right of liberty with the interest of the society in general. The Court has to state reasons for its order.[203]

Constitutional Validity

The mere fact that the Section makes a distinction between persons accused of graver offences and of lesser offences or that exceptions are created in favour of (a) young persons, (b) women, and (c) infirm persons does not make the Section constitutionally invalid being hit by Article 14 of the Constitution. The classification is based on intelligible differentia and has reasonable relation to the object of legislation in the matter of grant of bail.[204]

The Supreme Court has ruled in a number of cases that the object of granting bail is to secure the attendance of the accused before the Court at the time of inquiry or trial and not to punish him. Therefore, law favours grant of bail as a rule, and its refusal and exceptional cases.[205]

The observations of the Apex Court in *State of Rajasthan v. Bal Chand*,[206] sufficiently highlight the desirability of judicious approach towards granting bail to persons accused of a non-bailable offence. The Court *inter alia* observed:

The basic rule perhaps is tersely put as bail and not jail except where there are circumstances suggestive of fleeing from justice or thwarting the course of justice or creating other troubles in the shape of repeating offences or intimidating witnesses and the like, by the petitioner who seeks enlargement on bail from Court. It is true that the gravity of the offence involved is likely to induce the petitioner to avoid the course of justice and must weigh the Court when considering the question of bail. So, also the heinousness of the crime. . .

Broadly speaking, the Court or the police officer, while considering grant of bail in case of non-bailable offences, should refer to the following circumstances:

(i) the nature of accusation or charge;
(ii) the nature and character of evidence in support of the charge;
(iii) the severity of sentence which conviction will entail;
(iv) the possibility of the accused of fleeing or absconding on his release on bail;
(v) the apprehension of witnesses being tampered with or bribed or thr atened;
(vi) the protracted nature of the trial;
(vii) personal antecedents and conduct of the accused including his health, age, sex, family background, social status etc.
(viii) the circumstances under which the offence has been committed;
(ix) the large interest of public safety or State security and past conduct of the accused.[207]

Conditions on Bail

As per Section 437, if any person accused of an offence punishable with 7 years or more of imprisonment, or when the offence is against the State or against the human body or against property or; where the offences are of abetment of, conspiracy to, or attempt to commit any such offence as mentioned above. The Court and not the police officer to impose conditions as necessary in the circumstances in order to ensure that the accused shall attend the Court or not repeat the offence or otherwise not interfere with the course of justice.[208]

Cancellation of Bail

As per Section 437(5) any Court which has released a person on bail under Section 437(1) or 437(2), may direct that such person be arrested and commit him to custody. This basically cancels the bail. However, it must be noted that only the Court that has given the bail can cancel it. Thus, a bail given by a police officer cannot be cancelled by a Court under this Section. To do so the special power of High Court or Court of Session under Section 439 has to be invoked.

The new Section 439 explicitly gives the power to High Court and Court of Session to direct that any person who has been released on bail be arrested and to commit him to custody. The power given by Section 439 for cancellation has no riders. It is a discretionary power. It is not necessary that some new events should take place subsequent to the offender's release on bail for the Session judge to cancel his bail; however, the Court usually bases its decision of cancellation on subsequent events.

For example, in the case of *Surender Singh v. State of Bihar*,[209] Patna High Court pointed out that a bail may be cancelled on following grounds:

(i) When accused is found tampering with the evidence during the investigation or trial; or
(ii) If he commits a heinous offence during the period of bail; or
(iii) Where he absconds and delays the trial; or
(iv) Creates a serious law and order problem for the State; or
(v) If the Court finds that the accused has misused the privileges of bail.
(vi) When the life of accused itself, is in danger.

The basic criterion for cancellation of bail is interference or even an attempt to interfere with the due course of justice or any abuse of the indulgence/privilege granted to the accused.

(vi) Bail to require accused to appear before next appellate Court (Section 437A)[210]

To ensure presence of the person acquitted or discharged

Section 437A is inserted, which provides that before conclusion of the trial and before disposal of the appeal, the Court trying the offence or the Appellate Court, as the case may be, shall require the accused to execute bail bonds with sureties, to appear before the higher Court as and when such Court issues notice in respect of any appeal or petition filed against the judgment of the respective Court and such bail bonds shall be in force for six months. It further provides that if such accused fails to appear, the bond shall stand forfeited and the procedure under Section 446 shall apply.[211]

(vii) Direction for grant of bail to person apprehending arrest (Section 438)

Right to Anticipatory Bail

Section 438 deals with this right of the accused. Special powers have been conferred only on the High Court and Court of Session for directing a person on bail previous to his arrest, what is commonly known as anticipatory bail, imposing such conditions as the Court thinks fit. The order of anticipatory bail shall take effect at the time of arrest.[212]

This Section empowers the High Court and the Court of Session to grant anticipatory bail to a person who has a reasonable apprehension that he is likely to be arrested for accusation of having committed a non-cognizable offence.[213] Thus, anticipatory bail is a direction to release a person on bail issued even before he is arrested. The higher Court under this Section is to pass an order that the applicant for anticipatory bail be released on bail in the event he is arrested. Therefore, the order is operative only before the arrest of the applicant and not after he has already been arrested.[214]

Commenting on the necessity of the provision relating to grant of anticipatory bail to person who reasonably apprehended their arrest for non bailable offence, the law commission of India observed:

The necessity for granting anticipatory bail arises mainly because sometimes influential person try to implicate their rivals in false cases for the purpose of disgracing them or for other purposes by getting them detained in jail . . . apart from false cases, where there are reasonable grounds for holding that a person accused of an offence is not likely to abscond, or otherwise misuse his liberty while on bail, there seems no jurisdiction to require him first to submit to custody, remain in prison for some days and then apply for bail".[215]

Thus, the object of this provision is to see that the liberty of a person is not put in jeopardy on frivolous grounds at the instance of influential or irresponsible persons. However, with a view to ensure that the provision of anticipatory bail is not misused by unscrupulous applicants, the Section provides that Court should grant such bail only in exceptional cases and that too after issuing notice to the prosecution.[216] It should also record reasons for granting the anticipatory bail in writing.[217] The Court before granting anticipatory bail must ensure that the applicant would not abscond or hamper the cause of justice or otherwise misuse his liberty. Mere possibility of an accusation of some non bailable offence will not justify grant of anticipatory bail unless specific accusation based on reasonable ground to apprehend arrest are brought before the Court by the applicant.[218]

The term 'anticipatory bail' is really a misnomer, because what Section 438 contemplates is not anticipatory bail, but merely an order releasing the accused on bail in the event of his arrest. It is manifest that there can be no question of bail unless a person is under detention or custody.

The High Court or the Court of Session may, in its discretion, impose conditions including:

(a) A condition that the person shall make himself available for interrogation by a police officer as and when required;
(b) A condition that the person shall not make any inducement, threat or promise to any person for dissuading him from disclosing the facts of the case to the Court or to the police;
(c) A condition that the person shall not leave India without the previous permission of the Court;
(d) Such other conditions as deemed to be essential.[219]

In granting anticipatory bail the Court takes into account the following considerations:

(a) The nature and gravity of the accusation;
(b) The antecedents on the applicant including the fact as to whether he has previously been imprisoned upon a conviction by a Court in respect of a cognizable offence.
(c) The possibility of the accused to flee from justice;
(d) Whether the accusation has been made with the object of

injuring or humiliating the applicant by having him arrested.

Refusal of Anticipatory Bail

There are certain situations where such bail is normally not granted. These are:

- In case of dowry death or wife harassment.
- In case of economic offences.
- In case of atrocious crimes.

Cancellation of Anticipatory Bail

There is no specific provision that allows a Court to cancel the order of anticipatory bail. However, in several cases it has been held that when Section 438 permits granting anticipatory bail, it is implicit that the Court making such order is entitled upon appropriate considerations to cancel or recall the order.[220]

(viii) Special powers of the High Court or Court of Session regarding Bail

Section 439 gives an unfettered discretion on the High Court or Court of Session to admit an accused person to bail, but that discretion must be exercised judicially. The Section applies only to persons who are accused and not convicted persons. These Courts have discretion to grant bail without any restrictions or fetters and the power extends to grant of bail even in cases involving an offence punishable with death or imprisonment for life or imprisonment for a term of seven years or more. Normally, application for grant of bail under this Section should first be moved to the Sessions Court and it is only in exceptional or special circumstances that the High Court should be directly approached for this purpose.[221]

Section 439 empowers the higher Courts to order release of the accused on interim bail pending final disposal of his bail application.

Interim bail may be granted in the following cases:

(i) In trivial offences where bail is granted as a matter of fact/course;
(ii) In case of women, minors and children or aged persons of 70 years or more;
(iii) Persons seriously suffering from some incurable disease who need medical care;
(iv) Students who are taking some examination;

(v) Cases where in the accusation apparently appears to be mala fide etc.

Thus, from the above discussion it has been clearly stated that, at the present stage of civilisation, it has been universally accepted as a human value that a person accused of any offence should not be punished unless he has been a fair trial and his guilt has been proved in such trial. Fairness is a relative concept and therefore fairness in criminal trial could be measured only in relation to the gravity of the accusation, the time and resources which the society can reasonably afford to spend, the quality of available resources, the prevailing social values etc. It is very much clear that everyone is entitled in full equality to fair and public hearing by an independent and impartial tribunal in the determination of his rights and obligations of any criminal charge against him. Everyone charged with any offence has the right to be presumed innocent until proved guilty according to law. Our Courts have recognised that the primary object of criminal procedure is to ensure a fair trial of accused persons. Hence, it is known to us that the code of Criminal Procedure, 1973 provide number of rights for the protection of the accused.

Notes and References

1. P. Ramanatha Aiyar, *Concise Law Dictionary*, (2006).
2. *Directorate of Enforcement* v. *Deepak Mahajan*, AIR 1994 SC 1775, 1796.
3. *Amin* v. *State*, AIR 1958 All 293, 302.
4. *Veera Ibrahim* v. *State of Maharashtra*, AIR 1976 SC 1167 at 1169.
5. *Abraham Verghese* v. *State of Kerala*, AIR 1965 Ker 175, 176.
6. "Definition of accused", *Black Law Dictionary*.
7. "Definition of accused", *Law Lexicon*.
8. Vivek Jain, "Rights of Accused", National Law University, Orissa, available at *www.mightlylaws.in/511/rights_accused*.
9. Prof. R. Deb, "Rights of the Accused under the Law". Also see *Kishare Singh R. Dev.* v. *State of Rajasthan*, AIR 1981 SC 625.
10. "Indian Criminal Defence Manual – Rights of the accused and Exceptional circumstances", available at *www.wiki.ibj.org/index.php/india...*
11. R.V. Kelkar, *Criminal Procedure*. Dr. K.N. Chandrasekharan Pillai, 48 (2011).
12. *Ibid.*
13. *Avinash Madhukar Mukhedkar* v. *State of Maharashtra*, 1983 Cri LJ 1833 (Bom).
14. *Behary*, 71 WR Cr 3.
15. *K.V. Muhammad* v. *Chakkappayyan Kannan*, AIR 1943 Mad 218.
16. *Emperor* v. *Vimlabai Deshpande*, AIR 1946 PC 123.
17. *Ramprit*, AIR 1926 Punj 560.

18. Dr. Ashutosh, *Rights of Accused*, 12 (2013).
19. Sub-Section 1.
20. Sub-Section 2.
21. Sub-Section 3.
22. Sub-Section 4 substituted by Criminal Procedure Code (Amendment) Act, 2010 (41 of 2010), Section 3(b) for sub-Section 4 (w.e.f. 02.11.2010).
23. AIR 1974 SC 2092: (1975) 3 SCC 185: 1974 SCC (Cri) 803.
24. *Ibid.*
25. Inserted by Criminal Procedure Code (Amendment) Act, 2008.
26. Inserted by Criminal Procedure Code (Amendment) Act, 2008.
27. Rattanlal and Dhirajlal, *The Code of Criminal Procedure,* 70 (2012).
28. *Gopal Naidu*, (1922) 46 Mad 605: AIR 1923 Mad 528 (FB).
29. *Goolale Rasul,* (1903) 5 Bom LR 597. Also see *Gopal Naidu* v. *Emperor,* AIR 1923 Mad 523.
30. *Bolai De,* (1907) 35 Cal 361; *Durga Singh* v. *Md. Isa,* (1963) 1 Cri LJ 827.
31. *Ramaswami Ayyar,* AIR 1921 Mad 458.
32. *Kokul Tatwa* v. *Emperor*, AIR 1926 Pat 23.
33. *Kartar Singh* v. *State*, AIR 1956 Punj 122.
34. *Roshan Beevi* v. *Jt. Secy. to Govt. of T.N.,* 1984 Cri LJ 134 (FB) (Mad).
35. *Thaneil Victor* v. *State*, 1991 Cri LJ 2416 (Mad).
36. *Sheo Balak Dusadh* v. *Emperor*, AIR 1948 All 103.
37. *Dakhi Singh* v. *State*, AIR 1955 All 379.
38. *Supra* note 18 at 15.
39. *State of Maharashtra* v. *Christian Community W.C. of India*, AIR 2004 SC 7.
40. N.V. Paranjape, *The Code of Criminal Procedure*, 59 (2012).
41. *Ibid.*
42. *Madhu Limye* v. *State of Bihar*, AIR 1969 SC 1014.
43. *Govind Prasad* v. *State of West Bengal*, 1975 Cri LJ 1249 (Cal).
44. *Harikishan* v. *State of Maharashtra*, AIR 1962 SC 911, 914.
45. 1999 Cri LJ 274 (All).
46. *Rabindranath Prusty* v. *State of Orissa*, 1984 Cri LJ 1392 (Ori).
47. *Raghubir Singh* v. *State of Punjab*, AIR 1976 SC 91.
48. *Supra* note 18 at 17.
49. *Bhondar* v. *Emperor*, AIR 1931 Cal 601.
50. *Mahadeo* v. *State*, 1990 Cri LJ 858 (All).
51. Shailender Malik, *The Code of Criminal Procedure*, 56 (2011).
52. *Anant Kumar* v. *State of U.P.*, 1977 Cri LJ 1797.
53. 1993 Cri LJ 2266 (All).
54. *Ibid.*
55. Inserted by Code of Criminal Procedure (Amendment) Act, 2005.
56. *Supra* note 28 at 81.
57. Inserted by Criminal Procedure Code (Amendment) Act, 2005.
58. AIR 1974 SC 2092: 1975 Cri LJ 556.
59. 1995 Cri LJ 974 (Guj).
60. (1971) 2 SCC 76.
61. *Birbhadra* v. *District Magistrate, Ajamgarh,* AIR 1953 All 384.

62. *State of U.P.* v. *Ram Chandra*, AIR 1955 All 438; also see *Mulla Singh* v. *State*, AIR 1968 Al 132.
63. Inserted by Criminal Procedure Code (Amendment) Act, 2005.
64. *Supra* note 40 at 66.
65. *Khatri* v. *State of Bihar*, AIR 1981 SC 928.
66. *In t re, Nagendra Nath Chakravarti*, AIR 1924 Cal 476.
67. *Manoj* v. *State of M.P.*, (1999) 3 SCC 715.
68. *Sharifbai* v. *Abdul Rajak*, AIR 1961 Bom 62.
69. Inserted to Criminal Procedure Code (Amendment) Act, 2008.
70. *Jagdish Chander Bhatia* v. *State*, 1983 Cri LJ NOC 235 (Del).
71. *Mh. Ali* v. *Ram Swarup*, AIR 1965 All 161.
72. *Gangadharan* v. *Chellappan*, 1985 Cri LJ 1517.
73. *S.M. Sachdev* v. *State*, 1991 Cri LJ 300 (Del).
74. *Supra* note 18 at 23.
75. AIR 1954 SC 300.
76. *Amina Bewa* v. *Dukhmoni Dasi*, 1957 Cri LJ 669.
77. *Revanappa* v. *S.N. Ragunath*, 1983 Cri LJ 321 (Karn).
78. *Banarsi Lal* v. *Neelam*, AIR 1969 Del 304.
79. *Duryodhan Mohanta* v. *S. Mahanta*, 1992 Cri LJ 2231 (Cri).
80. *Emperor* v. *Balai Ghose*, AIR 1930 Cal 141 at 143.
81. *State of Bihar* v. *Kapil Singh*, AIR 1969 SC 53.
82. *Rabindranath* v. *State of Orissa*, 1984 Cri LJ 1392 (Ori).
83. *New Swadesh Mills Ahmedabad* v. *S.K. Rattan*, (1967) 9 Guj LR 364.
84. *State* v. *Tanman*, AIR 1960 SC 210.
85. *Supra* note 18 at 27.
86. *Supra* note 83.
87. *Supra* note 27 at 80.
88. *Ibid.*
89. *Id.*, at 81.
90. *Mohd. Suleman* v. *King Emperor*, 30 CWN 985, 987 (FB).
91. *Hari Om Prasad* v. *State of Bihar*, 1999 Cri LJ 4400 (Pat).
92. *Khatri (II)* v. *State of Bihar*, 1981 SCC (Cri) 228, 223; *D.G. and I.G. of Police* v. *Prem Sagar*, (1999) 5 SCC 700.
93. *Supra* note 51 at 681.
94. *State of Punjab* v. *Sarwan Singh*, 1981 Cri LJ 722.
95. *Supra* note 40 at 535-42.
96. *Harjiwan Laxman Patel* v. *State of Gujarat*, 1981 Guj LR 264 at 266.
97. *Nandini Satpathy* v. *P.L. Dani*, AIR 1978 SC 1025.
98. *M.N. Shreedharan* v. *State of Kerala*, 1981 Cri LJ 119.
99. Inserted by the Criminal Law (Amendment) Act, 2013 [Act No. 13 of 2013].
100. *Baliram* v. *Emperor*, ILR 1945 Nag 151.
101. *Pakala Narayanswami* v. *Emperor*, AIR 1939 PC 47.
102. *Aghnoo Nageria* v. *State of Bihar*, AIR 1966 SC 119.
103. *State of A.P.* v. *N. Venugopal*, AIR 1964 SC 33.
104. *Ranbir* v. *State of Punjab*, AIR 1973 SC 1409.
105. Inserted by the Criminal Law (Amendment) Act, 2013.
106. AIR 1964 SC 33.

107. *Rishi* v. *State of Bihar*, AIR 1955 Pat 425.
108. *Kuthu Goala* v. *State of Assam*, 1981 Cri LJ 424.
109. Inserted by the Criminal Law (Amendment) Act, 2013.
110. *P. Ranjangam* v. *State of Madras*, AIR 1959 Mad 294.
111. Inserted by Code of Criminal Procedure (Amendment) Act, 2005.
112. *Law Commission of India*, 14th Report, Vol. I, 587-600.
113. Fundamental Constitutional Rights as criminally accused person, available at *www.lawinfaboulder.com/criminal_con....*
114. *Moti Bai* v. *State*, AIR 1954 Raj 241.
115. *Kuthu Goala* v. *State of Assam*, 1981 Cri LJ 424 (Gau).
116. *Hansraj*, AIR 1956 SC 641.
117. *Supra* note 51 at 421.
118. 1995 Cri LJ 1231 (Raj).
119. AIR 1986 SC 911.
120. *T.R. Ganesan*, (1951) Mad 246.
121. *Supra* note 18 at 32.
122. *B. Singh* v. *State of Orissa*, 1990 Cri LJ 397 (Ori).
123. *Bigan Singh*, (1927) 6 Pat 691.
124. *Talab Haji Hussain* v. *State*, AIR 1958 SC 376 at 380.
125. *Ananta Singh* v. *State*, 1972 Cri LJ 1327 (Cal).
126. Vivek Jain, "Rights of Accused", *Mighty laws in Article for blog post-writing competition*, 2011.
127. *Supra* note 27 at 497.
128. *Gurbachan Singh* v. *State of Punjab*, AIR 1957 SC 623; *Brijendra Nath Kalay* v. *State*, 1994 Cri LJ 1194 (Cal).
129. *Gayadhar* v. *State*, 1985 Cri LJ (NOC) 108 (Ori).
130. *Sidharth Vashist* v. *State (NCT) of Delhi*, AIR 2010 SC 2352.
131. *Sheikh Mehebob* v. *State of Maharashtra*, AIR 2005 SC 1085.
132. *Gurbachan Singh* v. *State of Punjab*, AIR 1957 SC 623
133. *Rosy* v. *State of Kerala*, AIR 2000 SC 637.
134. *V.C. Shukla* v. *State (CBI)*, (1980) Supp SCC 92.
135. *Mannalal*, AIR 1967 Cal 478.
136. *Pratap Singh* v. *State of Rajasthan*, 1996 Cri LJ 4214 (Raj).
137. *Sheo Sankar*, 26 Cri LJ 62.
138. *Supra* note 27 at 508.
139. *Jaswant Rai* v. *State of Bombay*, AIR 1956 SC 575.
140. *Premgir* v. *Emperor*, AIR 1918 All 298.
141. *Supra* note 18 at 39.
142. *Supra* note 8.
143. *Debi Sah*, AIR 1943 Punj 359.
144. *Mohd. J. Rehman* v. *State of Assam*, 2005 Cri LJ 4245 (Gau).
145. *Bijoy*, AIR 1958 Cal 121.
146. *S.R. Chandra* v. *State of Karnataka*, (1978) 2 Kant LJ 459.
147. *Amritalal* v. *Suratha Lal*, AIR 1942 Cal 553.
148. *Vassiliadesh* v. *Vassiliades*, AIR 1945 PC 38.
149. State v. *Ravi Kant Sharma*, 2005 (2) SCC 347.
150. *Supra* note 18 at 43.
151. *Ibid.*

152. Neeraj Arora, "Plea Bargaining - A New Development in the Criminal Justice System", other laws, 18.12.2010.
153. Sourasubha, "Plea Bargaining - An analysis of the concept", available at www.legalserviceindia.com/articles/....
154. 2000 Cri LJ 384 at 386.
155. *Ibid.*
156. (2005) Cri LJ 2957.
157. *Supra* note 18 at 47.
158. *Ibid.*
159. *Idat*, p. 48.
160. AIR 1976 SC 2306.
161. *Shiv Mohan Singh* v. *State (Delhi Admn.)*, AIR 1977 SC 949.
162. *Mohammad Giasuddin* v. *State of A.P.*, AIR 1977 SC 1926.
163. 2002 Cri LJ 271 (All).
164. *Parichhat* v. *State of M.P.*, AIR 1972 SC 535.
165. *Keki Bejonji* v. *State of Bombay*, AIR 1961 SC 967.
166. *Shvaji* v. *State of Maharashtra*, AIR 1973 SC 2622.
167. 2002 Cri LJ 4330 at 4333 (SC).
168. AIR 2007 SC 848.
169. *Bidyanath P. Shrivastva* v. *State of Bihar*, AIR 1968 SC 1393.
170. *Jibach Shah* v. *State*, AIR 1965; *People's Ins. Co. Ltd.* v. *Sardar Sardul*, AIR 1962 Punj 101.
171. *Tukaram G. Gaokar* v. *R.N. Shukla*, AIR 1968 SC 1050.
172. (1978) 3 SCC 544.
173. *Supra* note 40 at 432.
174. 1999 Cri LJ 1438 (MP).
175. *Kochummihi C.R. Chettiar* v. *State of Kerala*, 1977 Cri LJ 1872.
176. *Shambhu* v. *State*, AIR 1956 All 633: 1956 Cri LJ 1179.
177. (1999) 4 SCC 421.
178. Inserted by Criminal Procedure Code (Amendment) Act, 2005.
179. *Supra* note 40 at 337.
180. *Natrajan* v. *State*, 1991 Cri LJ 2329 (Mad).
181. *Govind Prasad* v. *State of W.B.*, 1975 Cri LJ 1249, 1255.
182. "Article on Bail", available at www.legalhelplineindia.com/criminal....
183. *Ibid.*
184. *Chadayam Makki* v. *State of Kerala*, 1980 Cri LJ 1195.
185. AIR 2001 SC 1910.
186. *Supra* note 51 at 235.
187. *Babubhai P. Patel* v. *State of Gujarat*, AIR 1982 Guj 72.
188. *Rajnikant J. Patel and another* v. *I.O., Narcotic Control Bureau, New Delhi*, AIR 1990 SC 71.
189. Section 167(2-A) of Criminal Procedure Code.
190. 1982 Cri LJ 1103.
191. *Ramesh Kumar Ravi* v. *State of Bihar*, 1987 Cri LJ 1489 (Pat).
192. 1969 Cri LJ 1440.
193. Section 167 (5) of Criminal Procedure Code.
194. Section 167 (6) of Criminal Procedure Code. *Supra* note 11 at 73.
195. AIR 1979 SC 1377. See also *Khatri II* v. *State of Bihar*, (1981) 1 SCC 627.

196. *Hirender* v. *Thakur* v. *State of Maharashtra*, AIR 1994 SC 2623.
197. Inserted by Code of Criminal Procedure (Amendment) Act, 2008.
198. *Chowriappa Constructions, M/s* v. *M/s Embassy Constrns, and Devpt. P. Ltd.*, 2002 Cri LJ 3863.
199. *Afasr Khan* v. *State of Karnataka*, 1992 Cri LJ 1676 (Kant).
200. *Supra* note 51 at 618.
201. *Venkataramanappa* v. *State of Karnataka*, 1992 Cri LJ 2268.
202. *Supra* note 27 at 986.
203. *Mansab Ali* v. *Insan*, AIR 2003 SC 707.
204. *Shehat Ali* v. *State of Rajasthan*, 1992 Cri LJ 1335 (Raj).
205. *Sagri Bhagat* v. *State of Bihar*, AIR 1951 Pat 497.
206. AIR 1977 SC 2447.
207. *Supra* note 40 at 494.
208. *Ananth Kumar* v. *State of A.P.*, 1977 Cri LJ 1797 (AP).
209. 1990 Cri LJ 1904 (Pat).
210. Inserted by Criminal Procedure Code (Amendment) Act, 2008.
211. *Supra* note 18 at 66.
212. *Gurbaksh Singh Sibbia* v. *State of Punjab*, AIR 1980 SC 1632.
213. *Chandrashekhara Rao* v. *Kamla Kumari*, 1995 Cri LJ 3508 (AP).
214. *Balchand Jain* v. *State of M.P.*, AIR 1977 SC 366.
215. Law Commission of India, 41st Report, p. 321, para 39.9.
216. *Balchand Jain* v. *State of M.P.*, AIR 1977 SC 366.
217. *Pokar Ram* v. *State of Rajasthan*, AIR 1985 SC 969.
218. *Sajjan Kumar* v. *State*, 1993 Cri LJ 1493 (Del).
219. *Supra* note 11 at 117.
220. *Supra* note 157.
221. *Haji Alishar* v. *State of Rajasthan*, 1976 Cri LJ 1658 (Raj).

3

Rights of Accused and the Indian Constitution

The accused in India are provided with certain rights, the most basic of which are found in the Indian Constitution. The general theory behind these rights is that the government has enormous resources available to it for the prosecution of individuals, and individuals therefore are entitled to some protection from misuse of those powers by the government. Many admirers of India often go out of the way to depict India as the "world's largest democracy" and a "secular" State, which through its Constitution guarantees fundamental human rights to all Indians–the implication being that such rights are in practice as a matter of routine. The Constitution of India is one of the most right based Constitutions in the world. Drafted around the same time as the Universal Declaration of Human Rights 1948 was adopted, the Indian Constitution Captures the essence of human rights in its preamble and the Sections on Fundamental Rights and the Directive Principles of the State Policy. The Constitution of India is based on the principles that guided India's struggle against a colonial regime that consistently violated the civil, political, social, economic and cultural rights of the people of India. On 10th December, 1948, when the Constitution of India was in the making, the General Assembly proclaimed and adopted the Universal Declaration of Human Rights, which surely influenced the framing of India's Constitution. It is evident that the Constituent Assembly was mainly concerned with the welfare of the masses and to secure all persons basic human rights, is implicit from the prembular promise, fundamental rights, directive principles and various other provisions of the Constitution.

(A) RIGHTS OF ACCUSED AND FUNDAMENTAL RIGHTS GUARANTEED UNDER THE CONSTITUTION

The Indian Constitution bears the impact of the Universal Declaration of Human Rights and this has been recognized by the Supreme Court of India. while referring to the Fundamental rights contained in part III of the Constitution, Sikri, C.J. of the Supreme Court in *Kesavanand Bharti* v. *State of Kerala*:[1]

Observed

> "I am unable to held these provisions how that rights are not natural or inalienable rights. As a matter of fact, India was a party to the Universal Declaration of Rights . . . . And that Declaration describes some fundamental rights as inalienable". Earlier, in *Golak Nath* v. *State of Punjab*.[2] The Supreme Court observed:
>
> Fundamental rights are the modern name for what have been traditionally known as 'natural rights'.

The Constitution provides a number of rights to individuals in Part III which have been termed as "fundamental rights". The expression "fundamental" denotes that these rights are inherent in all the human personality and soul. These rights represent the basic values of a civilized society. These rights are therefore calculated to protect the dignity of the individuals and create condition in which every human being can develop his personality to the fullest extent.[3] In *State of West Bengal* v. *Subodh Gopal Bose*,[4] the Chief Justice Patanjali Shaatri has referred to fundamental rights as 'those great and basic rights which are recognized and guaranteed as the natural rights inherent in the status of a citizen of a free Country.

The rights of the accused are important because they protect the accused from unlawful search and seizure, unlawful arrests and illegal interrogations. It is also important that they are informed of their rights prior to questioning. This is done to prevent self incrimination. Fundamental rights as enacted in our Constitution not only recognize the dignity of the individual to which the preamble refers, but also recognize their necessity for full development of the individual and also for preserving the unity of India. Constitution of India confers on any person the right to practice, profess and propagate religion and confers on religious denominations the right to manage their own affairs in matters of religion. The unity of India, in the sense that India, not withstanding its divisions into several States is one Country, and all its inhabitants are the inhabitants of that one country, is provided for by making provisions for the protection of certain rights regarding freedom of speech etc. in part III of the Constitution pertaining to fundamental rights.[5]

Enforcement of Fundamental Rights

As it is very much clear to us that the mere declaration of rights is worthless without the will or the means to enforce them. The frames of our Constitution had the will and therefore they adopted the means, for such enforcement. To that end, it expressly declares any law violating fundamental rights to be *pro tanto* void.[6] Secondly, the Supreme Court was armed with the power to issue the historic writs of *habeas corpus*, *mandamus*, prohibition, *certiorari* and *quo warranto* for the enforcement of fundamental right.[7] And that provision was itself made a fundamental right. Further, the High Courts were also armed with the power to issue the same writs, not only for the enforcement of fundamental rights but also for any other purpose.[8]

The Fundamental Rights are not absolute rights

The absolute concept of liberty and equality are very difficult to achieve in modern welfare society. That is why the fundamental rights have been provided not in absolute terms. The form in which such rights have been provided is in the form of restriction which the government is expected to follow in the governance of the Country. However, the enjoyment of these rights is subjected to the interest of people. The State may, therefore, encroach on the domain of these rights for the common good or common interest.

Study of Articles 19 to 22, as contained in Part III of the Constitution of India, would reveal that even the Constitution has guaranteed certain rights to the accused. Article 19 of the Constitution guarantees certain freedoms to the citizens only and also the restrictions that may be imposed on them by the State. Article 20 deals with the protection in respect of conviction for offences under certain circumstances. Article 21 specifically deals with the protection of life and personal liberty. Article 22 provides for certain safeguards to the persons arrested or detained. The fundamental right to life, which Article 21 deals with, is the most precious human right and 'forms the arc of all other rights'.[9] Therefore, the present work start the study of topic i.e. rights of accused and Indian Constitution with respect to Articles 14, 19, 20, 21 and 22 of the Constitution.

(i) Right to equality, right to freedom for the accused under the Indian Constitution

Both these articles have a great relevance regarding the rights of accused. We have to discuss about these articles under the following heads:

(a) Right to equality and equal protection of law Article 14

The concept of equality has been held basic to the rule of law and is regarded as the most fundamental postulate of republicanism. In *Indira Nehru Gandhi* v. *Raj Narain*,[10] the majority of the Supreme Court has held that the right to equality conferred by Article 14 is a basic structure of the Constitution and an essential feature of democracy or rule of law. In *Secretary, H.S.E.B.* v. *Suresh*,[11] it has been held that the equality clause, embodied in Article 14, does not speak of mere formal equality before the law but embodies the concept of real and substantive equality which strikes at the inequalities arising on account of vast social and economic differentiation and is thus consequently an essential ingredient of social and economic justice.

Article 14 embodies the general principles of equality before law and prohibits unreasonable discrimination between persons. Article 14 declares that 'the State shall not deny to any person equality before the law or the equal protection of the laws within the territory of India'.

In *Chiranjit Lal* v. *Union of India*,[12] the Supreme Court stated that the equality before the law is guaranteed to all without regard to race, colour or nationality. The protection of Article 14 extends to both citizens and non citizens and to natural person as well as legal persons.

Article 14 of the Constitution embodies the principle of "non discrimination". Articles 21 and 14 are the heart of the chapter on fundamental rights. The Supreme Court in *M.G. Badappanavar* v. *State of Karnataka*[13] stated that "equality is a basic feature of the Constitution of India and any treatment of equals unequally or unequals as equals will be violation of basic structure of the Constitution of India".

(i) *Right to a fair trial*

Conducting a fair trial for those who are accused of criminal offences is the cornerstone of democracy. Conducting a fair trial is beneficial both to the accused as well as to the society. A conviction resulting from an unfair trial is contrary to our concept of justice.[14] Fair trial obviously would mean a trial before an impartial judge, a fair prosecutor and an atmosphere of judicial calm. Fair trial means a trial in which bias or prejudice for or against the accused, the witnesses or the cause which is being tried is eliminated.

In *Prem Shankar* v. *Delhi Administration*,[15] the Supreme Court has declared that hand cuffing is prima facie "inhuman, and, therefore unreasonable is over harsh and arbitrary." Accordingly, the Court has held that a rule requiring every undertrial person accused of a non bailable offence punishable with more than 3 years' prison term to be routinely handcuffed during transit from prison to Court for trial violates Articles 14, 19 and 21. The Court has declared it to be a constitutional mandate that no prisoner is to be handcuffed or fettered routinely or merely for the convenience of the custodian or the Courts. This distinction between classes of prisoners becomes constitutionally obsolete for this purpose as it cannot be assumed that a rich criminal or undertrial is any different from a poor undertrial in the matter of security risk. To be consistent with Articles 14 and 19, handcuffs must be the last refuge, not the routine regimen. Thus, the hand cuffing is violative of Articles 14 and 21 of the Constitution. Time and again, the Supreme Court has emphasised that Articles 14, 19 and 21 "are available to prisoners as well as freeman. Prison walls do not keep out fundamental rights."[16] In *Sunil Batra* v. *Delhi Adm.*,[17] the Court has observed:

We cannot be oblivious to the fact that the treatment of a human being which offends human dignity, imposes avoidable torture and reduces the man to the level of a beast would certainly be arbitrary and can be questioned under Article 14.

In *Kishor Singh* v. *State of Rajasthan*,[18] the Court emphasised that no solitary confinement and imposition of bar fetters should take place, "save in the rarest of rare cases and with strict adherence to procedural safeguards. Articles 14, 19 and 21 operate within the prisons". Human dignity is not to be ignored even in prisons.

(ii) Right to be presumed innocent

The presumption of innocence has been accepted as a central safeguard against the exercise of arbitrary power by public authorities. It means the prosecution has the ultimate burden of establishing guilt. If, at the conclusion of the case, there is any reasonable doubt on any element of the offence charged, an accused person must be acquitted. In India, a system of adversarial form of adjudication is followed which is also known as "accusatorial system" in case of criminal procedure and the underlying principle of this system is "presumption of innocent until proved guilty. The legal ethics of our criminal system is "let thousand of criminal's be let out but a single innocent should not be punished". Thus, as per Article 14 of the Constitution all people shall be equal before the Courts. Article 14 prohibits discrimination between one person and another.

(b) Freedom of Speech and Expression [Article 19(1) (a)]

Freedom of speech and expression is indispensable in a democracy. In *Romesh Thapper* v. *State of Madras*,[19] Patanjali Sastri, J., rightly observed that:

Freedom of speech and of the press laid at the foundation of all democratic organisations, for without free political discussion no public education, so essential for the proper functioning of the process of popular government, is possible. Article 19(1) (a) says that all citizens shall have the right to freedom of speech and expression. But this right is subject to limitations imposed under Article 19(2). Freedom of speech and expression means the right to express one's own convictions and opinions freely by words of mouth, writing, printing, pictures or any other mode. It thus includes the expression of one's ideas through any communicable medium or visible representation, such as, gesture, signs and the like.[20]

(i) Right of the convict to express himself

In *M. Hasan* v. *Government of A.P.*,[21] the Andhra Pradesh High Court held that refusal to journalist and videographers seeking interview with condemned prisoners amounted to deprivation of citizen's fundamental right to speech and expression under Article 19(1) (a). As far the exercise of fundamental rights concerned, the Court said, position of a condemned prisoner was on par with a free citizen. He had a right, the Court ruled, to give his ideas and was entitled to be interviewed or to be televised. In *Prabhu Dutt* v. *Union of India*,[22] the Supreme Court held that the press to interview prisoners sentenced to death. In *Francis Coralie Mullin* v. *Union Territory of Delhi*,[23] J. Bhagwati has observed: we think that the right to life includes the right to live with human dignity and all that goes along with it, namely, the bare necessaries of life such as adequate nutrition, clothing and shelter over the head and facilities for reading, writing and expressing oneself in diverse forms, freely moving about and mixing and commingling with fellow human beings". The Court further stated that the right of a detenu to have interviews with her friends and family members, Bhagwati J. held that personal liberty includes right to socialise with family members and friends as well as to have interviews with her friends. In *R. Rajagopal* v. *State of T.N.*,[24] the right to publish the life story of a condemned prisoner, in so far as, it appears from the public records, even without his consent or authorisation, has been held to be included in the freedom of the press guaranteed under Article 19(1)(a). No prior restraint upon such publication can be imposed.

Thus, it has been rightly said that these rights are great and basic rights which are recognised and guaranteed as the natural rights, inherent in the status of a citizen of a free country but not absolute in nature and uncontrolled in operation.

(ii) Protection in respect of conviction for offences [Article 20]

Article 20 provides protection in respect of conviction for offences. The protection contained in Article 20 is available to all persons, citizens or non-citizens. Article 20 of the Constitution generally provides for, no person shall be convicted of any offence except for violation of a law in force at the time of the commission of the Act charged as an offence, nor be subjected to a penalty greater than that might be inflicted under the law in force at the time of the commission of the offence.

- No person shall be prosecuted and punished for the same offence more than once.
- No person accused of any offence shall be compelled to be witness against himself.

(a) Protection given to person charged with a crime before a criminal Court, i.e. protection against ex-post facto law [Article 20(1)]

Clause (1) of Article 20 of the Indian Constitution says that "no person shall be convicted of any offence except for violation of a law in force at the time of the commission of the act charged as an offence, nor be subjected to a penalty greater than that which might have been inflicted under the law in force at the time of the commission of the offence. In *State of Maharashtra* v. *K.K.S. Ramaswamy*,[25] stated that immunity is thus provided to a person from being tried for an act, under a law enacted subsequently, which makes the act unlawful. This means that if an act is not an offence on the date of its commission, a law enacted in future cannot make it so.[26]

A legislature has power to enact a law and make it effective from an anterior date. But, it is a presumption that the legislature does not intend what is unjust. This is the rationale behind the rule against retrospectively. Laws are construed as operating only in cases or on facts which came into existence after the laws are passed unless the retrospective effect is clearly intended.[27] Article 20 states that no person shall be subjected to a penalty greater than that which he might have been inflicted under the law in force at the time of the commission of the offence. Thus, clause (1) of Article 20 makes provision for two things:

(i) No person is to be convicted of an offence except for violation of "a law in force" at the time of commission of the act charged as an offence. If an act is not an offence at the date of its commission, no future law can make it an offence. If such an act is made an offence from a date anterior to its making, it will hit Article 20(1) of the Constitution.[28] In other words, if an Act is not an offence on the date of its commission, a law made thereafter cannot make it so. Article 20(1) prohibits both pre-constitutional and post Constitution ex post facto laws imposing criminal liability.[29]
A trial under a procedure from what it was at the time of the commission of the offence or by a special Court constituted after the commission of the offence cannot *ipso facto* be held unconstitutional.[30]

(ii) The second part of clause (1) of Article 20 provides that no person shall be subjected to penalty greater than that which might have been inflicted under the law in force at the time of the commission of the offence. A penal statute which creates new offence is always prospective and a person can be punished for an offence committed by him in accordance with the law as it existed on the date on which the offence is committed. But an *ex post facto* law which only mollifies the rigour of a criminal law does not fall within the prohibition of Article 20(1) of the Constitution.[31] If a particular law makes a provision to that effect, the question whether such law is retrospective and, if so, to what extent depend upon the interpretation of the particular statutes, having regard to the well settled rules of interpretation as stated in *Dayal Singh* v. *State of Rajasthan*.[32]

The Supreme Court has held that if an amending Act reduces the punishment for an offence. There is no reason why the accused should not have the benefit of such reduced punishment.[33] In *Basheer* v. *State of Kerala*,[34] the Court has again held that if the amendments of the law are more beneficial to the accused and amount to mollification of the rigour of the law, they will apply retrospectively. In *Kedar Nath* v. *State of West Bengal*,[35] the accused committed an offence in 1947, which under the Act then in force was punishable by imprisonment or fine or both. The Act was amended in 1949 which enhanced the punishment for the same offence by an additional fine equivalent to the amount of money procured by the accused through the offence. The Supreme Court held that the enhanced punishment could not be application to the act committed by the accused in 1947 and hence set aside the additional fine imposed by the Amended Act. In *Ratanlal* v. *State of Punjab*,[36] a boy of 16 years was convicted for committing an offence of house trespass and outraging the modesty of a girl aged 7 years. The Magistrate sentenced him for 6 months' rigorous imprisonment and also imposed fine. After the judgment of Magistrate, the Probation of Offenders Act, 1958, came into force. It provided that a person below 21 years of age should not ordinarily be sentenced to imprisonment. The Supreme Court by a majority of 2 to 1 held that the rule of beneficial interpretation required that *ex post facto law* could be applied to reduce the punishment. So an *ex post facto law* which is beneficial to the accused is not prohibited by clause (1) of Article 20.

An *ex post facto law* which is enacted subsequent to some occurrence, i.e., the commission of some act or omission. *Ex post facto* laws are of following three kinds:

(a) A law which declares some act or omission as an offence

for the first time after the completion of that act or omission.[37]

(b) A law which enhances the punishment or penalty for an offence subsequent to the commission of that offence.[38]

(c) A law which prescribes a new and different procedure for the prosecution of an offence subsequent to the commission of that offence.[39]

In *Maru Ram* v. *Union of India*,[40] the Supreme Court held Section 433A of Criminal Procedure Code, 1973, as not violative of Article 20(1). This Section inserted by the Amendment Act of 1978 provided that a person sentenced to life imprisonment for an offence for which death was one of the punishments or where the death sentence was commuted to life imprisonment under Section 433 of the code, such person would not be released from prison unless he had served at least 14 years of imprisonment. Since Section 433A did not enlarge punishment retroactively and that it merely prescribed a minimum sentence of 14 years of imprisonment for a murderer, the Court held it not bad under Article 20(1).

(b) No person shall be prosecuted and punished for the same offence more than once

Double Jeopardy [Article 20(2)]

There are two Latin maxims '*nemo debet bis puniri*' (no one should be punished twice for one fault) and '*nemo debet bis vexari*' (no one ought to be vexed twice if it appears to the Court that it is for one and the same cause). The roots of double jeopardy are to be found in the above stated maxims. The rule against double jeopardy is a centuries old common law principle, which bars repeated criminal prosecution for the same offence. It is a procedural safeguard which bars a second trial then an accused person is either convicted or acquitted after a full fledged trial by a Court of competent jurisdiction. The core rule includes the old pleas in bar of jurisdiction namely autrefois acquit and autrefois convict. This doctrine aims to protect criminal defendants from the tedium and trauma of relitigation when a criminal charge has been adjudicated by a competent Court, that is final irrespective of the matter whether it takes the form of an acquittal or a conviction, and it may be pleaded in bar of a further prosecution when it is for the same offence. It is regarded as one of the most important fundamental as well as the human right against the repeated State prosecution for the same offence.

Double Jeopardy protection under Indian law

In India, the protection against the double jeopardy is a constitutional as well as a statutory guarantee. The principle has also been recognised under the provision of General Clauses Act. The Constitution of India recognise only autrefois convict, whereas the Code of Criminal Procedure, 1973 incorporates autrefois acquit as well. The rule against double jeopardy has been recognised as a fundamental right in the Constitution of India.[41]

Article 20(2) which run as "no person shall be prosecuted and punished for the same offence more than once". Under the provisions of the Indian Constitution, the conditions that have to be satisfied for raising the plea of autrefois convict are:

(a) There must be a person accused of an offence.
(b) The proceeding or the prosecution should have taken place before a 'Court' or 'judicial tribunal' in reference to the law which creates offences.
(c) The accused should be convicted in the earlier proceedings.

In *Kalawati* v. *Sate of H.P.*,[42] the appellant being accused of committing murder of her husband was prosecuted but acquitted by the District Judge. The State preferred on appeal against the acquittal. The accused contended that the appellate proceedings before the High Court against the acquittal by the District Judge, contravened Article 20(2). The Court held that appeal against the acquittal was not the second prosecution, but a continuation of the original prosecution and, therefore, Article 20(2) would not be attracted. Besides, there was no punishment for the offence in the earlier prosecution. The code of Criminal Procedure recognises both the pleas of auterfois acquit as well as auterfois convict. The conditions which should be satisfied for raising either of the pleas under the code are:

(a) that there should be previous conviction or acquittal;
(b) the conviction or acquittal must be by a competent Court having jurisdiction;
(c) the subsequent proceeding must be for the same offence.[43]

In fact, the principal reasons for protection of the doctrine of double jeopardy are two-fold, firstly, it afford protection be the citizens against the repeated prosecution is at one hand and secondly, it preserves the integrity of the criminal justice system. This rule serves the following purposes:

(a) reducing the risk of wrongful conviction;
(b) minimising the distress of the trial process;
(c) the need for finality;
(d) the need to encourage efficient investigation.

Thus, it is very much clear that the rule against double jeopardy is universally accepted principle for the protection of certain values within the criminal justice system. It serves many purposes such as preventing the arbitrary actions of the State against its subject, ensures finality in litigations etc., which are of great importance for the protection of human rights of the accused persons. It is a centuries old principle, which survived not by chance, but for many good reasons. Thus, existence of such a rule is inevitable for the integrity of the criminal justice system itself.[44]

(c) No person accused of an offence shall be compelled to be a witness against himself

Protection against self-incrimination [Article 20(3)]

Clause (3) of Article 20 provides: "No person accused of any offence shall be compelled to be a witness against himself". This clause is based on the maxim '*nemo tenetur prodere accussare seipsum*', which means that "no man is bound to accuse himself". Clause (3) of Article 20 follows the language of the Fifth Amendment of the American Constitution which lies down that "no person shall be compelled in any criminal case to be a witness against himself".[45] The characteristic features of common law criminal jurisprudence are that an accused must be presumed to be innocent till the contrary is proved; that it is the duty of the prosecution to establish the guilt of the accused; and that the accused need not make any admission or statement against his free will.

"... throughout the web of English Criminal Law, one golden thread is always to be seen that it is the duty of the prosecution to prove the prisoner's guilt".[46] The main provision regarding crime investigation and trial in the Indian Constitution is Article 20(3). It deals with the privilege against self incrimination. The privilege against 'self-incrimination is a fundamental canon of common law criminal jurisprudence'. Article 20(3) provides that no one is bound to criminate himself. Hence, although an accused person may of his own accord make a voluntary statement as to the charge against himself, a justice required that before receiving such statement from him to aware him that he is not obliged to say anything and that what he does say may be given in evidence against him. The privilege against self incrimination thus enables the maintenance of human privacy in the enforcement of criminal justice. It also goes with the maxim *Nemo Tenetur Seipsum Accusar* i.e., 'no man, not even the accused himself can be compelled to answer any question, which may tend to prove him guilty of a crime, he has been accused of'. If the confession from the accused is derived from any physical or moral compulsion (be it under hypnotic state of mind) it should stand to be rejected by the Court. The right against forced self incrimination, widely known as the right to silence is enshrined in the Code of Criminal Procedure and the Indian Constitution. In the Criminal Procedure Code the legislature has guarded a citizen's right against self incrimination. But where the accused makes a confession without any inducement, threat or promise Article 20(3) does not apply.

Ingredients constituting the provision . . .

This provision contains following ingredients:

(i) It is a right available to a person "accused of an offence".
(ii) It is a protection against "compulsion to be a witness".
(iii) It is a protection against such "compulsion resulting in his giving evidence "against himself".[47]

(i) Person accused of an offence

The words 'accused of an offence' make it clear that this right is only available to a person accused of an offence. A person is said to be an accused person against whom a formal accusation relating to the commission of an offence has been levelled which in normal course may result in his prosecution and conviction.[48] In *M.P. Sharma* v. *Satish Chandra*,[49] it was held that a person, whose name was mentioned as an accused in the first information report by the police and investigation was ordered by the Magistrate, could claim the protection of this guarantee. In *State of Bombay* v. *Kathi Kalu*

Oghad,[50] it has been clearly observed that a person cannot claim the privilege if at the time he made the statement he was not an accused but became an accused thereafter. What constitutes a formal accusation is rather flexible. To answer the question whether a person is accused or not at a particular time, it is necessary to make a reference to the nature and scope of the proceedings, the nature of the accusation and its probable consequence.[51]

Accusing a person of committing a crime in the first information report, or in formal compliant before a Magistrate, amounts to a formal accusation and the person concerned can claim the privilege. As the Supreme Court has observed in *R.B. Shah* v. *D.K. Guha,*[52] it is well settled that with the lodging of a first information report a person is accused of an offence within the meaning of Article 20(3)". The privilege in Article 20(3) is undoubtedly available at the trial stage in the Court room. But it is available even at the pre trial stage, i.e. during the course of police investigations if the person concerned can be regarded as an accused.

(ii) Protection against 'to be a witness'

The protection is against compulsion "to be a witness". In *M.P. Sharma* v. *Satish Chandra,*[53] the Supreme Court interpreted the expression "to be a witness" very widely so as to include oral, documentary and testimonial evidence. The prosecution under Article 20(3) covers not merely testimonial compulsion in a courtroom but also compelled testimony previously obtained – any compulsory process for production of evidentiary document which are reasonably likely to support the prosecution against him. The Court accepted the definition given in the Indian Evidence Act that a person can be 'a witness' not merely by giving oral evidence but also by producing documents or making intelligible gestures as in the case of a dumb witness or the like, if this interpretation of the phrase "to be a witness" adopted by the Court in *M.P. Sharma's* case was to be followed; the compulsory taking of finger impressions or specimen handwriting of an accused would come within the mischief of Article 20(3). This broad interpretation, it was thought, would certainly hamper the effective administration of crime and efficient administration of criminal justice.

(iii) Compulsion to give evidence "against himself"

The protection under Article 20(3) is available only against compulsion of the accused to give evidence against himself. Thus, if the accused voluntarily makes an oral statement or voluntarily produces documentary evidence, incriminatory in nature, Article 20(3) would not be attracted.[54] The term "compulsion" in the context of Article 20(3) means "duress". Thus, compulsion may take many forms. Person accused of an offence may be subjected to physical or mental torture. He may be starved or beaten and a confession may be extracted from him. By deceitful means he may be induced to believe that his son is being tortured in an adjoining room and by such inducement he may be compelled to make an incriminating statement.[55] Article 20(3) is not violated when an accused is compelled to stand up and show his face for the purpose of identification, for it does not amount to giving of testimony as the physical facts which are noticed speak for themselves.[56]

In *Re Palani Goundan*,[57] when the accused was taken to the doctor for medical examination to determine whether he was intoxicated or not, and the doctor recorded his observations of the physical features and other symptoms exhibited by the accused, and he was not compelled to give any evidence, the High Court held that the symptoms observed by the doctor could not be regarded as evidence obtained from the accused by compulsion. Compulsory taking of urine and blood samples from an accused is not hit by Article 20(3) as it is not testimonial compulsion.[58]

Admission of tape recorded evidence against the accused does not violate Article 20(3) when the conversation on his part was voluntary and there was no compulsion. The fact that the attaching of the tape recording instrument was unknown to the accused would not render the evidence of conversation inadmissible. The accused person's conversation is not extracted under duress or compulsion. Recording of conversation on tape was "a mechanical contrivance to play the role of an eavesdropper.[59]

(iv) Privilege against self-incrimination [Article 20(3)] and use of advanced scientific techniques for investigation[60]

In any criminal investigation, interrogation of the suspects and accused plays a vital role in extracting the truth from them. From time, immemorial several methods, most of which were based on some form of torture have been used by the investigating agencies to elicit information from the accused and the suspects. With the advancement of science and technology, sophisticated methods like Lie Detector or Polygraphy Tests, Brain Mapping and Narco Analysis or Truth Serum Tests, Brain Electrical Activation Profile

Test etc. have been developed which do away with the use of "third degree torture" by the police. These psychoanalytical tests are also used to interpret the behaviour of the criminal (or the suspect) and corroborate the investigating officers' observations. However, legal questions are raised about the validity of tests like Narco Analysis, lie detector etc., with some upholding its validity in the light of legal principles and others rejecting it as a blatant violation of constitutional provisions. It has been alleged that such tests are a blatant violation of the Article 20(3) of the Indian Constitution. However, in this age of ever increasing crime rate, such tests often render a lot of help to the investigation agencies and hence, it is high time to blend Article 20(3) with these tests.

According to the Court none of the tests violated Article 20(3) because "the tests of brain mapping and lie detector in which the map of the brain is the result or polygraph . . . cannot be said to be a statement made by the witness. At the most it can be called the information received or taken out from the witness". With regard to narco analysis while holding that the result of administration of serum is necessarily a statement nevertheless". "Unless it is shown to be incriminating to a person making it, it does not give rise to the protection under Article 20(3)". Several High Courts have taken similar views[61] and the issue is now pending before the Supreme Court.

Narco analysis and Article 20(3)

In *Selvi* v. *State of Karnataka*,[62] a three judge's bench of the Apex Court considered the questions relating to involuntary administration of narco analysis, polygraph examination and the Brain Electrical Activation Profile test for the improvement of investigation efforts in criminal cases. For this the Court pointed out that ordinarily evidence is classified into three broad categories – oral testimony, documents and material evidence. It noted that protective scope of Article 20(3) read with Section 161(2), Criminal Procedure Code, guards against the compulsory extraction of oral testimony, even at the stage of investigation with respect to the production of documents; the applicability of Article 20(3) is decided by the trial judge. But parties are obliged to produce documents in the first place. The compulsory extraction of material (or physical) evidence lies outside the protective scope of Article 20(3) of the Constitution. Narco analysis test includes substantial reliance on verbal statements by the test subject and hence its involuntary administration offends the 'right against self incrimination. The Court treated polygraph examination and BEAP Test as 'personal testimony'. All such tests including narco analysis test, according to the Court come within the scope of 'testimonial compulsion', thereby attracting the protective shield of Article 20(3). It is compulsory administration of the above tests which offends Article 20(3). Voluntary examination through these techniques is not covered by Article 20(3). For voluntary administration of the impugned test in the context of administration of criminal justice, the Court insisted on certain safeguards including those as suggested by the National Human Rights Commission in 2000. The guidelines of the above commission include taking consent of the accused, giving him access to lawyer, recording of consent before a Judicial Magistrate, and recording of lie detector test by an independent agency and recording full medical and factual narration of the manner of information received. The Court laid down the following guidelines for these tests:

1. No lie detector test should be administered except on the basis of consent of the accused. An option should be given to the accused whether he wishes to avail such test.
2. If the accused volunteers for a lie detector test, he should be given access to a lawyer and physical, emotional and legal implications of such a test should be explained to him by the police and his lawyer.
3. The consent should be recorded by a judicial Magistrate.
4. During the hearing before the Magistrate the person alleged to have agreed should be duly represented by a lawyer.
5. At the hearing the person in question should also be told in clear terms that the statement that if made shall not be a confidential statement to the Magistrate but will have the statement made to the police.
6. The Magistrate shall consider all factors relating to the detention including the length of detention and the nature of the interrogation.
7. The actual recording of the lie detector shall be done by an independent agency (such as hospital) and conducted in the presence of a lawyer.
8. A full medical and factual narration of the manner of the information received must be taken on record.

Thus, the picture is clear that, compulsory administration of the Narco analysis technique, as such amounts to "testimonial compulsion" and thereby triggers the protection of Article 20(3); that the test results of polygraph and BEAP/ Brain finger printing test amount to testimonial compulsion and therefore bar of Article 20(3) gets attracted to such tests; that, conducting DNA profiling of accused, expressly permitted by Sections 53, 54 of the Criminal Procedure Code, 1973, is not a testimonial act and therefore, bar under Article 20(3) does not apply to that Act. The Court as interpreter and protector of constitutional safeguards cannot permit involuntary administration of narco tests.[63] In the narco analysis test, the subject enters into a "twilight" stage i.e. a stage between consciousness and unconsciousness. In this stage, it becomes difficult for him to lie and his answers would be restricted to facts he is already aware of. Prior to the test, Court's permission and written consent of subject is secured which are mandatory for conducting the test. The test is conducted only in the presence of forensic and medical experts. In the case of *Nandini Sathpathy* v. *P.L. Dani*,[64] it is well established that the right to silence has been granted to the accused; no one can forcibly extract statements from the accused, who has the right to keep silent during the course of interrogation (investigation). By the administration of these tests, forcible intrusion into one's mind is being restored to, thereby nullifying the validity and legitimacy of the Right to silence. She claimed that she had a right of silence by virtue of Article 20(3) of the Constitution and Section 161(2) of Criminal Procedure Code. The Apex Court upheld her please.

In India, narco analysis was first used in 2002, in the *Godhra Carnage* case. It was also in the news after the famous Arun Bhatt kidnapping case in Gujarat wherein the accused had appeared before National Human Rights Commission and the Supreme Court of India against undergoing the narco analysis. It was again in the news in the Telgi Stamp paper scam when Abdul Karim Telgi was taken to the test in December, 2003. It was also used in famous *Nithari Village (Noida) serial killings*.[65]

Admissibility of DNA Technology in the Indian legal system

DNA test or 'DNA' profiling as popularly known as a technique in which a sample of DNA is run through a laboratory in order to generate information about it, looking specifically for DNA which could identify the source of the sample, or be used as a base of comparison between two samples. It becomes one of the most important technologies to be used in the forensic science.

DNA Test and the Indian Legal System

The application of DNA testing has been used in India for a long period of time. Sometimes, it has been used to resolve certain question which at one point of time becomes very difficult to resolve such as "has the crime been committed?", "How and when was the crime committed?", "who committed the crime?" The admissibility of the DNA evidence before the Court always depend on its accurate and proper collection, preservation and documentation which can satisfy the Court that the evidence which has been put in front it is reliable. Now what is the use of this material evidence in the investigation? The answer is very simple, that this material evidence help them in determining as to who was actually present at the place where the incident happened. The introduction of the DNA Technology has passed serious challenges to some legal and fundamental rights of an individual such as "right to privacy", 'right against self incrimination'. And this is the most important reason why Courts sometime are reluctant in accepting the evidences based on DNA technology. Right to privacy has been included under right to life and personal liberty, i.e. Article 21 and Article 20(3) provides about the right against self incrimination which protects an accused person in criminal cases from giving evidence against himself or evidence which can make him guilty. But it has been held by the Supreme Court on several occasions that right to life and personal liberty is not an absolute right. In *Kharak Singh* v. *State of U.P.*,[66] the Supreme Court held that right to privacy is not an absolute right as guaranteed under our Constitution. It can be subject to restriction. On this basis various Courts in the country have allowed DNA technology to be used in the investigation and in producing evidence. And it is on this basis the constitutionality of the laws affecting right to life and personal liberty are upheld by the Supreme Court which includes medical examination.[67]

In *Amrit Singh* v. *State of Punjab*,[68] the accused was charged for rape and murder of an eight year old girl. When the body of the child was recovered, some strands of hair were found in the closed fist of the child. The police wanted to analyse the hair found in the fist of the victim with that of hair of accused, but the accused refused to give the hair sample. The Supreme Court observed that the accused had protection against self incrimination not to give hair.

Thus, it is very much clear that in India 'Right against self-incrimination' finds a high place in legal system. The inter relationship between the 'right against self incrimination' and the 'right to fair trial' has been recognised in most jurisdiction as well as international human rights instruments. For example, the guarantee of 'presumption of innocence' bears a direct link to the 'right against self incrimination' since compelling the accused person to give evidence would place the burden of proving innocence on the accused instead of requiring the prosecution to prove guilt. Thus, the right to refusal to answer questions that may incriminate a person is a procedural safeguard which has gradually evolved in common law and bears a close relation to right to fair trial.

(iii) Rights of Accused and right to life and personal liberty: Article 21

Article 21 has given to the people of India as much they have wanted from it. It is quite clear that Articles 20, 21 and 22 of the Constitution of India guarantees right to life and personal liberty. These provisions ensure protection to person from arbitrary actions of the State. It has also been provided that State should take steps to ensure that citizens should be able to lead a meaningful life. More specifically provisions under Article 21 has been construed broadly by the Courts in various cases to ensure citizen's as well as non citizen's right to life with dignity.

(i) General introduction to protection of life and personal liberty

Article 21 provides "no person shall be deprived of his life or personal liberty except according to procedure established by law". This right has been held to be the heart of the Constitution, the most organic and progressive provision in our living Constitution, the foundation head of our laws.[69] Highlighting the paramount of the right to "life" and "personal liberty" a constitutional bench of the Supreme Court in *Kehar Singh* v. *Union of India*,[70] observed:

> To any civilised society, there can be no attributes more important than the life and personal liberty of its members . . . these twin attributes enjoy a fundamental ascendancy over all other attributes of the political and social order. . .

Article 21 secures two rights:

(a) Right to life

Right to life as given under Article 21 has been construed broadly by the Courts as an important right. It thus includes not only physical existence but include right to life with dignity. Thus, right to life does not merely mean the continuance of a person's animal existence, but a quality of life. It means 'the fullest opportunity to develop one's personality and potentiality to the highest level possible in the existing stage of our civilisation. Inevitably, it means the right to live decently as a member of a civilised society. It is to ensure all freedom and advantages that would go to make life agreeable. The right implies a reasonable standard of comfort and decency.[71] In *M. Nagaraj* v. *Union of India*,[72] the Court State that "the expression 'life' in Article 21 does not connote merely physical or animal existence. The right to life includes right to live with human dignity". In *Sunil Batra* v. *Delhi Administration*,[73] the Supreme Court held that the "right to life" included the right to lead a healthy life so as to enjoy all facilities of human body in their prime conditions. In *P. Rathinam* v. *Union of India*,[74] the Supreme Court has defined 'life' as follows:

> The right to live with human dignity and the same does not connote continued drudgery. It takes within its fold some of the fine graces of civilisation which makes life worth living and that the expanded concept of life would mean the tradition, culture and heritage of the person concerned.

In *Shantisar Builders* v. *Narayanan K. Totame*,[75] the Supreme Court has observed:

> The right to life under Article 21 would include the right to food, clothing, decent environment and reasonable accommodation to live in. . . .

(b) Right to personal liberty

The essence of Article 21 lies in guarantying person liberty to every citizen of India. "Personal liberty" includes all the freedom which is not included in Article 19. It means liberty of individuals, freedom from unwarranted arrest nor other physical coercion in any manner that does not fall under the ambit of legal justification. In *Kharak Singh* v. *State of U.P.*,[76] the Court observed:

> "Personal liberty" is used in Article 21 as a compendious term to include within itself all the varieties of rights which go to

> make up the 'personal liberty' of a man other than those dealt within the several clauses of Article 19(1). While Article 19(1) deals with particular species or attributes of that freedom, 'persona liberty' in Article 21 takes in and comprises the residue.

Personal liberty means nothing more than the liberty or the physical body – freedom from arrest and detention from false imprisonment of wrongful confinement. In *Maneka Gandhi* v. *Union of India*,[77] a seven judge bench of the expression "personal liberty" and give it the widest possible meaning. The Court held:

> The expression 'personal liberty' in Article 21 of the widest amplitude and it covers a variety of rights which go to constitute the personal liberty of a man and some of them have been raised to the status of distinct fundamental rights and given additional protection under Article 19. It may be noticed that while in *Kharak Singh* case, the freedoms of Article 19(1) were excluded from the scope of "personal liberty" of Article 21, according to *Maneka Gandhi* decision, they are within it and form part of "personal liberty". It follows that a law depriving a person of "personal liberty" has not only to stand the test of Article 21 but it must also stand the test of Article 19.

(ii) Accused's Rights and Article 21

The provisions of right to life and personal liberty under Article 21 also have been interpreted to include certain essentials rights relating to the accused. When read with Article 39A it would provide for the legal aid must be made available to the accused, a prisoner or any litigant who is poor or belongs to disadvantaged section of the society. It has also been read to uphold the rights of the prisoners, right to speedy trials, right against inhuman treatment, right to claim compensation for violation of fundamental rights and in larger context to include right to health and medical care. In *D.B.M. Patnaik* v. *State of Andhra Pradesh*,[78] some prisoners challenged some restrictions as violating their right under Article 21. The Supreme Court stated that a convict is not denuded of all his fundamental rights. Imprisonment after conviction is bound to curtail some of his rights, e.g., freedom of profession or movement, but certain other rights, e.g., the right to hold property could still be enjoyed by a prisoner. A convict could also claim that he should not be deprived of his life or personal liberty except according to the procedure established by law. Article 21 is of the widest amplitude and it covers a variety of rights regarding the accused person. It is quite known to us that the convicts are not by mere reason of their conviction deprived of all the fundamental rights which they otherwise possess. In *Babu Singh* v. *State of U.P.*,[79] it was held that 'refusal to grant bail' in a murder case without reasonable ground would amount to deprivation of personal liberty under Article 21. Court further stated that personal liberty of an accused or convict is fundamental and can be taken away only in accordance with the procedure established by law. In *Maneka Gandhi* v. *Union of India*,[80] it is now established after Maneka Gandhi case that 'procedure' for purpose of Article 21 has to be just, fair and reasonable.

(a) Criminal Justice after Maneka Gandhi case

Maneka Gandhi's case is having a profound but beneficial impact on the administration of criminal justice in India. The administration of criminal justice and the conditions prevailing in prisons have long been extremely deplorable and sub human; prisoners are mal treated; criminal trials are inordinately delayed: police brutality is legendary. Every day one hears news of police brutality, prison maladministration and inordinately long delay in trial of criminal case resulting in grave miscarriage of justice. In spite of the accent on socio-economic justice in the Constitution, precious little has been done so far to improve matters in the areas of criminal justice. Administration of criminal justice is a State matter. Fortunately, by reinterpreting Article 21 in *Maneka Gandhi's* case, and by giving up the sterile approach of Gopalan, the Supreme Court has found a potent tool to seek to improve matters, and to fill in the vacuum arising from governmental inaction and apathy to undertake reform, in the area of criminal justice. The Court has now been seeking to humanise and liberalise the administration of criminal justice. The Supreme Court has observed in *Sunil Batra II*[81] that thanks to Article 21, "human rights jurisprudence in India has a constitutional status and sweep . . . so that this Magna Carta may well toll the knell of human bondage beyond civilised limits".

Accordingly, since Maneka, the Supreme Court has in a number of cases tested various aspects of criminal justice and prison administration on this touchstone. The protection of Article 21 extends to all persons—persons accused of offences, undertrial prisoners, prisoners undergoing jail sentences etc. and, thus, all aspects of criminal justice fall under the umbrella of Articles 14, 19 and 21.[82] With the help of Article 21 our judiciary has done a marvellous job for securing the rights of accused. Let's make it more clear with the help of following heading:

(i) Right to a fair trial, a fair procedure and a fair investigation

Free and fair trial has been said to be the sine quo non of Article 21. It is said that justice should not be done but it should be seen to have been done. If the criminal trial is not free and fair and not free from bias, the judicial fairness and the criminal justice system would be at stake, shaking the confidence of the public in the system and woe would be the "rule of law". Article 21 envisages a fair trial, a fair procedure and a fair investigation. Such right extends not only to actual proceedings in Court but also includes within its sweep the preceding police investigation as well.[83] Although free and fair trial is *sine qua non* of Article 21, the apprehension of denial must be reasonable and not imaginary. Reasonableness would obviously depend on the facts and circumstances of a case and their evaluations by the Courts.[84] Conducting a fair trial for those who are accused of criminal offences is the cornerstone of democracy. Conducting a fair trial is beneficial both to the accused as well as to the society. A conviction resulting from an unfair trial is contrary to our concept of justice.[85] In *Zahira Habibulla H. Sheikh* v. *State of Gujarat*,[86] stated that fair trail obviously would mean a trial before an impartial judge, a fair prosecutor and an atmosphere of judicial calm. Fair trial means a trial in which bias or prejudice for or against the accused, the witnesses, or the cause which is being tried is eliminated. If the witnesses get threatened or are forced to give false evidence that also would not result in a fair trial. The failure to hear material witnesses is certainly denial of fair trial. Right to fair trial in a criminal prosecution is enshrined in Article 21. For example, Section 142 of the Evidence Act does not give power to the prosecution to put leading questions on the material part of the evidence which a witness intends to give against the accused. To do so infringes the right of the accused to have a fair trial which is enshrined in Article 21. This is not a curable irregularity.[87] Right to have a fair trial strictly in terms of the Juvenile Justice Act which would include procedural safeguard is a Fundamental right of the juvenile.[88] Thus, it may be said that right to fair trial, fair investigation is the important right in order to provide justice.

(ii) Right of accused against arrest

In *Joginder Kumar* v. *State of U.P.*,[89] the Apex Court has issued directions regarding arrest. The Court has emphasised that a police officer may have the power to arrest but justification for exercising the power is quite another matter. Arrest can cause incalculable harm to a person's reputation and self-esteem. Arrest should be made not merely on suspicion but only after a reasonable satisfaction reached after some investigation as to the genuineness and bonafides of the complaint and a reasonable belief as to the person's complicity and even as to the need to effect arrest. In *Lal Kamlendra P. Singh* v. *State of U.P.*,[90] the Court has now expressly said that arrest is not a must in all cases of cognizable offences. The Hon'ble Supreme Court in *D.K. Basu* v. *State of West Bengal*[91] laid down the following guidelines in case of arrest:

1. The police personnel carrying out the arrest and handling the interrogation of the arrestee should bear accurate, visible and clear identification and name tags with their designations. The particulars of all such police personnel who handle interrogation of the arrestee must be recorded in a register.
2. That the police officer carrying out the arrest of the arrestee shall prepare a memo of arrest at the time of arrest and such memo shall be attested by at least one witness, who may be either a member of the family of the arrestee or a respectable person of the locality from where the arrest is made. It shall also be counter signed by the arrestee and shall contain the time and date of arrest.
3. A person who has been arrested or detained and is being held in custody in a police station or interrogation centre or other lock up, shall be entitled to have one friend or relative or other person known to him or having interest in his welfare being informed, as soon as practicable, that he has been arrested and is being detained at the particular place, unless the attesting witness of the memo of arrest is himself such a friend or a relative of the arrestee.
4. The time, place of arrest and venue of custody of an arrestee must be notified by the police where the next friend or relative of the arrestee lives outside the district or town through the legal aid organisation in the district and

the police station of the area concerned telegraphically within a period of 8 to 12 hours after the arrest.

5. The person arrested must be made aware of this right to have someone informed of his arrest or detention as soon as he is put under arrest or is detained.
6. An entry must be made in the diary at the place of detention regarding the arrest of the person which shall also disclose the name and particular of the police officials in whose custody the arrestee is.
7. The arrestee should, where he so requests, be also examined at the time of his arrest and major and minor injuries, if any present on his/her body must be recorded at that time. The "Inspection Memo" must be signed both by the arrestee and the police officer affecting the arrest and the police officer affecting the arrest and a copy provided to the arrestee.
8. The arrestee should be subjected to medical examination every 48 hours during his detention in custody by a trained doctor on the panel of approved doctors appointed by the Director of Health Services of the concerned State or union territory. The Director of Health Services should prepare such a panel for all Tehsils and Districts as well.
9. Copies of all the documents including the memo of arrest, referred to above, should be sent to the Illaqa Magistrate for his record.
10. The arrestee may be permitted to meet his lawyer during interrogation, though not throughout the interrogation.
11. A police control room should be provided at all district and State headquarters, where information regarding the arrest and the place of custody of the arrestee shall be communicated by the officer causing the arrest, within 12 hours of effecting the arrest and at the police control room it should be displayed conspicuously on the notice board of the police control room.

The accused has the right to be treated decently while he is in custody. He must be provided with good food and drink, clothing as necessary as well as sleeping and washing facilities. The accused cannot be "punished" or treated as guilty while he awaits trial. While detained, the accused retains the right to Court access and to a legal aid.[92]

(iii) Right to free legal aid

Legal aid is the provision of assistance to people otherwise unable to afford legal representation and access to the Court system. Legal aid is regarded as central in providing access to justice by ensuring equality before the law, the right to counsel and the right to a fair trial. Legal aid has a close relationship with the welfare State and the provision of legal aid by a State is influenced by attitudes towards welfare. Legal aid is a welfare provision by the State to people who could otherwise not afford access to the legal system.

Article 39A of the Constitution, provides for equal justice and free legal aid. It directs the State to ensure that the operation of the legal system promote justice, on a basis of equal opportunities and shall, in particular provide free legal aid, by suitable legislation schemes or in any other way, to ensure that opportunities for securing justice are not denied to any citizen by reason of economic or other disabilities. This Article also emphasises that free legal service is an inalienable element of 'reasonable, fair and just procedure for a person accused of an offence and it must be held implicit in the guarantee of Article 21 of the Constitution. On the other hand in the civil side Order XXXIII Rule 18 of the Code of Civil Procedure, 1908 provided that the State and central governments may make supplementary provisions as it thinks fit for providing free legal services to those who have been permitted to sue as an indigent person.[93]

In *M.H. Hoskot* v. *State of Maharashtra*,[94] the Supreme Court laid down that right to free legal aid at the cost of the State to an accused, who could not afford legal services for reasons of poverty, indigence or incommunicado situation, was part of fair, just and reasonable procedure implicit in Article 21. Free legal aid to the indigent has been declared to be "a State's duty and not government charity". *Hussainara Khatoon* v. *Home Secretary Bihar*,[95] the Supreme Court held that a procedure which does not make available legal services to an accused person who is too poor to afford legal services cannot possibly be regarded as 'reasonable, fair and just, and therefore implicit under Article 21 of the Constitution. In *Khatri* v. *State of Bihar*,[96] the Supreme Court directed the State of Bihar that it cannot avoid its constitutional obligation to provide free legal services to a poor accused by pleading financial or administrative inability. The constitutional obligation to provide free legal services to an indigent accused does not arise only when the trial commences but also attaches when he is for the first time produced before the Magistrate.

That is the stage at which an accused person needs competent legal advice and representation. It is further held that the Magistrate or the Session Judge, before whom the accused appears, is under an obligation to inform the accused that if he is unable to engage a lawyer, he is entitled to obtain free legal services at the cost of the State.[97] The Supreme Court has taken a big innovative step forward in humanising the administration of criminal justice by suggesting that free legal aid be provided by the State to poor prisoner facing a prison sentence. The main question for the Court to consider in Suk Das was whether this fundamental right could be denied lawfully to an accused person if he does not apply for free legal aid. The Court has now pointed out that the bulks of the Indian people living in rural areas are illiterate and are not aware of their rights. Even literate people do not know what their rights are under the law. In this circumstances, it would make a mockery of legal aid if it were to be left to a poor, ignorant and illiterate accused to ask for free legal service. "Legal aid would be an idle formality if it was to depend upon a specific application by such poor or ignorant person for such legal assistance".

The Supreme Court has now clarified that free legal assistance at the cost of the State is a fundamental right of a person accused of an offence involving jeopardy to his life or personal liberty.

(iv) Right to speedy trial

Speedy trial as such is not mentioned as specific fundamental right in the Constitution. The Criminal Procedure Code does not guarantee specifically any right to speedy trial. Nor is there any provision prescribing the maximum period for which a Magistrate can keep an undertrial in jail without trial. Nevertheless, the Supreme Court has recognised the same to be implicit in the spectrum of Article 21 and has derived the right of an accused to a speedy trial from Article 21. It is well settled that the right to speedy trial in all criminal prosecutions is an inalienable right under Article 21 of the Constitution. The right is applicable not only to the actual proceedings in Court but also includes within its sweep the proceeding police investigations as well. In every case, where the right to speedy trial is alleged to have been infringed, the Court has to perform the balancing act upon taking into consideration all the attendant circumstances and determine in each case whether the right to speedy trial has been denied in a given case.[98] A procedure cannot be reasonable, fair or just unless it ensures a speedy trial for determination of the guilt of the person deprived of his liberty. In *Hussainara Khatoon (No. 1)* v. *Home Secretary, State of Bihar*,[99] it was brought to the notice of the Supreme Court that an alarming large number of men, women, children including, were kept in prisons for years awaiting trial in Courts of law. The offences with which they were charged were trivial and if proved would not have warranted punishment for more than a few months, perhaps for a year or two. But, they were deprived of their freedom for periods ranging for three to ten years, without their trial having yet commenced. The Court took a serious note of the situation and observed that it was a crying shame on the judicial system which permitted incarceration of men and women for such long periods of time without trials. These persons were denied human rights and were languishing in jails for years for offences which perhaps they might ultimately be found not to have committed. Reiterating the above view with approval in *Hussainara Khatoon (No. II)* v. *Home Secretary, State of Bihar*,[100] the Court held that detention of undertrial prisoners, in jail for period longer than what they could have been sentenced if convicted, was illegal as being in violation of Article 21. The Court, thus, ordered the release from jail of all those undertrial prisoners who had been in jail for longer period than what for which they could have been sentenced had they been convicted. The Apex Court in *Pradeep Kumar Verma* v. *State of Bihar*,[101] having noticed that people in India were simply disgusted with the State of affairs and were fast losing faith in the judiciary because of the inordinate delay in disposal of cases, required the authorities to do the needful in the matter urgently to ensure speedy disposal of cases, "before the situation goes totally out of control" and if the people's faith in the judiciary was to remain. In *A.R. Antulay* v. *R.S. Nayak*,[102] a Constitution bench of five learned judges of the Supreme Court dealt with the question of "the right to speedy trial" and laid down certain guidelines for the speedy trial of offences, which may be summarised as follows:

(a) Fair, just and reasonable procedure implicit in Article 21 creates a right in the accused to be tried speedily.
(b) Right to speedy trial flowing from Article 21 encompasses all the stages, namely, the stage of investigation, inquiry, appeal, and revision and re trial.
(c) The concerns underling the right to speedy trial from the point of view of the accused are:
    (i) The period of remand and pre conviction detention

should be as short as possible. In other words, the accused should not be subjected to unnecessary or long incarceration prior to the conviction;

(ii) The worry, anxiety, expense and disturbance to his vocation and peace, resulting from an unduly prolonged investigation, inquiry or trial should be minimum; and

(iii) Undue delay may well result in impairment of the ability of the accused to defend himself, whether on account of death, disappearance or non availability of witnesses or otherwise.

(d) Where the right to speedy trial is alleged to have been infringed, the first question to be put and answered is who is responsible for the delay? Proceedings taken by either party in good faith, to vindicate their rights, and interest, as perceived by them, cannot be treated as delaying tactics nor can the time taken in pursuing such proceedings be counted towards delay.

(e) While determining whether undue delay has occurred, one must have regard to all the attendant circumstances, including nature of offence, number of accused and witnesses, the work load of the Court concerned, prevailing local conditions and so on – what is called the systematic delays?

(f) Each and every delay does not necessarily prejudice the accused. However, inordinately long delay may be taken as presumptive proof of prejudice.

(g) An accused's plea of denial of speedy trial cannot be defeated by saying that the accused did at no time demand a speedy trial.

(h) Ultimately, the Court has to balance and weigh the several relevant factors – balancing test or balancing process – and determine in each case whether the right to speedy trial has been denied in a given case.

(i) Ordinarily speaking, where the Court comes to the conclusion that right to speedy trial of an accused has been infringed, the charges or the conviction, as the case may be, shall be quashed. In a given case, however, the Court may make such other appropriate order if the quashing of proceedings is not in the interest of justice.

(j) It is neither advisable nor practicable to fix any time limit for trial of offences. In every case of complaint of denial of right of speedy trial, it is primarily for the prosecution to justify and explain the delay.

(k) An objection based on denial of right to speedy trial and for relief on that account, should first be addressed to the High Court. Even if the High Court entertains such a plea, ordinarily, it should not stay the proceedings except in case of grave and exceptional nature. Such proceedings in High Court must, however, be disposed of on a priority basis.

In *Common Cause, a Registered Society* v. *Union of India*,[103] holding that the very pendency of criminal proceedings for long periods by itself operated as an engine of oppression, the Supreme Court issued appropriate directions for the release on bail or the discharge of the accused persons and closure of such cases. Speedy trial is thus "an integral and essential part of the fundamental right to life and liberty enshrined in Article 21".[104] In *Kadra Pahadiya* v. *State of Bihar*,[105] several under trials were languishing in jail for 8 years without their trial having made any progress. The Supreme Court commented: "it is a crying shame upon our adjudicatory system which keeps men in jail for years on end without a trial". In *Union of India* v. *Ashok K. Mitra*,[106] there was delay in trial but it was not attributable only to the prosecution and the respondent himself had contributed to the delay. Refusing to quash the prosecution in the instant case, the Court observed that the respondent could not be allowed to take advantage of his own wrong and take shelter under "speedy trial" to escape from prosecution.

(v) Right against solitary confinement and long pre trial confinement

It has been held that a convict is not wholly denuded of his fundamental rights and his conviction does not reduce him into a non person whose rights are subject to the whims of the prisoner administration. Therefore, the imposition of any major punishment within the prison system is conditional upon the observance of procedural safeguards.[107] In *Sunil Batra* v. *Delhi Administration*,[108] the Supreme Court observed that if by imposing solitary confinement there is total deprivation of camaraderie (friendship) amongst co-prisoners coming ling and talking and being talked to, it would offend Article 21 of the Constitution. The liberty to move, mix, mingle, talk, share company with co-prisoners if substantially curtailed would be violative of Article 21 unless curtailment has the backing of law. Thus, the punishment of solitary confinement was regarded as violative of Article 21.

Right against pre-trial confinement

A very grievous aspect of the present day administration of criminal justice is the long pre-trial incarceration of the accused persons. The poor persons have to languish in prisons awaiting trial because there is no one to post bail for them. This perpetrates great injustice on the accused person and jeopardises his personal liberty. Thousands of accused persons languish in jails awaiting trial for their offences.[109] Sometimes an undertrial may remain in prison for much longer than even the maximum prison sentence which can be awarded to him on conviction for the offence of which he is accused. This adversely affects the rights of the under trials who are presumed to be innocent till proven guilty. This also leads to overcrowding in prisons. One reason for this state of affairs is the irrational law regarding bail which insists on financial security from the accused and their sureties and thus, the poor and indigent persons cannot be released on bail as they are unable to provide financial security. Consequently, they have to remain in prison awaiting their trail. Thus even persons accused of bailable offences are unable to secure bail. The Supreme Court has criticised long incarceration of under trials, and has sought to rectify, the deplorable situation. Commenting on the deplorable situation, the Court has observed:

> "It is a crying shame on the judicial system which permits incarceration of men and women for such long periods of time without trial. . ."

The Court has declared that after the 'dynamic' interpretation of Article 21 in Maneka Gandhi, there is little doubt that any procedure which keeps such large numbers of people behind bars without trial so long cannot possibly be regarded as "reasonable, just and fair" so as to be in conformity with Article 21.

(vi) Right to Bail

The Supreme Court has diagnosed the root cause for long pre trial incarceration to be the present day unsatisfactory and irrational rules of bail which insist merely on financial security from the accused and their sureties. The Court has characterised, the system of bail in India as 'antiquated'. It is oppressive and weighted against the poor. Improvement of the system is very necessary as the Court insists in *Babu Singh* v. *State of U.P.*,[110] the Supreme Court held that "refusal to grant bail" to an accused person without reasonable grounds would amount to deprivation of his "personal liberty" under Article 21. The Court has made the constructive suggestion to change legal provisions for bail so that these provisions need no longer be based merely on financial sureties but that other factors should also be taken into account so that the poor can get their release from the prison pending their trial. The Court has laid down that even under the law as it exists, if the trial Court feels satisfied that an accused has his roots in the community and he is not likely to abscond, it can safely release him on his personal bond without sureties. The Court has emphasised: ". . . the issue of one of liberty, justice, public safety and burden on the public treasury, all of which insist that a developed jurisprudence of bail is integral to a socially sensitive judicial process. . ."

Imposing unjust or harsh conditions, while granting bail, is violative of Article 21.[111] Ordinarily in cases under TADA, release of under trials on bail is extremely restricted. But the Supreme Court has ruled that even in TADA cases, where there is no prospect of a trial being concluded within a reasonable time, release on bail may be necessary as this can be taken to be embedded in the right to speedy trial under Article 21.

Anticipatory bail is a statutory right and it does not arise out of Article 21. Anticipatory bail cannot be granted as a matter of right as it cannot be considered as an essential ingredient of Article 21.[112] In *Mantoo Majumdar* v. *State of Bihar*,[113] the Apex Court once again upheld the under trials right to personal liberty, and ordered the release of the petitioners on their own bond and without sureties as they had spent six years awaiting their trial, in prison. The Court deplored the delay in police investigation and the mechanical operation of the remand process by the Magistrate insensitive to the personal liberty of under trials, and the Magistrate failure to monitor the detention of the under trials remanded by them to prison.

(vii) Right against handcuffing of undertrials

In *Prem Shankar* v. *Delhi Administration*,[114] the Supreme Court added yet another projectile in its armoury to be used against the war for prison reform and prisoners rights. In that case the validity of certain clauses of Punjab Police Rules were Challenged as violation of Articles 14, 19 and 21 of the Constitution. Krishna Iyer clearly stated that every undertrial who was accused of non-bailable offence punishable with more than three years jail term would be handcuffed, were violative of Articles 14, 19 and 21 of the Constitution. Handcuffing should be resorted to only when there is 'clear and present danger of escape, breaking out the police control and for this there must be clear material, not merely an assumption. His lordship said:

> "Handcuffing is *prima facie* inhuman and, therefore, unreasonable, is over harsh and at the first flush, arbitrary. Absent fair procedure and objective monitoring, to inflict 'irons' is to resort to zoological strategies repugnant to Article 21 . . .". According to Krishna Iyer, J., Article 21 now "the sanctuary of human values prescribes fair procedure and forbids barbarities, punitive or processual". While conceding that prevention of escape of a prisoner was in public interest and reasonable, fair and just, Iyer, J. asserted that "insurance against escape does not compulsorily require handcuffing".[115] In *Khatri* v. *State of Bihar*,[116] the Court has declared it to be a constitutional mandate that no prisoner is to be handcuffed or fettered routinely or merely for the convenience of the custodian or the Courts. The distinction between classes of prisoners becomes constitutionally obsolete for this purpose as it cannot be assumed that a rich criminal or undertrial is any different from a poor undertrial in the matter of security risk. To be consistent with Articles 14 and 19, handcuffs must be the last refuge, not the routine regimen. Handcuffing of the accused by the police while in police custody violates Article 21 of the constitution. In *Citizens for Democracy through its president* v. *State of Assam*,[117] the Court has directed that "handcuffs or other fetters shall not be forced on a prisoner convicted or under trial while lodged in a jail anywhere in the country or while transporting or in transit from one jail to another or from jail to Court and back". The police and jail authorities, on their own, shall have no authority to direct handcuffing of any one without the order of a Magistrate for the purpose.

(viii) Rights against Bar Fetters

In *Sunil Batra* v. *Delhi Administration*,[118] the Supreme Court laid down that the treatment of a human being which offended human dignity, imposed avoidable torture and reduced the man to the level of a beast, would certainly be arbitrary and could be questioned under Articles 21 and 14. The Court held that continuously keeping a prisoner in fetters day and night reduces the prisoner from a human being to an animal and that this treatment was cruel and unusual that the use of bar fetters was against the spirit of the Constitution. In *Charles Shobraj* v. *Supdnt. Central Jail, Tihar,*[119] the Supreme Court recognised that the 'right to life' is more than a mere animal existence. Even in prison a person is required to be treated with dignity and one enjoys all the rights specified in Articles 19 and 21. Sobhraj alleged that ever since he was lodged in Tihar Central Jail, he was put in bar fetters and the fetters were retained continuously for 24 hours a day. The Court held Section 56 of the Prison Act, 1894 did not permit the use of bar fetters for an unusually long period, day and night and that too when the prisoner was confined in secure cells from where escape was somewhat inconceivable. The Court thus ordered the removal of the bar fetters.

(ix) Right to Appeal

Any person who feels aggrieved by any judgment passed by the Court may prefer an appeal in a superior Court if an appeal is provided against that judgment. Appeal is "the judicial examination of the decision by a higher Court of the decision of an inferior Court. A right of appeal is not a natural or inherent right. It is well settled that an appeal is a creature of statute and there is no right of appeal unless it is given clearly and in express terms by a statute. Whereas sometimes an appeal is a matter of rights, sometimes it depends upon discretion of the Court to which such appeal lies. In *M.H. Hoskot* v. *State of Maharashtra,*[120] it was stated that as a part of the concept of 'fair procedure' in Article 21, the Supreme Court has emphasised that one right of appeal from the Sessions Court to the High Court is essential where criminal conviction is brought about with long loss of liberty.

(x) Right against inhuman treatment and Third Degree methods

The Supreme Court in several cases has taken a serious note of the inhuman treatment to the prisoners and has issued appropriate directions to prison and police authorities for safeguarding the rights of the prisoners and person in police lockup, particularly of women and children. The incidents of torture, assault, injury and deaths in police custody have been said to be the worst form of human rights violation.[121] In *Kishore Singh* v. *State of Rajasthan*,[122] the Court held that the use of "third degree" methods by the police was violative of Article 21. Imposing "solitary confinement" for a long period from 8 to 11 months, or putting bar fetters on the prisoners in jail on flimsy gourds like "loitering in the prison", "behaving insolently and in an uncivilised manner", "tearing of his history ticket", the Court said must be regarded as barbarous and against human dignity and hence violative of Articles 14, 19 and 21.

Krishna Iyer, J. speaking for the Court observed that human dignity is a clear value of our Constitution not to be bartered away for mere apprehension entertained by jail officials. Torture and ill treatment of women suspects in police lockups has been held to be violative of Article 21 of the Constitution. The Court gave detailed instruction to concern authorities for providing security and safety in police lockup and particularly to women suspects. Female suspects should be kept in separate police lockups and not in the same in which male accused are detained and should be guarded by female constables. The Court directed the I.G. Prisons and State Board of Legal Aid Advice Committee to provide legal assistance to the poor and indigent accused (male and female) whether they are under trial or convicted prisoners.[123]

(xi) Right against Custodial Violence – police atrocities

Torture in custody, it is held, flouts, the basic rights of the citizens, and is an affront to human dignity. It tarnishes the image of any civilised nation. Unless stern measures are taken, civilisation would risk the consequences of leading towards total decay, resulting in anarchy and authoritarianism, reminiscent of barbarism.[124] Life or personal liberty includes a right to live with human dignity. There is an inbuilt guarantee against torture or assault by the State or its functionaries. Torture, assault and death in custody raise serious questions about the credibility of the rule of law and administration of the criminal justice system. There has been increase in instances of custodial violence/torture attributed to misuse of police machinery by those at the helm of affairs to settle personal scores.[125] In number of cases the Supreme Court has condemned police brutality and torture on prisoners, accused person and under trials. In this connection, the Supreme Court has observed in *Raghubir Singh* v. *State of Haryana*,[126] that:

> We are deeply disturbed by the diabolical recurrence of police torture resulting in a terrible scare in the minds of common

citizens that their lives and liberty are under a new peril when the guardians of the law gore human rights to death.

The Supreme Court has stressed that police torture is "disastrous to our human rights awareness and humanist constitutional order". The Court has squarely placed the responsibility to remedy the situation on the State. In the words of the Court: "the states, at the highest administrative and political levels, we hope, will organise special strategies to prevent and punish brutality by police methodology. Otherwise, the credibility of the rule of law in our Republic *vis-à-vis* the people of the country will deteriorate".

In *Francis Coralie Mullin* v. *Union Territory of Delhi*,[127] the Supreme Court has condemned cruelty or torture as being violative of Article 21 in the following words:

> ". . . any form of torture or cruel, inhuman or degrading treatment would be offensive to human dignity and constitute an inroad into this right to live and it would, on this view, be prohibited by Article 21 unless it is in accordance with the procedure prescribed by law, but no law which authorises and no procedure prescribed by law, which leads to such torture or cruel, in human or degrading element can never stand the test of reasonableness and non arbitrariness it would be plainly unconstitutional and void as being violative of Articles 14 and 21. It would be seen that there is implicit in Article 21 the right to protection against torture or cruel, inhuman or degrading treatment which is enunciated in Article 5 of the Universal Declaration of Human Rights and guaranteed by Article 7 of the International Covenant on Civil and political rights."

The incidents of brutal police behaviour towards persons detained on suspicion of having committed a crime are a common occurrence in India. There has been public outcry from time to time against custodial deaths. The Supreme Court has now ruled that it is well recognised right under Article 21 that a person detained lawfully by the police is entitled to be treated with dignity befitting a human being and that legal detention does not mean that he could be tortured or beaten up. If it is found that the police have ill treated a detenu, he would be entitled to monetary compensation under Article 21.[128]

The Court has given an expensive definition of "torture". According to the Court, "torture is not merely physical but may even consist of mental and psychological torture calculated to create fright to make her submit to the demands of the police".[129] Explaining that the problem is assuming alarming propositions, the Supreme Court in *Dalbir Singh* v. *State of U.P.*,[130] expressing their anguish, observed:

> . . . it is merely on account of the devilish devices adopted by those at the helm of affairs who proclaim from roof tops to be the defenders of democracy, and protectors of people's rights and yet do not hesitate to condescend behind the screen to let loose their men in uniform to settle personal scores, feigning ignorance of what happens and pretending to be peace loving puritans and saviours of citizens' rights.

In *Afzal* v. *State of Haryana*,[131] the Supreme Court condemned the illegal detention and confinement in police custody of innocent children belonging to the family of the accused on condition that they would be released only on surrender of the accused. The Court held this needless harassment of the innocent people for detecting the crimes as violative of Article 21.

(xii) Undertrials not to be kept with convicts

In *Sunil Batra (No. II)* v. *Delhi Administration*,[132] it was brought to the notice of the Supreme Court that a substantial number of undertrial prisoners, presumably innocent until convicted, were kept in Tihar jail with convicts. The Court condemned this practice as a "custodial perversity" which offended the test of reasonableness in Article 19 and fairness in Article 21. It was held that these undertrial prisoners by contamination were being made criminals. The Court observed:

> "How cruel would it be if one went to a hospital for a check-up and by being kept along with contagious cases came home with a new disease."

The Court then lay down that the undertrial should be kept separate from the convicts, the hardened criminals, whose guilt had been proved.

(xii) Right against delayed execution

A principle evolved by the Supreme Court in relation to death sentences is that if there is prolonged delay in execution of a death sentence then it would be an "unjust, unfair and unreasonable way" so as to offend Article 21.[133]

In *Vatheeswaran* v. *State of T.N.*,[134] the Court thought that the delay of two years would make it unreasonable to execute death sentence. The cause of delay was immaterial. The accused himself may be responsible for the delay. In such a case, the appropriate relief would be to vacate the death sentence and substitute life imprisonment instead. In *Sher Singh* v. *State of Punjab*,[135] the three judge bench of the Court agreed with this view that prolonged delay in the execution of a death sentence should be allowed to be executed or should be converted into sentence of imprisonment. Prolonged detention to await the execution of a sentence of death is an unjust, unfair and unreasonable procedure and the only way to undo the wrong is to quash the death sentence. However, the Court held that this cannot be applied as a rule in every case and each case should be decided on its own facts. The Court should consider whether the delay was due to the conduct of the convict (where he pursues series of legal remedies), the nature of offence, its impact on the society, its likelihood of repetition, before deciding to commute the death penalty into a sentence of life imprisonment. In the instant case the delay was found to be due to the conduct of the convict and therefore it was held that the death sentence was not liable to be quashed. Accordingly, the Court overruled the decision in *Vatheeswaran's* case. Finally, in *Triveni Ben* v. *State of Gujarat*,[136] a five judge bench of the Supreme Court has set the matter at rest and held that undue long delay in execution of the death sentence will entitle the condemned person to approach the Court for conversion of death sentence into life imprisonment, but before doing so the Court will examine the nature of the delay and circumstances of the case. No fixed period could be held to make the sentence of death in executable. In the present case the death penalty of the accused was converted into life imprisonment. Finally, the Court would, while deciding the question, consider the nature of the offence, circumstances in which the offence was committed, besides it would be open to the Court to examine or consider any circumstances after the final verdict was pronounced, if it was considered relevant.

In *Shivaji Jaising Babar* v. *State of Maharashtra*,[137] the Supreme Court, on the ground of delay for more than four years in the disposal of the mercy petition by the President under Article 72, held that Justice demanded modification of the sentence of death and commuted it to imprisonment for life.

(xiv) Right to write a book

A person detained in preventive detention wrote a scientific book, but the government refused permission to him to send it to his wife for publication. The Supreme Court in *State of Maharashtra* v. *Prabhakar Pandurang*,[138] held it to be an infringement of detenu's personal liberty as under Article 21 prohibiting a person from writing a book without there being any legal provision to that effect would be unconstitutional.

(xv) Right against public hanging

The Rajasthan High Court, by an order directed the execution of the death sentence of an accused by public hanging at the Stadium Ground or Ramlila Ground of Jaipur. It was also directed that execution should be done after giving widespread publicity through media. On receipt of the certified copy of the above order, the Supreme Court in *Attorney General of India* v. *Lachma Devi*,[139] held that the direction for execution of the death sentence was unconstitutional and violative of Article 21. It was further made clear that death by public hanging would be a barbaric practice. Jail Manual of no State in the country makes provisions for execution of death sentence by public hanging. The Court expressed that although the crime of which the accused had been found to be guilty was barbaric and a disgrace and shame on any civilised society which no society should tolerate, but a barbaric crime should not have to be visited with a barbaric penalty.

(xvi) Right against Illegal Detention

In *Joginder Kumar* v. *State of U.P.*,[140] the petitioner was detained by the police officer and his whereabouts were not told to his family members for a period of 5 days. Taking serious note of the police high handedness and illegal detention of a free citizen, the Supreme Court laid down the following guidelines governing arrest of a person during investigation:

1. An arrested person being held in custody is entitled, if he so requests to have one friend, relative or other person, who is known to him or likely to take an interest in his welfare, told as far as is practicable that he has been arrested and where he is being detained.

2. The police officer shall inform the arrested person when he is brought to the police station of this right.
3. An entry shall be required to be made in the diary as to who was informed of the arrest.

These protections from illegal arrest, the Court held, must be held to flow from Article 21 and 22(1) and enforced strictly.

Thus, it is rightly said that the scope of Article 21 have been expands over the years through judicial pronouncements over the years. Right to life and personal liberty are the most precious fundamental right. The provision of Article 21 ensures protection to citizens from arbitrary action of the State. It has also been provided that State should take steps to ensure that citizens should be able to lead a meaningful life. Article 21 has been construed broadly by the Courts in various cases to ensure citizen's right to live with dignity. Article 21 guarantees protection against the executive and legislative actions. The provisions under Article 21 mean that a personal liberty and person's life can only be disputed if that person has committed a crime.

(xvii) Right of the accused against death penalty

The Indian Criminal Justice System provides both deterrent and reformative punishments. A sentence of death can only be awarded in the "rarest of rare" cases. It may thus seem that the normal sentence for murder or culpable homicide amounting to murder is no longer a sentence of death but imprisonment for life. In choosing between the sentence of death and life imprisonment, the Court must show the high degree of concern and sensitivity that is only for special reasons to be recorded in the judgment, can a sentence of death be awarded and this is 'in rarest of the rare cases. It is conceded that the death penalty is barbaric, cruel, inhuman and opposed to civilised social norms and values and it is disproportionately excessive and therefore violative of principles of equality, freedom and right to life and personal liberty. The Supreme Court of India has unequivocally handed down some questions to be asked and answered when awarding a sentence of death, viz.:

(a) is there something uncommon about the crime which rendered a sentence of imprisonment for life inadequate and gave cause for the death sentence?
(b) are the circumstances of the crime such that there is no alternative but to impose the death sentence even after

according maximum weight to the mitigating circumstances which speak in favour of the offender?[141]

The legal approach in India thus seems to be more reformative than deterrent punishment. In recent times there have been consistent endeavours to provide orientation programmes to the convicts in the jails thus enabling them to rehabilitate or resocialise themselves after completing the conviction period.

(xviii) Right to seek Amnesty, Clemency, Pardon, Commutation

Article 72 of the Constitution of India creates mercy jurisdiction of the executive head, that is the President of India, to grant pardons, reprieves respites or remissions of punishments or to suspend, remit or commute the sentence of any person convicted of any offence where the sentence or punishment is by a Court Martial, or where the sentence is a sentence of death. Similar powers are conferred on the Governor of a State which extends to matters with respect to which the legislature of the State has powers to make laws. It may be *mutatis mutandi* clear that the President of India alone has the Executive power to grant pardons, reprieves, respites in all cases where the sentence is a sentence of death and both the President and the Governor have concurrent powers in respect of suspensions, remission and commutation of the sentence of death. It may be made clear that powers conferred on the Executive Heads are not judicial in nature but they are to be exercised in the exercise of executive functions. A pardon is an act of grace and it cannot be demanded as a matter of right. The effect of a pardon is to clear the convict of infancy. It is a power of executive character and the convict has no right to insist on an oral hearing before the President. However, the scope of pardoning power is judicially determinable when the Executive Head rejects the mercy petition on the ground that he could not go into the merits of the conviction granted by the Courts, as stated in *Kehar Singh* v. *Union of India*.[142] In *Moru Ram* v. *Union of India*,[143] Chief Justice, R.S. Pathak stated, "we are of opinion that the President is entitled to go in to the merits of the case notwithstanding that it has been judicially concluded by the consideration given to it by the Court". It may thus seem that the President of India has to give reasons if he refuses to entertain a pardon petition otherwise such action of Executive Head would be subject to judicial review.

(iv) Safeguards available to accused against arbitrary arrest and detention: Article 22

According to Article 21 no person can be deprived of his life or personal liberty except according to procedure established by law. This means that a person can be deprived of his life or personal liberty provided his deprivation was brought about in accordance with the procedure prescribed by law. Article 22 provides those procedural requirements which must be adopted and included in any procedure enacted by the legislature. If these procedural requirements are not complied with, it would then be deprivation of personal liberty which is not in accordance with the procedure established by law. Thus, Article 22 prescribes the minimum procedural requirements that must be included in any law enacted by the legislature in accordance with which a person may be deprived of his life and personal liberty.

Article 22 deals with two separate matters:

(i) persons arrested under the ordinary law of crimes; and
(ii) Persons detained under the law of 'preventive detention'.

Object behind Article 22

The safeguards are provided with a view to avoid any miscarriage of justice. It is to correct or check the use of power by the executive in arresting or detaining a person.

Who can claim Article 22?

The safeguards contained in Article 22 can be claimed by every person whether a citizen or a non citizen. Even a foreigner can claim these safeguards. However, these safeguards are not available to an enemy alien.

Article 22 applies to arrests, otherwise than under a warrant of a Court, made on the allegation or accusation of an actual, suspected or apprehended, commission by the person of any offence, criminal or quasi criminal in nature or some act prejudicial to the State or public interest.[144] The protection of the individual from oppression and abuse by the police and other enforcement officers is a major interest in a free society. Arrest and detention in police lockup may be very traumatic for a person. It can cause him incalculable harm by way of loss of his reputation. Denying a person of his liberty is a serious matter. The Supreme Court has clarified in *Joginder Kumar* v. *State of Uttar Pradesh*,[145] that no arrest can be made because it is lawful for the police officer to do so. The existence of the power of arrest is one thing, the justification for its exercise is quite another. The police officer must be able to justify the arrest apart from his power to do so. Accordingly, the Court has laid down the following guidelines in this regard for the police to follow:

> No arrest can be made in a routine manner on a mere allegation of commission of an offence made against a person. It would be prudent for a police officer in the interest of protection of the constitutional rights of a citizen and perhaps in his own interest that no arrest should be made without a reasonable satisfaction reached after some investigation as to the genuineness and bonafide of a complaint and a reasonable belief both as to the person's complicity and even so as to the need to effect arrest.

Article 22 guarantees the minimum rights which any person who is arrested will enjoy. Clause (1) and (2) of Article 22 ensure the following four safeguards for a person who is arrested:

1. He is not to be detained in custody without being informed, as soon as may be, of the grounds of his arrest [Article 22(1)].
2. He shall not be denied the right to consult, and to be defended by a legal practitioner of his choice [Article 22(2)].
3. A person arrested and detained in custody is to be produced before the nearest Magistrate within a period of twenty four hours of his arrest excluding the time necessary for the journey from the place of arrest to the Magistrate's Court [Article 22(2)].
4. No such person is to be detained in custody beyond this period without the authority of a Magistrate [Article 22(2)].

All these rights are without any qualifications and are therefore, in absolute terms. There are however, two exceptions to the universal application of the rights guaranteed under the first two clauses of Article 22. These relate to:

1. Any person who is for the time being an enemy alien; or
2. Any person who is arrested or detained under any law providing for preventive detention. The first exception was accepted by the constituent assembly without any

opposition as it embodied a sound principle. For instance, if India were at war with another country, considerations of national security may demand the arrest and detention of a person who is the citizen of the enemy country. He may not be given the rights guaranteed under Article 22(1) and (2). But no such easy justification is available for the second exception which provides for preventive detention even during normal times. Discussion on this clause in the constituent assembly was stormy and acrimonious.

The reasons for the introduction of such a clause were explained by Ambedkar thus:

> "It has to be recognised that in the present circumstances of the country, it may be necessary for the executive to detain a person who is tampering either with public order or with the Defence Services of the country. In such case, I do not think that the exigency of the liberty of the individual shall be placed above the interests of the State". Ambedkar explanations, however, failed to satisfy a considerable section of the Assembly who criticised the provision in strong terms. Replying to the debate, Ambedkar laid emphasis on the special safeguards embodied in the Constitution even when a person is arrested and detained under a preventive detention law. He said:

> If all of us follow purely constitutional method to achieve our objective, I think the situation would have been different and probably the necessity of having preventive detention might not be there at all. But I think in making a law we ought to take into consideration the worst and not the best. There may be many parties and persons who may not be patient enough to follow constitutional methods but are impatient in reaching their objective and if for that purpose they resort to unconstitutional methods, then there may be a large number of people who may have to be detained by the executive to prepare the cases and do all that is necessary to satisfy the elaborate legal procedure prescribed. Is it practicable?[146]

(i) ***Rights of arrested persons under Article 22***

Following are the rights available to the accused person against arbitrary arrest:

(a) The right to be informed 'as soon as' may be of ground of arrest

Any arrested person cannot be detained in custody without being informed, as soon as may be, of the grounds of his arrest. Such communications of grounds would enable him to make preparations for his release. The words, 'as soon as may be' occurring in Article 22(1) make it clear that there should not be unexplained delay. If information is delayed, there must be some reasonable grounds justified by circumstances.[147] Information about the grounds of arrest is mandatory under Article 21(1).[148] The Supreme Court has said about this rule in *State of M.P.* v. *Shobharam*,[149] in other words, a person's personal liberty cannot be curtailed by arrest without informing him, as soon as is possible, why he is arrested". The reason behind the rule requiring communication of grounds to the person arrested is to enable him to prepare his defence, and to move the Court for bail, or for a writ of habeas corpus. Failure to inform the person arrested of the reasons for his arrest would entitle him to be released. It is an imperative requirement. The object is to enable the person arrested to know as to why and for what offence he has been arrested. It is to afford him the earliest opportunity to remove any mistake or misapprehension or misunderstanding in the mind of the authority making the arrest.[150] It was further held that the Court can go into the sufficiency or otherwise of the grounds so furnished. The detention becomes unlawful if the grounds furnished are not proper and sufficient.[151] For the purposes of this rule, it is not necessary to furnish him with full details of the offence, but the information should be sufficient to enable him to understand why he has been arrested and to give him an idea of the offence which he is alleged to have committed. The grounds given to the arrested person should be intelligible.[152]

(b) The right to consult and to be represented by a lawyer of his own choice

Clause (1) of Article 22 further provides that the person arrested, "shall not be denied the right to consult and to be defended by a legal practitioner of his choice". The right to consult and be defended by a legal practitioner of his choice is guaranteed with a view to enable the detenue to prepare for his defence. This right belongs to the arrested person not only at the pre trial stage, but also at the trial before a criminal Court or before a special tribunal and whether the arrest is made under the general law or under a special statute. This is mandatory.[153] In *Joginder Kumar* v. *State of U.P.*,[154] the Supreme Court has ruled that the right of arrested person to have someone informed about his arrest and to consult privately with his lawyer were inherent in Articles 21 and 22. Thus, the right to consult the lawyer means the right to consult him, away from the hearing of the police.[155] The right to be defended by a legal practitioner cannot be excluded by a statute because of the constitutional mandate under Article 22(1).

In order to effectuate the right to consult a lawyer of his choice properly and reasonably, it is necessary that such legal practitioner is allowed the facility to consult the accused without the hearing of the police. A Court cannot therefore direct consultation between the accused and his counsel in the presence of police.[156] The police may, however be present so as to ensure that the accused does not abscond from custody, or do anything which may be objectionable otherwise. The right to consult a legal practitioner starts right from the day of arrest. According to Iyer, J. in *Nandini Satpathy* v. *P.L. Dani*,[157] Article 22(1) does not mean that a person who is not under arrest or custody can be denied the right to consult an advocate of his choice. The spirit and sense of Article 22(1) does not mean that a person who is not under arrest or custody can be denied the right to consult an advocate of his choice. The spirit and sense of Article 22(1) is that it is fundamental to the rule of law that the services of a lawyer shall be available for consultation to any accused person under "circumstances of near custodial interrogation". Moreover, the right against self incrimination is best promoted by conceding to the accused the right to consult a legal practitioner of his choice. Reading Articles 20(3) and 22(1) together, it will be prudent for the police to permit the advocate of the accused, if there be one, to be present at the time he is examined. If an accused person expressed the wish to have his lawyer by his side when his examination goes on, this facility should not be denied to him.

(c) The right to be produced before a Magistrate within 24 hours

The arrested person must be produced before a Magistrate within 24 hours of his arrest. It thus ensures that a judicial mind is applied immediately to the legal authority of the person making the arrest and regularity of the procedure adopted by him. This is a mandatory provision.[158] Where a person is arrested by a Magistrate without warrant, it is not sufficient for purposes of Article 22(2) to produce the person arrested before the same Magistrate who arrested him. The reason is that such a Magistrate could not apply a judicial mind to the facts of the case as he would be like a judge in his own cause. The policy of the law is that the Magistrate before whom a prisoner is produced must be in a position to bring an independent judgment to bear on the matter.[159] The Magistrate is not to act mechanically but should apply judicial mind to see whether the arrest of the person produced before him is legal, regular and in accordance with law. Otherwise, the protection afforded by Article 22(2) would be meaningless. The provision for production of an arrested man before a Magistrate is not to be treated as a mere formality but as purposeful and designed to enable the person arrested to be released on bail, or other provision made for his proper custody pending investigation into the offences with which he is charged pending an enquiry or trial. In *Bhim Singh* v. *State of J & K*,[160] the Supreme Court has criticised in very strong terms the conduct of a Magistrate who passed an order remanding the accused to police custody without the accused having been produced before him personally. The Magistrate was not concerned that the person whom he was remanding to custody had not been produced before him. The Magistrate acted in a very casual way. The Supreme Court considered it a great pity that the Magistrate acted without any sense of responsibility of genuine concern for the liberty of the subject. The police officer acted deliberately and mala fide and the Magistrate aided him either by colluding with him or by his casual attitude, this certainly was a gross violation of the constitutional rights of the accused under Articles 21 and 22(2) and the Court ordered the State to pay Rs. 50,000/- to the concerned person as monetary compensation. The requirement to produce an arrested person before a Magistrate may come to an end if he is released on bail. In *C.B.I.* v. *Anupam J. Kulkarni*,[161] stated that the "nearest Magistrate" means the Magistrate found to be nearest to the place of arrest. It is immaterial whether the Magistrate has or does not have jurisdiction to try the case or that the Magistrate sits in a Court or not, at the time the arrested person is produced before him. In *Khatri* v. *State of Bihar*,[162] it has been strongly urged by the Supreme Court that the State and police authorities should see to that, this constitutional and legal requirement to produce an arrested person before a judicial Magistrate within 24 hours of the arrest, must be scrupulously observed.

(d) No person to be detained in custody beyond 24 hours without the authority of Magistrate

Clause (2) of Article 22 mandates that the arrested person shall not be detained in custody beyond the stated period of 24 hours without the authority of a Magistrate. It would mean that if there is failure to produce the arrested person before the nearest Magistrate within 24 hours, it would make the detention illegal. This means that if there is necessity of detention beyond 24 hours it is only possible under judicial custody. A person was arrested in Bombay on a warrant issued by the speaker of the U.P. Legislative Assembly and was taken to Lucknow in custody to be produced before the speaker to answer a charge of breach of privilege of the house. He was not produced before a Magistrate within 24 hours of his arrest. The Supreme Court held in *Gunpati* v. *Nafisul Hasan*,[163] that this was a clear breach of the provisions of Article 22(2) and hence the petitioner was released.

(ii) Right against Preventive Detention

Preventive detention means detention of a person without trial and conviction by a Court, but merely on suspicion in the mind of an executive authority. Preventive detention is fundamentally and qualitatively different from imprisonment after trial and conviction in a criminal Court. Preventive detention and prosecution for an offence are not synonymous. In conviction, an accused is sought to be punished for a past act. The offence has to be proved in the Court beyond reasonable doubt. In preventive detention, on the other hand, a person is detained without trial in the subjective satisfaction of the executive to prevent him for committing an undesirable act in future. The idea is not to punish him for his past acts. "In preventive detention, the past act is merely the material for inference about the future course of probable conduct on the part of the detenu". In *Rajesh Gulati* v. *Government NCT of Delhi*,[164] preventive detention is thus preventive, not punitive, in theory. Preventive detention is not to punish an individual for any wrong done by him, but at curtailing his liberty, with a view to preventing him from committing certain injurious activities in future. As the Supreme Court has observed in *State of T.N.* v. *Senthil Kumar*,[165] whereas punitive incarceration is after trial on the allegations made against a person, preventive detention is without trial into the allegations made against him". Preventive detention has not been unknown in other democratic countries like Britain, United States of America and Canada, but only as a war time, and not a peace time, measure. In India, the Constitution itself visualises the possibility of a law of preventive detention. In spite of all the emphasis on individual liberty, it has been found necessary in India to resort to preventive detention during peace time because of unstable law and order situation in the country.[166]

Necessity of such provision

The justification for preventive detention is suspicion or reasonable apprehension, reasonable probability, of the impending commission of an act prejudicial to the State. The object is to prevent the abuse of freedom by anti social and subversive elements. In *A.K. Gopalan* v. *State of Madras*,[167] Patanjali Shastri, J., explaining the necessity of this provision said: "The sinister looking feature, so strangely out of place in democratic Constitution, which invests personal liberty with the sacrosanctity of a fundamental right, and so incompatible with the promises of its preamble, is doubtless designed to prevent the abuse of freedom by anti social and subversive elements which might imperil the national welfare of the infant republic".

Dr. Ambedkar explained the significance of the provision of Clauses (4) to (7) of Article 22 relating to preventive detention. He said that by virtue of the various entries in the legislative lists, the union and the states already possessed complete powers to legislate on preventive detention. The intention of these constitutional provisions was actually to curtail these powers and render them subject to certain specific limitations. In the absence of such a provision, Dr. Ambedkar pointed out the legislature might make any kind of law for preventive detention.

(i) Safeguards against arrest or detention made under a law providing for preventive detention [Articles 22(4) to (7)]

Clauses (4) to (7) of Article 22 contain the procedural requirements which one to be complied with when a person is detained under a law providing for preventive detention. These are as follows:

(a) No detention beyond three months unless such detention is approved by the Advisory Board;

(b) The detaining authority must communicate, as soon as may be, to the detenu, the grounds of such detention;

(c) The detenu must be afforded the earliest opportunity of making a representation against the order of detention;
(d) No detention beyond the maximum period prescribed under a law made by Parliament under clause 7(b).[168]

(a) No detention beyond three months without review by Advisory Board [Article 22(4) (a)]

Article 22(4) (a) makes provision for an Advisory Board for examining the desirability and sufficiency of detention of a person beyond the period of three months. Under this clause no detention can be made beyond three months. This limit can be exceeded beyond three months if an Advisory Board reports that there are sufficient reasons for detention beyond three months. The Government cannot detain a person beyond three months if the Advisory Board has not reported for such extended detention. If the Advisory Board does not report before the expiry of three months, detention cannot be extended and if extended, it will be illegal.[169] Sub clause (a) of clause (4) of Article 22 provides that a law providing for preventive detention shall not authorise the detention of a person for a longer period than three months except in the following cases:

(a) Where an Advisory Board, before the expiration of the stated period of three months, reports that in its opinion, there is sufficient cause for such detention.
(b) Where a person is detained in accordance with the provisions of any law made by Parliament under sub clauses (a) and (b) of clause (7).

A provision for an Advisory Board is not necessary where the detention is for less than three months.[170] The opinion of an Advisory Board confirming the detention must be obtained before the expiry of the first three months of detention. The order of confirmation passed after three months of the date of detention, though the opinion of the Advisory Board had been received, would be invalid and violative of Article 22(4) (a).[171]

Advisory Board

The function of the Advisory Boards is merely to report on the point whether there is sufficient cause for the detention. It is to provide a safeguard against misuse of the power of preventive detention. The Board is to judge whether the detention is justified and not arbitrary. Its duty is to report about the sufficiency of the detention. The board is not concerned as to how long the person should be detained.

The 44th Constitutional Amendment enacted by Parliament in 1978, amended Articles 22(4) to (7) so as to introduce therein a few more safeguard for the detenu as follows:

(a) the maximum period for which a person may be detained without obtaining the opinion of the advisory board has been reduced from 3 to 2 months;
(b) no person is to be kept in detention beyond two months unless the advisory board reports that in its opinion there is sufficient cause for such detention;
(c) an advisory board is to consist of a chairman and not less than two other members;
(d) the chairman of the board has to be a serving judge of the appropriate High Court and the other members may be serving or retired High Court judges;
(e) the board is to be constituted in accordance with the recommendations of the Chief Justice of the appropriate High Court;
(f) no person is to be kept in preventive detention beyond the maximum period prescribed by any law made by Parliament;

The reason for making the above changes in the composition of the advisory board is to make the board independent of the executive so that it may look into a case of preventive detention objectively. But these constitutional amendments have not yet been effectuated and Articles 22(4) to (7) still continues to be as they were before the 44th amendment.[172]

(i) Procedure before the Advisory Board

Clause 7(c) of Article 22 imposes that Parliament may, by law, prescribe the procedure to be followed by the Advisory Board in an inquiry under Article 22(4)(a). It has, however, been held that the Board submitting its report without hearing the detenu and examining his witness violates Article 22. Further, that the failure to produce the detenu before the board, due to the wilful refusal of the detenu himself is equally violative of these provisions.[173] But, the detenu cannot claim to be represented by a legal practitioner before the board. However, if the detaining authority or the Government takes the aid of a legal practitioner or adviser before the Board, the detenu must be allowed the same facility.[174] The detenu cannot claim the right of cross examination before the Advisory Board.[175]

(ii) Confirmation of the detention order

From the wording of Article 22(4), the Supreme Court has spelled out the rule that not only the advisory board should report within three months of the date of detention order that, in its opinion, there is sufficient cause for the detention of the detenu, but also the government should itself confirm and extend the period of detention (beyond three months) within the three months time limit. Failure on the part of the government to do so will render the detention invalid as soon as three months elapse and any subsequent action by the government cannot have the effect of extending the period of detention beyond three months. While confirming the order of detention, the government has not only to peruse the report of the advisory board, but apply its mind to the material on record.[176] It is also necessary that the order of confirmation be in writing and be communicated to the detenu. The detenu whose freedom is in jeopardy is entitled to know the result of his representation. But lack of communication to him is merely an irregularity and it does not invalidate an otherwise valid detention.[177]

(b) Communication of grounds to the detenu

Clause 5 of Article 22 involves an obligation on the government to communicate to the detenu the grounds of detention. For the compliance of this requirement, the ground of detention should be very clear and easily understandable. There must be a rational connection between the grounds stated by the government and the object which are to be prevented under the law providing for preventive detention.[178] Where the grounds of detention related to publication of a defamation of a judge of a High Court and had nothing to do with the purpose of public order or other objects of the statute, the grounds were irrelevant which would invalidate the detention.[179] It has been held that the grounds furnished to the detenu must not be "vague", "irrelevant" or "non-existent", or based on extraneous consideration.[180] These must be self explanatory and self sufficient and the copies of documents referred to in the grounds, must be supplied. In *Sophia Gulam Mohd. Bham* v. *State of Maharashtra*,[181] when the order of detention was passed on ground that when detenu was held at airport and on his search, being taken he was found in possession of diamonds which he was trying to smuggle out of India and the documents were seized from the premises which revealed to the detaining authority the link between smugglers of diamonds and the detenu and it was concluded that the detenue was a "carrier" of goods for those smugglers, however, copies of these documents were not supplied to the detenu, the Supreme Court held that the order of detention illegal as depriving the detenu from making effective representation. In *Surjeet Singh* v. *Union of India*,[182] where the detenu did not know sufficient English to understand the grounds communicated to him, it was held that service of grounds in English was no sufficient compliance with the requirement contained in Article 22(5). Simply by reason that the detenu signed in English, did not mean that he could understand the grounds. If the grounds are only verbally explained to the detenu and nothing in writing is left with him in a language which he understands, it has been held that the purpose of Article 22(5) is not served. Where a detenu is totally illiterate, it is necessary that the grounds of detention should be explained to him as early as possible in the language he understands so that he can avail of the statutory right of making representation under Article 22(5).[183] In *Lallubhai Jogibhai Patel* v. *Union of India*,[184] the detenu did not know English but the grounds were drawn in English and the detaining order stated that the police inspector, while serving the grounds of detention to the detenu, fully explained the grounds in Gujarati, which he could follow, but no translation of the grounds in Gujarati was given to him, it was held that there was no sufficient compliance of Article 22(5). Article 22(5) run as follows:

> When any person is detained in pursuance of an order made under any law providing for preventive detention, the authority making the order shall, as soon as may be, communicate to such person the grounds on which the order has been made and shall afford him the earliest opportunity of making a representation against the order.

Article 22(5) has two limbs. One, the detaining authority is to communicate to the detenu the grounds of his detention 'as soon as may be'. Two, the detenu is to be afforded 'the earliest opportunity of making a representation against the order of detention. This is natural justice woven into the fabric of preventive detention by the Constitution. In *Madhab Roy* v. *State of W.B.*,[185] it was stated that the detention order becomes bad if any factual components constituting the real grounds for detention are not fairly and fully put across to the detenu, the reason being that if some facts are held back from him, his right to make an effective representation against his detention is infringed. The Supreme Court has emphasised that Article 22(5) vests a real and not an imaginary or illusory right in the detenu. The communication of facts is the cornerstone of his right of representation and an order of detention passed on uncommunicated material is unfair and illegal. In *Nandoli Mohamed Rafeeq* v. *Union of India*,[186] it was held that the detenu can make an effective representation only after reading and understanding the contents of all documents. Where the document supplied was in Tamil, a language which was not known to the detenu, he is deprived of the right to make an effective representation.

The Amended National Security Act, 1984

In earlier cases, the inclusion of even a single irrelevant or obscure ground in the detention order was held to be invasion of the detenu's constitutional right under Article 22(5). For example, in *Fogla and S.K. Jatil* v. *State of W.B.*,[187] the Supreme Court set aside the order of detention on the ground that one of the reasons for detention was not communicated to the detenu. To nullify the effect of these decisions, the National Security Act, was amended in 1984. In the amended NSA, it has been provided that a detention order made under the Act, for which two or more grounds have been communicated to the detenu, would not be deemed to be invalid or inoperative, merely because some of the grounds are found to be vague, non-existent, not relevant, unconnected or invalid. The detention order has been held to be valid even if one of the grounds was found to be bad and unsustainable if the remaining grounds are sufficient to sustain the detention.[188] It is done by applying the principle of severability.

(c) Right of the detenu to make a representation against the order of detention [Article 22(5)]

The detenu has a constitutional right to make a representation against the order of detention. This right of making the representation is dependent upon receiving the grounds on which the detention order has been passed. Therefore, the grounds are to be communicated "as soon as may be" and an "earliest opportunity" for making representation is mandatory given to him. Thus, clause 5 of Article 22 enjoins the detaining authority to afford the detenu the earliest opportunity to make a representation against the order of detention. The right to make a representation implies that the detenu should have such information as will enable him to make a representation. All the basic and material facts which influenced the detaining authority to order detention must be communicated to the detenu. If there are any statements and documents referred to in the grounds, they must also be communicated to him.[189] Non communication to the detenu that he has right to make representation to the detaining authority amounts to infraction of his right under Article 22(5).[190] In *Vakil Singh* v. *State of J & K*,[191] it has been clarified that grounds for the purposes of Article 22(5) mean materials on which the order of detention was primarily based, that is to say all primary facts though not subsidiary facts or evidential details.

It has thus been made clear that the Court has a duty to see whether non supply of any document is in any way prejudicial to the case of the detenu.[192] The right to make a representation does not include in it the right to be heard orally or an oral interview in respect of the representation. It is implicit in Article 22(5) that the representation must be a written representation through the jail authorities or through any other mode which the detenu thinks fit.[193] Grounds were served on a detenu in the English language which he did not know. He asked for a Hindi version of the grounds which was not supplied to him. Quashing his detention, the Supreme Court emphasised that to enable the detenu to make an effective representation, he should have knowledge of the grounds of detention. Communication envisages bringing home to the detenu effective knowledge of the facts and circumstances on which the order was based. To a person not conversant with the English language, the grounds must be explained in language which he understands.[194] A smuggler detained under COFEPOSA challenged his detention on several grounds of which one proved to be fatal, viz., the detaining authority had not severed on the detenu copies of several documents on which the authority had relied in the grounds of detention. The points of this case in deep concern were expressed by the Supreme Court for the upholding of personal liberty. The Court ruled that, in the instant case, continued detention of the petitioner became illegal because of non compliance with statutory and constitutional requirements.[195]

(d) No detention beyond the maximum period prescribed under a law made by parliament under clause 7(b)

Article 22(4) (a) says that no person can be detained beyond the maximum period prescribed by any law made by Parliament. Under Article 22(7) (b), Parliament may by law prescribe the maximum period of detention for which any person can be detained. This provision has been held to be merely permissive, and it does not oblige Parliament to prescribe any maximum period of detention. It has also been held that it is not necessary for Parliament to fix the maximum period for detention in terms of years, months or days. It is valid to fix such period in terms of a specific event, as for example, until the expiry of the emergency proclaimed under Article 352.[196] Clause 7 of Article 22 confers power on Parliament to make a law prescribing the maximum period for which any person may, in any class or classes for cases, be detained under any law providing for preventive detention. Section 14A of the National Security Act, 1980, prescribes a maximum period of twelve months for which a person can be detained under the Act.

(e) No right to disclose of certain facts [Article 22(6)]

Clause 6 of Article 22 is an exception to clause (5). Clause 6 provides: "Nothing in clause (5) shall require the authority making any such order as is referred to in that clause to disclose facts which such authority considers be against the public interest to disclose". The facts which cannot be required to be disclosed are those which the detaining authority considers to be against public interest to disclose. It is, therefore, for the detaining authority, in the exercise of its discretion, to decide what facts cannot be disclosed. For example, the detenu is not entitled to the disclosure of confidential sources of information used in the ground for making of the order of detention.[197]

Consideration of the Representation

Article 22(5) imposes an obligation on the government to consider the representation of the detenu as expeditiously as possible and without inordinate delay.[198] Right to liberty under Article 21 depends upon a proper consideration of the representation, after full and independent application of mind on the representation and on the relevant documents.[199]

Thus, from the above discussion regarding the rights of the accused and the Constitution of India, it is quite clear that the Constitution of India is one of the most rights based Constitution in the world. A Constitution is the vehicle of a nation's progress. It is a legal and social document. The highest law of the land, the

Constitution is the repository and source of all legal powers. It is intended to serve the needs of the days when it was enacted and also to meet the needs of the changing conditions in new circumstances. A Constitution is thus, said to be a living and organic document, which of all instruments has the greatest claim to be construed broadly and liberally. Part III of the Indian Constitution secures to the people of India fundamental basic and natural rights. The chapter is known as the Bill of Rights for the people of India. The Constitution not only declares these fundamental rights but it also provides a speedy remedy for the enforcement of these rights and the remedy for their enforcement is itself declared a fundamental right. Fundamental rights as enacted in our Constitution not only recognise the dignity of the individual to which the preamble refers, but also recognise their necessity for the full development of the individual and also for preserving the Union of India. The unity of India is also emphasised by granting equality before law or the equal protection of the laws within the territory of India; by prohibiting discrimination against citizens on the grounds of religion, race, caste, sex or place of birth, and by providing for equality of opportunity. The fundamental rights help not only in protection but also the prevention of gross violations of human rights. They emphasise on the fundamental unity of India by guaranteeing to all citizens the access and use of the same facilities, irrespective of background. Some fundamental rights apply for persons of any nationality whereas others are available only to the citizens of India. Specially, Articles 20 and 21 of the Constitution of India provide the basis for human rights of an accused under the Indian criminal jurisprudence. These rights mentioned in two articles cannot be suspended even in the proclamation of emergency. The rights of accused has been realised and establish both internationally and nationally throughout various countries. In India specifically keeping in mind this growing debates and the current worsening position of the criminal justice system; the Supreme Court of India has by way of interpretation found and laid down various mandates towards the rights and fairness to the accused like right against inhuman treatment, torture or degrading punishment under the police or judicial custody, right to have a fair trial, a fair procedure and a fair investigation, right against arbitrary and illegal arrest, right to free legal aid and speedy trial, etc. In other words it has been impliedly incorporated that innocent until proved guilty and hence the person must and should be provided with not just the rights under Articles 21 and 20 but with those rights as well that improves the life and dignity mandate.

Notes and References

1. AIR 1973 SC 1461, 1536.
2. AIR 1967 SC 1643, 1656.
3. Dr. H.O. Agarwal, *International Law and Human Rights*, 885 (15th Edition).
4. AIR 1954 SC 92.
5. Dr. Ashutosh, *Rights of Accused*, 142 (2013).
6. Article 13 of the Constitution.
7. Article 32 of the Constitution.
8. Article 226 of the Constitution.
9. Vivek Jain, "Rights of Accused", available at *www.mightylaws.in/511/rights*.
10. AIR 1975 SC 2999.
11. AIR 1999 SC 1160.
12. AIR 1951 SC 41.
13. AIR 2001 SC 260 at 264.
14. *State of Punjab* v. *Baldev Singh*, AIR 1999 SC 2378.
15. AIR 1980 SC 1535.
16. *T.V Vetheeswaran* v. *State of Tamil Nadu*, AIR 1983 SC 361, 362.
17. AIR 1980 SC 1579 (II).
18. AIR 1981 SC 625.
19. AIR 1950 SC 124.
20. Dr. J.N. Pandey, *The Constitutional Law of India*, 172 (2012).
21. AIR 1998 AP 35.
22. AIR 1982 SC 6.
23. AIR 1981 SC 746.
24. AIR 1995 SC 264. Also see *Khushwant Singh* v. *Maneka Gandhi*, AIR 2002 Del 58.
25. AIR 1977 SC 2091.
26. *Soni D. Babubhai* v. *State of Gujarat*, AIR 1991 SC 2173.
27. *Maxwell on Interpretation of Statutes*, 215 (12th Edition).
28. *Chief Inspector of Mines* v. *K.C. Thapar*, AIR 1961 SC 838.
29. *Rao Shiva B. Singh* v. *State of Vindhya Pradesh*, AIR 1953 SC 394.
30. *Shiv Bahadur Singh* v. *State of Vindhya Pradesh*, AIR 1963 SC 394. Also see *Union of India* v. *Sukumar Pyne*, AIR 1966 SC 1206.
31. *Rattan Lal* v. *State of Punjab*, AIR 1965 SC 444.
32. AIR 2004 SC 2608.
33. *T. Barai* v. *Henry Ah Hoc*, AIR 1983 SC 150.
34. AIR 2004 SC 2757.
35. AIR 1953 SC 404.
36. AIR 1965 SC 444.
37. *Kanaiyalal* v. *Indumati*, AIR 1958 SC 444.
38. *Kedar Nath* v. *State of West Bengal*, AIR 1953 SC 404.
39. *Shiv Bahadur* v. *State of Vindhya Pradesh*, AIR 1953 SC 394.

40. AIR 1980 SC 2147.
41. Vijoy Vivekanandan, "The Conceptual Analysis of the Principle of Double Jeopardy", available at *www.lawcollegedehradun.com/lawreview*.
42. AIR 1953 SC 131.
43. *Ibid.*
44. *Supra* note 40.
45. *P. Ranjangam* v. *State of Madras*, AIR 1959 Mad 294.
46. *Woolmington* v. *DPP*, (1935) AC 462 is a famous House of Lords case in English law, where the presumption of innocence was first articulated in the common wealth by Viscount Sankey.
47. Article 20—Constitution of India, available at *www.lawzonline.com/bareacts/ Indian*.
48. *Narayan Lal* v. *M.P. Mistry*, AIR 1961 SC 29.
49. AIR 1954 SC 300.
50. AIR 1961 SC 1808.
51. *Ambalal* V. *Choksi* v. *State of Maharashtra*, AIR 1966 Bom 243.
52. AIR 1973 SC 1196.
53. AIR 1954 SC 300.
54. *Dastagir* v. *State of Madras*, AIR 1960 SC 756.
55. *Yusufalli* v. *State of Maharashtra*, AIR 1968 SC 147.
56. *Pakhar Singh* v. *State of Punjab*,
57. AIR 1958 Punj 204. AIR 1957 Mad 546.
58. *Subhaya Gounder* v. *Bhoopala*, AIR 1959 Mad 396.
59. *R.M. Malkani* v. *State of Maharashtra*, AIR 1973 SC 157.
60. Article 20(3) of Constitution of the India and Narco Analysis, available at www.legalserviceindia.com/article/.... See also Harshit Khare, "Self-incrimination: A Study", February 23, 2010.
61. *Dinesh Dalmia* v. *State*, 2006 (3) Cri LJ 2401. See also *Abhay Singh* v. *State of U.P.*, 2009 Cri LJ 2189.
62. AIR 2010 SC 1974.
63. Prof. Narender Kumar, *Constitutional Law of India*, 305 (2011).
64. AIR 1978 SC 1025.
65. Sonakshi Verma, "Article on the Concept of Narco analysis in view of constitutional law".
66. AIR 1963 SC 1295.
67. Article on "Admissibility of DNA Technology in the Indian Legal System . . ., available at *www.legallyindia.com/esayblog/adm*.
68. AIR 1956 All 341.
69. *I.R. Coelho* v. *State of T.N.*, AIR 2007 SC 861.
70. AIR 1989 SC 653.
71. *Confd. of Ex-Servicemen Asso.* v. *Union of India*, (2006) 8 SCC 399.
72. AIR 2007 SC 71 (CB).
73. AIR 1978 SC 1675.
74. AIR 1984 SC 1844.
75. AIR 1990 SC 630.
76. AIR 1963 SC 1295.
77. AIR 1978 SC 597.
78. AIR 1974 SC 2092.

79. AIR 1978 SC 527.
80. AIR 1978 SC 597.
81. *Sunil Batra* v. *Delhi Administration (II)*, AIR 1980 SC 1579.
82. M.P. Jain, *Indian Constitution Law*, (2011).
83. *Vakil Prasad Singh* v. *State of Bihar*, (2009) 3 SCC 355.
84. *DLF Power Limited* v. *Central Coalfields Ltd.*, AIR 2009 SC 2189.
85. *State of Punjab* v. *Baldev Singh*, AIR 1999 SC 2378.
86. AIR 2004 SC 3114.
87. *Varkey Joseph* v. *State of Kerala*, AIR 1993 SC 1892.
88. *Pratap Singh* v. *State of Jharkhand*, (2005) 3 SCC 551.
89. AIR 1994 SC 1349.
90. (2009) 4 SCC 437.
91. AIR 1997 SC 610.
92. *Ibid.*
93. Article on "Legal Aid in India - expert lawyer, India", available at www.expertlawyer.in/legal-aid-in.
94. AIR 1978 SC 1548.
95. AIR 1979 SC 1369.
96. AIR 1981 SC 928.
97. *Suk Das* v. *Union territory of Arunachal Pradesh*, AIR 1986 SC 991.
98. *Supra* note 81 at 1198.
99. AIR 1979 SC 1360.
100. AIR 1979 SC 1369.
101. AIR 2007 SC 3057.
102. AIR 1992 SC 1701.
103. AIR 1996 SC 1619.
104. *State of Maharashtra* v. *Champalal*, AIR 1981 SC 1675.
105. AIR 1981 SC 939.
106. AIR 1995 SC 1976.
107. *State of Maharashtra* v. *Prabhakar Pandurang*, AIR 1966 SC 424.
108. AIR 1978 SC 1675.
109. The Law Commission has in its 77th and 78th reported on this matter. It has said that the matter of reducing delay and arrears in trial Courts is of "the greatest importance" to which "the highest priority" ought to be given.
110. AIR 1978 SC 527.
111. *Gurbaksh Singh Sibbia* v. *State of Punjab*, AIR 1980 SC 1632.
112. *State of M.P.* v. *Ram Kishan Balothia*, AIR 1995 SC 1198.
113. AIR 1980 SC 846.
114. AIR 1980 SC 1535.
115. *Id.*, at 1542.
116. AIR 1981 SC 1068; also see, *Sunil Gupta* v. *State of M.P.*, AIR 1955 SC 31.
117. AIR 1996 SC 2193.
118. AIR 1978 SC 1675.
119. AIR 1978 SC 514.
120. AIR 1978 SC 1548.
121. Justice A.S. Anand, "Third Degree Methods, Criminal Act", *The Tribune*, December 11, 2000.

122. AIR 1981 SC 625; also see *Rama Murthy* v. *State of Karnataka*, AIR 1997 SC 1739.
123. *Sheela Barse* v. *State of Maharashtra*, (1993) 2 SCC 96.
124. *Smt. Shakila Abdul G. Khan* v. *V.R. Dhokle*, JT 2003 SC 282.
125. *Munshi Singh Gautam* v. *State of M.P.*, (2005) 9 SCC 631.
126. AIR 1980 SC 1087, 1088.
127. AIR 1981 SC 746.
128. *Mohan Lal Sharma* v. *State of U.P.*, (1989) 2 SCC 314.
129. *Arvinder Singh Bagga* v. *State of U.P.*, AIR 1995 SC 117.
130. AIR 2009 SC 1674.
131. AIR 1996 SC 2326.
132. AIR 1980 SC 1579.
133. *Earl Pratt* v. *Att. Gen. of Jamaica*, (1994) 2 AC 1.
134. AIR 1983 SC 361, 362.
135. AIR 1983 SC 465.
136. AIR 1989 SC 1335.
137. AIR 1991 SC 2147. See also *Daya Singh* v. *Union of India*, AIR 1991 SC 1548.
138. AIR 1966 SC 424.
139. AIR 1986 SC 467.
140. AIR 1994 SC 1349.
141. *Bachan Singh* v. *State of Punjab*, (1982) 3 SCC 24. See also *Machhi Singh* v. *State of Punjab*, (1983) 3 SCC 470.
142. (1989) 1 SCC 204, 217.
143. (1981) 1 SCC 107.
144. *State of M.P.* v. *Shobharam*, AIR 1966 SC 1910.
145. AIR 1994 SC 1349: (1994) 4 SCC 260.
146. Arvind Kumar, "Essay on Protection against Arrest and Detention as per Indian Constitution", available at *www.preventivearticles.com/201111...*
147. *Tarapada De* v. *State of W.B.*, AIR 1951 SC 174.
148. *Hansmukh* v. *State of Gujarat*, AIR 1981 SC 28.
149. AIR 1966 SC 1910.
150. In *Re Madhu Limaye*, AIR 1969 SC 1014.
151. *Ibid.*
152. *Vimal* v. *State of U.P.*, AIR 1956 All 56.
153. *State of M.P.* v. *Shobharam*, AIR 1966 SC 1910.
154. AIR 1994 SC 1349.
155. *Moti Bai* v. *State of Rajasthan*, AIR 1954 Raj 241.
156. *Jose Poothrikkayil* v. *Union of India*, 2009 (2) KLJ 381.
157. AIR 1978 SC 1025.
158. *State of U.P.* v. *Abdul Samad*, AIR 1962 SC 1506.
159. *Hariharanand* v. *Jailor*, AIR 1954 All 601.
160. AIR 1986 SC 424.
161. AIR 1992 SC 1768.
162. AIR 1981 SC 928.
163. AIR 1954 SC 636.
164. (2002) 6 Scale 142.
165. AIR 1999 SC 971.

166. *Supra* note 81 at 1256.
167. AIR 1950 SC 27.
168. *Supra* note 62 at 368.
169. *Abdul Latif* v. *B.K. Jha,* AIR 1987 SC 725.
170. *Ujjal* v. *State of W.B.*, AIR 1972 SC 1446.
171. *S. Mukharji* v. *State of W.B.*, AIR 1972 SC 1356.
172. Section 3 of the Constitution (Forty fourth Amendment) Act, 1978.
173. *State of Punjab* v. *Sukhpal Singh,* AIR 1990 SC 231.
174. *Phillipa Anne Duke* v. *State of T.N.*, AIR 1982 SC 1178.
175. *A.K. Roy* v. *Union of India,* AIR 1982 SC 710.
176. *Nandlal* v. *State of Punjab*, AIR 1981 SC 2041.
177. *Deb Sadhan Roy* v. *State of W.B.*, AIR 1972 SC 1924.
178. *Darpan Kumar Sharma* v. *State of T.N.*, AIR 2003 SC 971.
179. *Sodhi Shamsher Singh* v. *State of Pepsu*, AIR 1954 SC 276.
180. *Kishori Mohan* v. *State of W.B.*, AIR 1972 SC 1749.
181. AIR 1999 SC 3051.
182. AIR 1981 SC 1153.
183. *Kubic Darinsz* v. *Union of India*, AIR 1990 SC 605.
184. AIR 1981 SC 728.
185. AIR 1975 SC 255.
186. (2004) 12 SCC 218, 219.
187. AIR 1975 SC 245.
188. *D. Anuradha* v. *Joint Secretary*, (2006) 5 SCC 142.
189. *State of Maharashtra* v. *Zubair Haji Qasim*, AIR 2008 SC 2825.
190. *State of Maharashtra* v. *S.S. Acharya,* AIR 2000 SC 250.
191. AIR 1974 SC 2337.
192. *J. Abdul Hakeem* v. *State of T.N.*, AIR 2005 SC 3677.
193. *Devji Vallabhbhai* v. *Administrator, Goa, Daman and Diu*, AIR 1982 SC 1029.
194. *State of Maharashtra* v. *Bhaurao P. Gawande,* AIR 2008 SC 1705.
195. *Icchu Devi* v. *Union of India,* AIR 1980 SC 1983.
196. *Sunil Fulchand Singh* v. *Union of India*, AIR 2000 SC 1023.
197. *State of Rajasthan* v. *Shamsher Singh,* AIR 1985 SC 1091.
198. *D. Anuradha* v. *Joint Secretary*, (2006) 5 SCC 142.
199. *A.C. Razia* v. *Government of Kerala,* AIR 2003 SC 2222.

4

Rights of the Accused and the Indian Evidence Act, 1872

The Adversarial System is a fundamental principle of criminal jurisprudence. It is based on the precinct that through a process of fair hearing and adducing of evidence, the truth of the matter will eventually emerge. As such, the Indian Evidence Act includes certain provisions which uphold the adversarial principles and grant certain protections to the accused in its endeavour to make the criminal justice system reasonably fair to the accused. The enactment and adoption of the Indian Evidence Act was a path breaking judicial measure introduced in India, which changed the entire system of concepts pertaining to admissibility of evidences in the Indian Courts of law. Until then, the rules of evidence were based on the traditional legal systems of different social groups and communities of India and were different for different people depending on caste, religious, faith and social position. The Indian Evidence Act introduced a new standard set of law applicable to all Indians. As it is very much clearly stated in *Ram Jas* v. *Surendra Nath*,[1] the law of evidence does not affect substantive rights of parties but only lays down the law for facilitating the course of justice. The Evidence Act lays down the rules of evidence for the purposes of the guidance of the Courts. It is procedural law which provides, *inter alia*, how a fact is to be proved. In the leading case of *Kishore Singh Ravinder Dev* v. *State of*

Rajasthan,[2] it was held that the laws of India i.e. constitutional, evidentiary and procedural have made elaborate provisions for safeguarding the rights of accused with the view to protect his dignity as a human being and giving him benefits of a just, fair and impartial trial. An accused have certain rights during the course of any investigation, enquiry or trial of offence with which he is charged. The soul of criminal justice system is adversarial system which provides with a prospect for the parties to case, advance and present their arguments, gather and submit evidence, call and question witness and control the information presented conferring to the law and legal procedure.

The Act applies uniformly to civil and criminal proceedings. Yet its provisions can be classified into those applicable only to civil proceedings, those applicable only to criminal proceedings and those applicable to both. In civil matters standards of proof go by probabilities, but in criminal matters there must be more certainty and proof beyond reasonable doubt. In criminal matters the degree of proof is stricter and where circumstantial evidence is the only basis, proof cannot be in the realm of surmises and conjectures. Certain provisions of the Act are typically applicable only to criminal matters, for example, those connected with confessions. Certain others are typically applicable to civil matters only, for example, provisions as to estoppel.

I. PROTECTION TO ACCUSED AVAILABLE UNDER INDIAN EVIDENCE ACT, 1872

Section 4 of the Act talks about presumptions of fact and such presumptions may well be against the accused, making this provision stand in contradiction adversarial principles to a certain extent. However, facts which the Court 'may presume' at its discretion, as well as facts which it 'shall presume' according to specific provisions of the Act, are rebuttable; and evidence may be produced to disprove them, thereby granting an aspect of fairness to the accused which overrides these seemingly inquisitorial provisions. Moreover, such presumptions are based on natural logical inferences and per se are not unfair as stated in *Gitika Bagechi* v. *Shubhabrata Bagechi*,[3] 'conclusive proof', as mentioned under this section is irrbuttable; however, the aspect of fairness to the accused is maintained since nothing can be 'Conclusive proof' of anything unless that primary fact is *prima facie* 'proved', and hence the element of irrebuttable presumption is of a secondary nature.

The only exception of this rule regarding 'conclusive proof' is in Section 112, which talks of the legitimacy of children.

(a) Rights of accused relating to confession

In the law of criminal evidence, a confession is a statement by a suspect in crime which is adverse to that person. Some secondary authorities, such as Black's Law Dictionary, define a confession in more narrow terms, e.g. as "a statement admitting or acknowledging all facts necessary for conviction of a crime", which would be distinct from a mere admission of certain facts that, if true, would still not, by themselves, satisfy all the elements of the offence. Confessions were first developed in the Roman Catholic Church under the Sacrament of Penance, where the confession of a sin is considered to be enough to absolve oneself. This aspect concerning moral guilt has been carried on in various legislative codes, in which a criminal is considered worse if he does not confess to his crimes. Confessions obtained under torture have often been considered to be not objective enough, since the use of such means may lead to the suspect in confessing anything. However, when the confession reveal secret only known to the perpetrator (such as the location of the body or murder weapon), the confession is reliable. Confession evidence can be considered, arguably, the best piece of evidence of guilt in the criminal justice system.[4] Confession is a direct admission or acknowledgement of his guilt by a person who has committed a crime. It may be judicial or extra judicial. "Confession" in common acceptance means and implies acknowledgment of guilt confession in Section 25 of the Indian Evidence Act (1 of 1872), means, as in Section 24 of the same Act, a 'confession made by an accused person' which it is proposed to prove against him to establish an offence, "confessio facta in judicio, Omni probatione major est" is of great importance, which means "A confession made in Court is of greater effect than any proof".[5] The definition of "admission" as given in Section 17 becomes applicable to confession also. Section 17 defines "admission" as "a statement oral or documentary, which suggests any inference as to any fact in issue or relevant fact". If such a statement is made by a party to a civil proceeding it will be called an "admission" and if it is made by a party charged with a crime it will be called a "confession".[6] Thus, in terms of the Act, a confession is a statement made by a person charged with a crime suggesting an inference as to any facts in issue or as to relevant facts. The inference that the statement should suggest should be that he is guilty of the crime.

Form of Confession

A confession may occur in any form. It may be made to the Court itself, when it will be known as judicial confession or to anybody outside the Court, in such case it is called an extra judicial confession. It may even consist of conversation to oneself which may be produced in evidence if overheard by another. For example, in *Sahoo* v. *State of U.P.*,[7] the accused who was charged with the murder of his daughter-in-law with whom he was always quarrelling was seen on the day of the murder going out of the home, saying words to the effect: "I have finished her and with her the daily quarrels".

The statement was held to be a confession relevant in evidence, for it is not necessary for the relevancy of a confession that it should be communicated to some other person.

Extra Judicial confession must be voluntary

It has always been the fundamental principle of the Courts that a prisoner's confession outside the Court is only admissible if it is voluntary. In deciding whether an admission is voluntary the Court had been at pain to hold that even the most gentle threats or slight inducements will taint a confession.[8] Whether the accused was a freeman when he confessed is one of the relevant factors. The value of the confession is determined by the veracity of the person to whom the confession is made and who appears to testify to it.[9] It is stated that an extra judicial confession is, in the very nature of things a weak piece of evidence. There should be no difficulty in rejecting it if it lacks in probability.[10]

(i) Confession caused by inducement, threat or promise, when irrelevant in criminal proceedings [Section 24]

A confession made by an accused person is irrelevant in a criminal proceeding, if the making of the confession appears to the Court to have been caused by any inducement, threat or promise having reference to the charge against the accused person, proceeding from a person in authority and sufficient, in the opinion of the Court, to give the accused person grounds, which would appear to him reasonable, for supposing that by making it he would gain any advantage or avoid any evil of temporal nature in reference to the proceeding against him.

Thus, it is quite clear that a confession should be free and voluntary. If it proceeds from remorse and a desire to make reparation for the crime, it is admissible. If it flows from hope or fear, excited by a person in authority, it is inadmissible. The ground for not receiving such evidence is that it would not be safe to receive a statement made under any influence or fear. Where the prisoner is only told to tell the truth without exciting any hope or fear in him, his statement cannot be regarded as being made in response to any threat or promise. Where a prisoner was told by a constable that he need not say anything to criminate himself, but what he did say would be taken down and used in evidence against him, it was held that such words did not amount to any threat or promise to induce the prisoner to confess.[11] In *Satbir Singh* v. *State of Punjab*,[12] it was stated that, whether a particular confession attracts the frown of Section 24 of the Evidence Act, the question has to be considered from the point of view of the confessing accused as to how the inducement, threat or promise proceedings from a person in authority would operate in his mind". It is for the prosecution to prove affirmatively that the confession was free and voluntary.[13] It is sufficient for the purpose of excluding a confession that the confession appear to have been the result of an inducement, even if it is not proved that the inducement reached the accused.[14] Where the accused was told by the Magistrate, "tell me where the things are and I will be favourable to you", or "if you do not tell the truth you may get yourself into trouble and it will be worse for you" or "if you make a clear breast of it, I will see you acquitted", and a sailor's confession in response to the captain's words that "if you do not tell me, I will give you to the police". Confession obtained in response to these statements was held to be irrelevant.

Thus, it is necessary for the confession to be excluded from evidence that the accused should labour under influence that in reference to the charge in question his position would be better or worse according as he confesses or not. Mere moral or spiritual inducements or exhortations will not vitiate a confession. For example, where the accused is told, "be sure to tell the truth", or "you have committed one sin, do not commit another and tell the truth", a confession made in response to this is valid. In *Selvi* v. *State of Karnataka*,[15] stated that protection against self incrimination is available even at the stage of investigation. It ensures that the statements have been made by the person accused voluntarily and therefore they are reliable. The burden is on the accused to show that his confessional statement is irrelevant because it attracts the bar of Section 24 but such burden is not as high as on the prosecution. Once the accused is able to establish facts which create a reasonable doubt that the confession was not voluntary, the burden would be shifted to the prosecution to show that the confession was voluntary and also satisfied all the requirements of relevancy.

(ii) Confession to police

(a) Confession to police officer not to be proved [Section 25]

This Section simply provides that no confession made to a police officer, shall be proved as against a person accused of any offence.

The principle upon which the rejection of confession made by an accused to a police officer or while in the custody of such officer is founded is that a confession thus made or obtained is untrustworthy. The broad ground for not admitting confessions made to police officer is to avoid the danger of admitting a false confession. A police officer, on receiving information of the occurrence of a dacoity or other offence of a serious character, failing to discover the real culprits often endeavours to secure himself against any charge of neglect by implicating person who are innocent. The police officer in order to secure conviction in a case very often puts the person so arrested to severe torture and makes him to confess a guilt without having committed it and when such steps are taken there is impunity for the real offender and great encouragement to crime. A police officer who is armed with large powers, may willingly excite terrors in their minds and extort false and involuntary confession; and his duty to investigate criminal cases and to detect offenders and to bring them to justice may make him feel tempted to obtain confession from accused persons by threat, promise or other improper influence. On these grounds confessions made to police officers and those made while the accused is in custody of police officers are excluded from evidence.

In Section 25 criterion for excluding the confession is the answer to the question as to whom the confession was made? If the answer is that it was made to a police officer, the law says that such confession should be absolutely excluded from evidence, because the person to whom it was made is not to be relied on for proving such confession and he is moreover suspected of employing coercion for obtaining confession.[16]

Reasons for exclusion of confession to police

Another variety of confessions that are under the Evidence Act regarded as involuntary are those made to a police personnel. Section 25 expressly declares that such confessions shall not be proved. Such confessions cannot even be used to corroborate any other evidence.[17]

If confessions to police were allowed to be proved in evidence, the police would torture the accused and thus force him to confess to a crime which he might not have committed. A confession so obtained would naturally be unreliable. It would not be voluntary. Such a confession will be irrelevant whatever may be its form, direct, express, implied or inferred from conduct.[18] The reasons for which this policy was adopted when the Act was passed in 1872 are probably still valid. Goswami, J. of the Supreme Court noted:[19]

> The archaic attempt to secure confessions by hook or by Crook seems to be the be-all and end-all of the police investigation. The police should remember that confession may not always be a short cut to solution. Instead of trying to "start" from a confession they should strive to "arrive" at it. Else, when they are busy on their short route to success, good evidence may disappear due to inattention to the real clues. Once a confession is obtained, there is often flagging of zeal for a full and through investigation with a view to establish the case de hors the confession. It is often a sad experience to find that on the confession, later, being inadmissible for one reason or other the case fondles in the Court.

Effect of Police Presence

The mere presence of the policeman should not have this effect. Where the confession is being given to someone else and the policeman is only casually present and overhears it that will not destroy the voluntary nature of the confession. But where that person is a secret agent of the police deputed for the very purpose of receiving a confession, it will suffer from the blemish of being a confession to police.[20]

In *Sita Ram* v. *State*,[21] the accused left a letter recording his confession near the dead body of the victim with the avowed object that it should be discovered by the police, the Supreme Court held that confession to be relevant. There was not even the shadow of a policeman when the letter was being written and planted. This principle of exclusion applies only to statement which amount to a confession. If a statement falls short of a confession, that is, it does not admit the guilt in terms or substantially all the facts which constitute the offence, it will be admissible even if made to a policeman. A confessional statement made by a person to the police even before he is accused of any offence is equally irrelevant. The Section clearly says that such a statement cannot be proved against any person accused of any offence. This means that even if the accusation is subsequent to the statement, the statement cannot be proved.[22]

Who is police officer?

A police officer means for this purpose a member of the regular police force, but the Supreme Court has held that the expression would include any person who is clothed with the powers of a police officer. Thus, excise inspector and sub inspectors enjoying police powers were held to be police officers.[23] A special legislation may change the system of excluding police confessions. For example, under the Terrorists and Disruptive Activities (Prevention) Act, 1987, (Section 15) confessional statements were not excluded from evidence on the ground that the persons making them were in police custody.[24]

(iii) Confession by accused while in custody of police not to be proved against him [Section 26]

No confession made by any person whilst he is in the custody of a police officer, unless it is made in the immediate presence of a magistrate, shall be proved as against such person.

Confession in police custody

No confession is made to anybody while the person making it is in police custody is provable. The Section will come into play when the person in police custody is in conversation with any person other than a police officer and confesses to his guilt. The Section is based upon the same fear, namely, that the police would torture the accused and force him to confess, if not to the police officer himself, at least to someone else. The confession made to a police officer or to anyone else while the accused is in police custody is not different in kind and quality. Both are likely to suffer from the blemish of not being free and voluntary. Statements made to TV and press reporters by the accused person in the presence of police and also in police custody were held to be inadmissible.[25] Police custody means police control even if it be exercised in a home, in an open place or in the course of a journey and not necessarily in the walls of a prison.

Presence of magistrate

The Section recognises one exception if the accused confesses while in police custody but in the immediate presence of a Magistrate, the confession will be valid. The presence of a Magistrate rules out the possibility of torture thereby making the confession free, voluntary and reliable. The fact that the advice of a counsel was not available at the time when the accused was recording his confession to a Magistrate would not destroy its value.[26]

Immediate presence of the Magistrate means his presence in the same room where the confession is being recorded. His presence in the adjoining room cannot afford the same degree of protection against torture.[27] A confession made while the accused is in judicial custody or lock up will be relevant, even if the accused is being guarded by policeman.[28]

(iv) How much of information received from accused may be proved [Section 27]

This Section provided that when any fact is deposed to as discovered in consequence of any information received from a person accused of any offence, in the custody of the police officer, so much of such information, whether it amounts to a confession or not, as relates distinctly to the fact thereby discovered, may be proved.

Section 27 of the Act is founded on the principle that if the confession of the accused is supported by the discovery of a fact then it may be presumed to be true and not to have been extracted. It comes into operation only:

(a) If and when certain facts are deposed to as discovered in consequence of information received from an accused person in police custody, and
(b) If the information relates distinctly to the fact discovered.

This Section is based on the view that if a fact is actually discovered in consequence of information given, some guarantee is afforded thereby that the information was true and accordingly can be safely allowed to given in evidence. But clearly the extent of the information admissible must depend on the exact nature of the fact discovered to which such information is required to relate. Section 27 lays down that when at any trial, evidence is led to the effect that some fact was discovered in consequence of the information given by the accused of an offence in custody of the police officer, so much of the information as relates to the facts discovered by that information, may be proved irrespective of the facts whether that information amounts to confession or not.

Article 20(3) of the Constitution and Section 27

Article 20(3) of the Constitution reads as "no person accused of an offence shall be compelled to be a witness against himself". The information given under Section 27 may be either voluntary or extracted from him by compulsion. Article 20(3) of the Constitution embodies the principle of protection against compulsion of self incriminating and the protection afforded under that Article extends to compelled testimony previously obtained from him. Information given to the police by the accused is certainly testimony previously obtained from him for that is intended to be used in a Court of law. If that information is not voluntary but is compelled testimony, Article 20(3) prohibits the user of the said evidence in Court. Section 27 of the Evidence Act, and Article 20(3) of the Constitution may be reconciled. Information voluntarily received from an accused relating distinctly to the fact thereby discovered is not hit by Article 20(3) and is relevant under Section 27. Information obtained by compulsion was not admissible, under Article 20(3) they must be excluded from evidence for otherwise the accused would be compelled to be a witness against himself. Article 20(3) applies to discoveries under Section 27, Evidence Act, if these discoveries are the results of compulsion. The scope of Section 27 Evidence Act is thus restricted by Article 20(3) of the Constitution and the discoveries which follow a confession brought about by compelling an accused person cannot be used against him.[29]

Confessions to police and consequential discoveries

Under the Evidence Act, there are two situations in which confessions to police are admitted in evidence. One is when the statement is made in the immediate presence of a Magistrate, and the second, when the statement leads to the discovery of a fact connected with the crime. The discovery assures the truth of the statement and makes it reliable even if it was extorted. In order to assure genuineness of recoveries, it has become a matter of practice that recoveries should be affected in the presence of witnesses. The Section is quite apparently laid out as a proviso or an exception to the preceding Section which deals with confessions in police custody and other involuntary confessions. In *Aftab Ahamed Ansari* v. *State of Uttaranchal*,[30] the accused voluntarily disclosed the place where he had kept the clothes of the deceased. They were recovered from there in the state of blood stained. The voluntary disclosure was relevant as a confession and discovery under Section 27.

Thus, it is very much clear that the accused has the right to remain silent. The confession must be made by the accused voluntarily, a confession given by an accused under the police restraint is not valid, a confession given under any inducement, threat or promise is inadmissible. Confession must be taken into consideration as a whole. It is against the principle of justice to accept part of the confession into consideration, and to exclude the other part of it. A confession must be used either as a whole or not at all. Confession is really a very valuable piece of evidence. By the confession, the innocence of the accused is rebutted. Being the confession is made by the accused himself, he is estopped to contradict it. At the same time, it reduces the burden of proof from the prosecution. It also reduces work load of the Court, and lengthy procedure. If the facts of the confession and the relevant facts are inconsistent with each other, then also the confession given by the accused must be inadmissible.

(b) Right of accused to claims that his case comes within any of the recognised exceptions

Section 105 provides for burden of proving that case of accused comes within exceptions.

When a person is accused of any offence, the burden of proving the existence of circumstances bringing the case within any of the General Exceptions in the Indian Penal Code (45 of 1860) or within any special exception or proviso contained in any other part of the same code, or in any law defining the offence, is upon him and the Court shall presume the absence of such circumstances.

Section 105 applies only to criminal trials. The cardinal principle that the accused is entitled to get the benefit of reasonable doubt is the base of Section 105. The meaning of this Section is that, it is not for the prosecution to examine all possible defences which might be put forward on behalf of an accused person and to prove that none of them applies. But at the conclusion of all the evidence it is incumbent upon the prosecution to have proved their case.

In *Vijayee Singh* v. *State of U.P.*,[31] it was observed that if the prosecution has discharged its duty to prove the guilt of accused, the accused may raise the plea of exception either by pleading the same specifically or by relying on probability. He may adduce evidence in support of his plea directly or may rely on prosecution case itself or he can indirectly introduce such circumstances by way of cross examination and also rely on the probabilities and other circumstances. Then the original presumption against the accused regarding the non existence of circumstances in favour of his plea get displaced and on an examination of the material if a reasonable doubt arises the benefit of it should go to the accused.

Illustrations

A, accused of murder, alleges that, by reason of unsoundness of mind he did not know the nature of the Act.

The burden of proof is on A.

The general principles relating to burden of proof in criminal cases are these two:

> Firstly, that the Court presumes that the accused is innocent and, therefore, prosecution must prove that he is guilty, and secondly, that once the prosecution has proved beyond a reasonable doubt that the accused is guilty and he takes any defence, such as insanity, the burden of proving that fact lies on him. This is what Section 105 provides: it says that if the accused claims that his case comes within any of the recognised exceptions, the burden of proving that lies on him.

Presumption of innocence

Every person accused of a crime is always presumed to be innocent, so that burden lies upon the prosecution to establish beyond a reasonable doubt that all the ingredients of the offence with which the accused is charged are made out. Thus, prosecution has to prove every ingredient in the crime. The decision of the House of Lords in *Woolmington* v. *Director of Public Prosecutions*,[32] that at the end of the evidence it is not for the prisoner to establish his innocence, but for the prosecution to establish his guilt". In *Gandap Bhimanna* v. *State of Hyderabad*,[33] it was held that it is for the prosecution to prove beyond reasonable doubt that the accused committed the offence; it is not for the Court to speculate that as to how the crime has been committed. If the evidence is of such nature that conclusion cannot be arrived the benefit of doubt should be given to the accused therefore in case of *Rama* v. *The State of Hyderabad*,[34] as the evidence was not conclusive enough to conclude who started the fight or how the quarrel began the benefit of doubt was provided to the accused. The Supreme Court has recognised that a person has a profound right not to be convicted of an offence which is not established by the evidential standard of proof beyond reasonable doubt.[35] Where the accused remained silent and offered no explanation the Supreme Court refused to draw the inference that he must be guilty. "We are unable to draw any such inference. It is for the prosecution to prove its case affirmatively and it cannot gain any strength from the conduct of the accused in remaining silent".[36] Where the accused gave an explanation which was afterward found to be false, even that has been held not to be a proof of his guilt.[37] Section 105 clearly casts the burden of proving a defence or any of the exceptions upon the accused. Everybody is presumed to be sane.

In reference to the burden that lies on the accused to prove his defence, the Supreme Court laid down certain principles, which are restated by Fazal Ali, J. in *Rabindra Kumar Dey* v. *State of Orissa*.[38]

In our opinion three cardinal principles of criminal jurisprudence are well settled, namely:

(a) That the onus lies affirmatively on the prosecution to prove its case beyond reasonable doubt and it cannot derive any benefit from weakness or falsity of the defence version while proving its case;
(b) That in a criminal trial the accused must be presume to be innocent unless he is proved to be guilty; and
(c) That the onus of the prosecution never shifts.

(c) Right of accused and the burden of proof

Section 114 provides that Court may presume existence of certain facts. The Court may presume the existence of any fact which it thinks likely to have happened regard being had to the common course of natural events, human conduct and public and private business, in their relation to the facts of the particular case.

In this context, the principle of 'fairness' to the accused seems to be set on volatile bases, as such a wide and pervasive allowance to make any presumption of fact may leave the accused at the mercy of the judge and not justice. However, the effect of this provision is to clarify that Courts of justice are to use their own common sense and experience while considering facts. The nine illustrations to Section

114 are mainly 'presumption of law'. The main difference between presumption of law and those of fact is that the former applies to a class for which conditions are fixed and uniform; whereas the latter applies to individual cases, the conditions of which are fluctuating. Additionally, presumptions are not evidence or proof; they only go on to show on whom the burden of proof lays.[39] The following statement made by Justice Krishna Iyer in *Krishanlal* v. *State of Haryana*,[40] perhaps most succinctly justifies the drawing of presumption by the Court while maintaining fairness to the accused: "to forsake vital considerations . . . is to sacrifice common sense in favour of an artificial concoction called judicial probability. A socially sensitised judge is better statutory armour . . . than long clauses of a complex Section". There also lies a rule of prudence in the Indian Evidence Act, 1872 in Section 114 illustration (b). That an acompliance is an unworthy of credit, unless he is corroborated with material facts. It is called a rule of prudence because it can well understood that a person who has given statements against his/her own friend in the crime is unworthy of trust so his statements cannot be considered as a good piece of evidence, which is again seems to be tilted on the side of the accused. Illustration (h) (Refusal to answer questions) says that if a man refuses to answer a question, which he is not compelled to answer by law, the Court may presume that the answer given, would be unfavourable to him.[41]

(d) Rights of accused and Privileged Communications

Fairness needs to flow from every corner, this seems to be the agenda of the Indian Evidence Act, 1872 as Sections 122 and 126 also talks about communication during marriage and professional communication respectively now these two Sections clearly focuses on the communication done or exchange of information based on trust. Therefore, in accordance with Section 122 of Indian Evidence Act; no person who is or has been married shall be permitted to disclose any such communication made to him during marriage by any person to whom he or she is or has been married unless there is a consent from him/her or representative of the same or if the proceedings is against one married person prosecuted for the crime against other.

This protects the accused from flowing of any information made by him to the married counterpart on the bond of trust. Similarly, Section 126 states that no barrister, attorney or vakil shall at any time disclose any information made to him by his/her client unless there is an express consent on the side of the person. This section is based upon the principle that if communication to legal adviser were not privileged, a man would be deterred from fully disclosing his case, so as to obtain proper professional aid in a matter which he is likely to be thrown into litigation. So for instance, an accused made any statement to his pleader that he has committed the murder now he wants the pleader to defend him so this communication will be protected from disclosure.

Sections 151 and 152 of the Indian Evidence Act are also very meaningful and important when it comes to fair trial of the accused as these two sections focuses on the questions that are being asked during a case proceeding and they prohibit any indecent, scandalous or any question that has been put to annoy or insult, unless, it is necessary to ask or is very related to the fact in issue because as the decision of the case is unstable so any such kind of question put to the accused can be harmful the dignity of that person if the decision stand in his acquittal, so this will violate the right to life with human dignity of the person guaranteed by Article 21 of the Constitution of India. Therefore, these two Sections are essential when it comes to the fairness of trial of the accused or the protection of the accused. So the criminal justice system prevailing in India is to its extent pro-accused with some restriction limiting the concept of fairness.[42]

Thus, it is quite clear from the above discussion that the Indian Evidence Act guarantees the fairness to the accused of any offence during the investigation or trial. The Indian Evidence Act includes certain provisions which uphold the rights and protection to the accused so that to make it possible to reach at just, fair and reasonable justice.

Notes and References

1. AIR 1980 All 385, 388.
2. AIR 1981 SC 625.
3. AIR 1996 Cal 246.
4. Available at *http://en.wikipedia.org/wiki/confession_(law)*.
5. P. Ramanatha Aiyar, *Concise Law Dictionary*, (2006).
6. *Sahoo* v. *State of U.P.*, AIR 1966 SC 40.
7. AIR 1966 SC 40.
8. *Mohd. Azad* v. *State of W.B.*, AIR 2009 SC 1037.
9. *Chattar Singh* v. *State of Haryana,* AIR 2009 SC 378.
10. *Jagta* v. *State of Haryana*, AIR 1974 SC 1545.
11. *R* v. *Baldry,* (1852) 2 Den CC 430.
12. (1977) 2 SCC 263.

13. *Reathu* v. *State of U.P.*, AIR 1956 SC 56.
14. *Pyare Lal Bhargava* v. *State of Rajasthan*, AIR 1963 SC 1094.
15. AIR 2010 SC 1974.
16. Batuk Lal, *The Law of Evidence*, 172 (19th Edition).
17. *Gulam Haider* v. *State of Maharashtra,* 1980 SCC (Cri) 145.
18. *Narayanrao* v. *State of A.P.*, AIR 1957 SC 737.
19. *Dagdu* v. *State of Maharashtra*, AIR 1977 SC 1579.
20. *Pandru Khadia* v. *State of Orissa,* 1992 Cri LJ 762 (Ori).
21. (1966) Supp SCR 265.
22. *Bheru Singh* v. *State of Rajasthan*, (1994) 2 SCC 467.
23. *Raja R. Jaiswal* v. *State of Bihar*, AIR 1964 SC 828.
24. *State of Maharashtra* v. *Bharat Chaganlal*, AIR 2002 SC 409.
25. *State (NCT of Delhi)* v. *Navjot Sandhu*, (2005) 11 SCC 600.
26. *Sarkar Mardi* v. *State of W.B.*, 1992 Cri LJ 367 (Cal).
27. *Niko Ram* v. *State of H.P.*, AIR 1972 SC 2077.
28. *Iman Din* v. *Emperor*, AIR 1934 Lah 76.
29. *Supra* note 16 at 185, 193.
30. AIR 2010 SC 773.
31. AIR 1990 SC 1459.
32. (1935) AC 462. See also *Bhikari* v. *State,* AIR 1966 SC 1.
33. (1956) Hyd 636.
34. (1952) Hyd 354.
35. *State of U.P.* v. *Krishna Gopal*, AIR 1987 SC 2154.
36. *Nagappa Dondiba* v. *State of Karnataka*, AIR 1980 SC 1753.
37. *Shankarlal* v. *State of Maharashtra*, AIR 1981 SC 765.
38. (1976) 4 SCC 233.
39. *Sodhi Transport Corporation* v. *State of U.P.*, AIR 1986 SC 1099.
40. AIR 1980 SC 1952.
41. Avtar Singh, *Principles of the Law of Evidence*, 466 (2011).
42. Sarthak Sharma, "Protection of the alleged in Indian Criminal Justice System", April 26, 2011.

5

Rights of Accused (Prisoners) in Jail

Crime is the outcome of a diseased mind and jail must have an environment of hospital for treatment and care.

—Mahatma Gandhi

Prisons, as a formal agency of the criminal justice administration, have a unique role in a democratic society. They are deployed, both for incarceration of convicts, as well as for providing custodial care to the under trials. In India prisons constitute the largest area of penal administration. Jails are essentially State subjects. Today, the prisons agency is said to be in a state of crisis. They are marked by subhuman material conditions, overcrowding, and lack of sensitivity, weak motivation and rampant corruption amongst the prison functionaries. The main reasons for such a state of affairs are:

First, priority accorded to prisons at political and social levels, second, lack of transparency and visibility of the prison system in public eyes and third, inadequate training and orientation of the prison officials. Imprisonment as a mode of dealing with offenders has been in vogue since time immemorial. Though the foundations of the contemporary prison administration in India were laid during the British period, the system has drastically changed over the years, especially since the dawn of independence. Prisonisation symbolises a system of punishment and also a sort of institutional placement of under trials and suspects during the period of trial. Since there cannot be a society without crime and criminals, the institution of prison is indispensable for every country. Thus, prison may serve to deter the offender as it may be used as a method of retribution or vengeance by making the life of the offender miserable and difficult. The isolated life in prison and incapacity of inmates to repeat crime while in the prison fulfils the preventive purpose of punishment. It also helps in keeping crime under control by elimination of criminals from the society. That apart, prison may also serve as an institution for the reformation and rehabilitation of offenders. It, therefore, follows that whatever be the object of punishment, the prison serves to keep offenders under custody and control.

OBJECTIVES OF PRISON

As in the year 1920, the Indian jail committee had unequivocally declared that the reformation and rehabilitation of offenders was the ultimate objective of prison administration. This declaration subsequently found its echo in the proceedings of various prison reform committees, appointed by the central and State governments under international influence. In 1864, the second commission of inquiry into Jail Management and Discipline was appointed. While recommending the commission made some specific suggestions regarding security and custody of prisoners, improvement of diets, clothing, bedding and medical care, rehabilitation of prisoners and also made suggestions as to the inmate management staff management, etc. It is the Prisons Act, 1894 on the basis of which the present Jail Management and Administration is operating in India.[1]

In a number of judgments on various aspects of prison administration, the Supreme Court of India has laid down three broad principles:

(i) A person in prison does not become a non person.
(ii) A person in prison is entitled to all human rights within the limitations of imprisonment.
(iii) There is no justification in aggravating the suffering already inherent in the process of incarceration.

Prison system which is a method of handling criminals was the result of historic accidents. Segregating criminals from society to protect it is an acknowledged necessity of every civilised State. Yet, unduly harsh treatment is not favoured by civilised states.

PRISON SYSTEM MUST AIM AT REFORMATION

Prison deprives liberty. Even while doing this, prison system must aim at reformation. Liberty has always been one of the most cherished possessions of man. It has many nuances. This personal autonomy extends beyond animal existence. This theme is highlighted in *Munn* v. *Illinois*,[2] Blackstone said:

> Personal liberty includes the power of locomotion of changing situation, or removing one's person to whatsoever place one's inclination may direct, without imprisonment or restraint unless by due course of law.

But, that is not to say that restraint of liberty is not permissible. It becomes not only permissible, but necessary because of need to protect society. The changing crime scenario must be reckoned.[3]

GUIDING PRINCIPLES FOR AN IDEAL PERSON

The A.N. Mulla Committee on jail reforms while proposing the Model Prison Manual laid down the guiding principles as under:

> The purpose and justification of a sentence of imprisonment is to protect society against crime. The punishment inherent in imprisonment primarily consists in deprivation of liberty involving compulsory confinement and consequent segregation from normal society. In carrying out the punishment, the prison administration should aim at ensuring the return of an offender in society not only willing but also able to lead a well adjusted and self supporting life.

Imprisonment and other measures which results in cutting off an offender from the outside world are afflictive by the very fact of taking away from him the right of self determination. Therefore, the prison system should not, except incidental to justifiable segregation as maintenance of discipline, aggravate the suffering inherent in such a situation".

Therefore, in this scenario the consequence of punishing a man for an offence committed by him should not indirectly result in such person's almost certain permanent exile from the country in which he has made his home or brings about his permanent separation from his wife and child.[4] Therefore, Justice Krishna Iyer rightly observed that deprivation of a personal freedom must be goal oriented and humanely restorative, apart from being deterrent. The insulated years behind the incentive bars must possess a hospital, if correction is a social purpose, as Gandhi Ji often insisted. In prison treatment must, therefore, be geared to psychic healing, release of stresses, restoration of self respect and cultural normalisation apart from training to adopt oneself to the life outside.[5] When the Courts sentence a person to a term of imprisonment they deprive him of his liberty but not his other freedoms: Prisoners are still 'persons' entitled to all constitutional rights unless their liberty has been constitutionally curtailed by procedures that satisfy all the requirements of due process. Thus, a prisoner is not wholly stripped of constitutional protections when he is imprisoned for crime. There is no iron curtain drawn between the Constitution and the prisons.

RIGHTS OF THE ACCUSED (PRISONERS IN JAIL)

The Indian Socio-Legal system is based on non-violence, mutual respect and human dignity of the individual. If a person commits any crime, it does not mean that by committing a crime, he ceases to be a human being and that he can be deprived of those aspects of life which constitutes human dignity. A convict lodged in a prison is not denuded of all his fundamental rights though it is true that he does not enjoy all the fundamental rights like other persons because of the fetters imposed on him in accordance with the law. The following rights include those expressly recognised under the various Indian laws governing prisoners, Supreme Court and High Court rulings as well as those recommended by expert committees. Each category lists the corresponding duties of the prison staff and other officers of the Criminal Justice System. The broad categories of rights are not exhaustive as this field is still developing.[6]

1. Right to be lodged appropriately based on proper classification

All female prisoners have the right to be lodged away from the direct contact and vision of all male prisoners, either in separate prisons or in a separate building of the same prison complex. As per Section 27(3), Prison Act, 1894, both male and female under trial prisoner have right to be lodged separately from male and female convicts respectively. First time under trial and convict prisoners involved in minor offences have the right to be lodged separately from habitual criminal and those involved in serious offences. Civil prisoners have the right to be lodged separately from criminal prisoners. In *Rakesh Kaushik* v. *B.L. Vig, Superintendent Central Jail,*

Delhi,[7] stated that inequality and discrimination on the basis of social and financial status of prisoners is prohibited. Affluent criminals cannot be treated with luxury while lowly indigents are treated as pariahs.

2. Special rights of young prisoners to be segregated from adult prisoners[8]

(i) All offenders under the age of 21 have the right to be lodged separately from all adult prisoners and the Jail officials are duty bound to ensure that no adult prisoner is allowed into his ward after sunset on any ground whatsoever.

(ii) Young offenders also have the right not to be transferred into any adult ward as punishment.

(iii) Prisoners under the age of 21 who have not arrived at the age of puberty have the right to be lodged separately from those who have.

3. Rights of Women Prisoners

Two basic protections for women are:

(i) A woman prisoner admitted to jail can be searched for prohibited items and injuries only by a matron appointed for the jail under the orders of the medical officer and only with strict regard to decency and away from the view of all male officers and prisoners.[9]

(ii) Every woman prisoner has the right to be examined and treated as far as possible only by a lady doctor and lady assistant even when she is taken to a hospital outside the jail.

In general, a female prisoner is in greater need of privacy, seclusion, medical and psychiatric care; facilities which are generally inadequate for all prisoners, males or females. There is the problem of young children's placement when the mother is serving a jail term. The prison rules permit children of five to six years to stay with their prisoner mothers but the problem of slightly older children. All the committees, the jail Committees of 1919-20 and 1980-83 and National Expert Committee on women prisoners, 1986-87 included, have been recommending and reiterating quite vehemently the need for separate prisons for women prisoners but, till date, this ideal remains far from being fulfilled. According to information available, there are only four separate prisons for women prisoners in the whole country, one each in Andhra Pradesh, Maharashtra, Tamil Nadu and Uttar Pradesh. There are two more prisons for women, one each in Bihar and Rajasthan, but they form part of the Central Prisons where male prisoners are also confined. Besides recommending separate institutions/annexes the committee of 1980-83 recommended that the staff for these institutions and annexes shall comprise women employees only.[10] The same approach to protect women is reflected in the following recommendations of the committee:

(a) All police investigations involving women must be carried out in the presence of a relative of the accused or her lawyer and of a lady staff member. Women should not be called to the police station for investigation.
(b) Police personnel should treat women with due courtesy and dignity during investigation and while they are in police custody.
(c) Women kept in police lock up should invariably be under the charge of a woman official and while in transit they should always be accompanied by women escorts.
(d) Bail should be liberally granted to women undertrial prisoners.
(e) The probation of offenders Act should be extensively used for the benefit of women offenders in order to keep them away from prison as far as possible.[11]

One of the problems which women prisoners face within the four walls of jail is the maintenance of their children. The Supreme Court in *R.D. Upadhyay* v. *State of A.P.*,[12] observed as under:

Women under trials/convicts if living in jail with their children, the jail conditions are not conducive and State has an obligation to look after welfare of children and to provide for social, educational and cultural development of children.

4. Right to healthy environment and timely medical services

(i) Every prisoner has the right to a clean and sanitised environment in the jail free from any kind of disease ridden or disease causing atmosphere. It is the responsibility of the medical officer of the jail to ensure that the environment of the jail is sanitised.[13]
(ii) It is the responsibility of the medical officers and the

superintendent to ensure that prisoner suffering from contagious disease like tuberculosis are separated from the healthy population and treated appropriately so that the infection does not spread to other healthy prisoners.[14]

(iii) Every prisoner has the right to be attended to and treated for any disease from which he/she is suffering at the time of admission to the jail or which he/she contracts while in jail.

(iv) A prisoner has the right not to be forcibly discharged from the jail against his/her will if he/she is suffering from any acute or dangerous disease and until the medical officer certifies that he/she is fit to be discharged.[15]

(v) Every prisoner has the right to be medically examined by the medical officer before being transferred to any other jail. He/she can be transferred only once the medical officer certifies that the prisoner is free from any serious illness which would otherwise have rendered transfer dangerous.[16]

(vi) Every prisoner confined to a solitary cell, either as punishment or for any other reason, has the right to be visited and examined by a medical officer or medical subordinate at least once in a day.[17]

(vii) Prisoners, who are undergoing rigorous imprisonment as part of their sentences or are engaged in hard labour on their own, have the right to be medically examined by the medical officer from time to time and their weight examined and recorded in their history tickets once in every fortnight by the medical officer.[18]

(viii) If the medical officer after any periodical examination of any such prisoner is of the opinion that the prisoner is not fit for the particular kind of hard labour, then he shall not be employed for such labour but shall be placed on such other kind of labour as the medical officer may consider suitable for him.[19]

(ix) The superintendent has the power to send a prisoner for special treatment to a hospital or asylum outside the jail if the condition of the prisoner so demands.[20]

5. Right to have interviews with one's lawyer

(i) Every prisoner has the right to have interviews with his/her lawyer at any reasonable hour after taking appointment from the superintendent. The conversation can be within the sight but outside the earshot of any officer, if the officer is deputed to be present there.[21]

In *Prabha Dutt* v. *Union of India*,[22] the Supreme Court held that it would be a part of fundamental freedom of the press to interview prisoners sentenced to death. In this case the Court directed the superintendent of the Tihar Jail to permit the Chief Reporter of the Hindustan Times Newspaper to interview, Ranga and Billa, the two death sentence convicts, under Article 19(1) (a) as they were willing to be interviewed. In *Francis Coralie Mullin* v. *Union Territory of Delhi*,[23] the Supreme Court held that a detenue has a fundamental right to have interview with his legal advisor and family members and that it is a part of his fundamental right under Article 21. In *Sheela Barse* v. *State of Maharashtra*,[24] it was observed that the interviews of the prisoners become necessary as otherwise the correct information may not be collected but such access has to be controlled and regulated. The pressmen are not entitled to uncontrolled interview. It was also stated that those who receive permission to have interviews will have to agree to abide by reasonable restrictions as contained in Jail Manual, and therefore, permission granted by the Court would be subject to provisions contained in the Jail Manual itself. The Supreme Court has ruled that lawyers, nominated by the District Magistrate, Sessions Judge, High Court and the Supreme Court will be given all facilities for interviews, visits and confidential communication with prisoners, subject to discipline and other security considerations.[25]

6. Right against being detained for more than the period for sentence imposed by the Court

(i) All prisoners have the right not to be detained for a day more than what the trial Court has mentioned in the sentence. The Supreme Court held that the inaction of the concerned authorities to take steps to release insane prisoners who become sane and in keeping them in jail for 20 to 37 years would be violative of Article 21 of the Constitution.[26] In *Ram Dass Ram* v. *State of Bihar*,[27] the Supreme Court held that detention of an accused in jail for 8 years even after his acquittal violates Article 21 of the Constitution. In *Sant Bir* v. *State of Bihar*,[28] the Supreme Court held that detention of a prisoner as a criminal lunatic, though he had become perfectly sane and fit for discharge for a period over 16 years without any justification violates the protection under Article 21. In *Hussainara Khatoon (I to VI)* v. *Home Secretary, Home Secretary*,[29] the Supreme Court held that judicial custody of an undertrial prisoner beyond the period of maximum imprisonment possible on his conviction for the offence would contravene the mandate under Article 21 and he further held that the practice of keeping lunatics and persons of unsound mind along with ordinary prisoners in ordinary jails also violates Article 21 of the Constitution. In *Dhananjay Sharma* v. *State of Haryana*,[30] the Supreme Court held that right to compensation for illegal detention is a fundamental right under Article 21. In *Rudal Shah* v. *State of Bihar*,[31] one of the pioneering decisions awarding monetary compensation for violation of fundamental rights, the Supreme Court held that the illegal detention of a person after his acquittal in trial, for 14 long years violated his fundamental right under Article 21. The Court probably for the first time had awarded a monetary compensation of Rs. 30,000 to the person illegally detained.

7. Right to protection against being forced into sexual activities

In the isolated and unprotected environment of a prison, instances of prisoners being forced to sexual activities (including rape and sodomy) by fellow inmates and prison staff are very high. In addition to causing physical injury and severe psychological trauma to the prisoners, it carries a potential high risk of transferring sexually transmitted disease including HIV/AIDS.

Since prisons are required to provide a safe environment:

(i) All prisoners have the right to be protected by the prison officials for being forced into any form of sexual activity by staff or fellow inmates.

(ii) They have the right to approach the jailer, the prison doctor and the superintendent against any such aggression who then have to ensure that it is not repeated and that the aggressor is dealt with appropriately, as necessitated.

(iii) If the aggression does not stop even then, the prisoner has the right to complain about this to the District Magistrate or the Session Judge at the earliest.[32]

8. Right to free legal service

(i) It is the fundamental right of all poor and indigent prisoners to be provided with free legal aid in the prosecution of their case at different levels of their trial.

(ii) The Magistrate is duty bound to offer the facility to the accused the moment he/she is produced before him or for the first time even if the accused has not asked for it out of ignorance. In *Madhav Hariwardhan Rao Hoskot* v. *State of Maharashtra*,[33] the Apex Court laid down that Article 21, read with Articles 39A and 142, requires, *inter alia*, that where a prisoner is disabled from engaging a lawyer on reasonable grounds, such as, indigence or incommunicado situation, the Court shall, if the circumstances of the case, the gravity of the sentence and the ends of justice so require, assign a competent counsel for the prisoner's defence, provided the party does not object to that lawyer. The Supreme Court has interpreted this object of rendering equal justice and free legal aid, as a part and parcel of Article 21 in numerous judgments rendered by it. In *Kavita* v. *State of Maharashtra*,[34] the Court held that Article 21 imbibes in itself the right to legal assistance. In *Nandlal Bajaj* v. *State of Punjab*,[35] the Supreme Court held that denial of legal assistance to a detenue violates Article 21. In *Khatri* v. *State of Bihar*,[36] popularly known as the Bhagalpur Blinding case also the Supreme Court held that the right to legal aid under Article 39A is implicit under Article 21. In *Kadra Pehadiya* v. *State of Bihar*,[37] the Supreme Court specifically declared that the right to legal assistance of under trial prisoners in the form of a competent lawyer at State's expense is part of their fundamental right under Article 21. The legal aid must be made available from the stage of first production before the Magistrate and not only when the trial commences, because "the jeopardy to his personal liberty arises as soon as a person is arrested and produced before a Magistrate".

(iii) Where the accused is not in a position to defend him/herself, the Magistrate is duty bound to appoint a committed and competent lawyer having sufficient experience in criminal matters for the defence of the accused at the expense of government.

(iv) The Magistrate is duty bound to refer such cases to the District Legal Services Authority.

(v) The Government cannot plead financial or administrative inability in any such situation.

(vi) If the prisoner wishes to appeal he/she may present a petition of appeal and copies accompanying the same to the superintendent or the officer in charge of the jail who is duty bound to forward the petition of appeal and copies thereof to the proper Appellate Court within the period of limitation.

9. Right against arbitrary use of handcuffs and fetters

(i) The Supreme Court has ruled that no prisoner shall be handcuffed or fettered routinely or merely for the convenience of the escort. Even in extreme circumstances, where handcuffs have to be put on prisoners, the escorting party shall record the reason for doing so in writing and take the Court's permission either before and or if that is not possible than soon after.[38]

(ii) Further, no bar fetters can be imposed on the prisoners for the short or for excessively long periods, unless permitted by the Trial Court. The Court declared that handcuffing of only the ordinary prisoners and leaving the better class prisoners is arbitrary. The Court further held that the distinction between ordinary and better class prisoners or the one based on the nature of offence or sentence insofar as handcuffing is concerned, is arbitrary and violates the fundamental rights of the prisoners under Article 21. Thus, the Supreme Court through its numerous liberal interpretations laid down the principle that handcuffing a prisoner is an exception and not a rule in criminal cases.[39] The Court issued a general direction that such handcuffing should be resorted to only with the permission of the Magistrate concerned granted after being satisfied that a particular prisoner is likely to jump jail or break out the custody.[40]

The Court laid down following set of conditions precedent for placing bar fetters on prisoners, which are applicable to all prisoners:

(a) Absolute necessity for fetters;
(b) Special reasons why no other alternative but fetter will alone secure custodial assurance;
(c) Record of those reasons contemporaneously in extenso;
(d) The basic conditions of dangerousness must be well grounded and recorded;
(e) All these are conditions precedent to 'irons' save in a great emergency;
(f) Before preventive or punitive irons (both are inflictions of bodily pain) natural justice in its minimal form shall be complied with (both *audi alteram* and the *nemo judex* rules);
(g) The fetters shall be removed at the earliest opportunity;
(h) There shall be a daily review of the absolute need for the fetters, none being conceivable for nocturnal manacles, etc.
(i) If it is found that the fetters must continue beyond a day, it shall be held illegal unless an outside agency like the district Magistrate or Sessions Judge, on materials placed, directs it continuance.[41]

10. Right against torture, cruel and degrading punishment

(i) The Supreme Court has ruled that the right to life and liberty guaranteed under Article 21 of the Constitution of India includes the right to use every faculty or limb through which life is enjoyed. Hence, cruel, inhuman, degrading treatment, or punishment is not permissible.[42]
(ii) Therefore, all prisoners have the right not to be harmed physically or psychologically while they are in jail either by the jail staff or by any of their fellow inmates. But at the same time, the prisoners are duty bound to follow the rules of the jail in order to maintain discipline and order in the jail.
(iii) In case any prisoner is harmed by a fellow inmate or jail staff without any ground whatsoever, then he/she has the right to complain to the immediate superior authority that is then duty bound to undertake an inquiry into the incident.

In *Nilabati Behra* v. *State of Orissa*,[43] the Supreme Court found that the petitioner's son was killed in police custody due to torture by the police, when he was arrested on a charge of petty theft. The Supreme Court deprecated the barbaric act of the police and declared that any person, whose fundamental rights have been violated by State action, can move either the High Court under Article 226 or the Supreme Court under Article 32 for monetary compensation.

In *D.K. Basu* v. *State of West Bengal*,[44] the Supreme Court took cognizance of the fact of custodial violence and its adverse impact on the right to life and personal liberty of the persons taken into police custody. In this case, the Supreme Court acting on a public interest litigation, held that custodial deaths, any form of torture or cruel or inhuman and degrading treatment, in custody, fall within inhibition of Article 21 whether they occur during investigation, interrogation or otherwise.

ABU Kasab Case

In a recent high profile judgment, delivered in *Kasab's* case, the Supreme Court while reiterating and affirming the earlier law on the subject, directed all the magistrates in the country to faithfully discharge the duty and obligation of making the accused fully aware, at the time of his first production, that it is his right to consult and be defended by a legal practitioner and in case he has no means to engage a lawyer of his choice, that one would be provided to him for legal aid at the expense of the State. It was also observed that this right flows from Articles 21 and 22(1) of the Constitution and needs to be strictly enforced.

11. Right to bail

(i) Where the person is arrested for a bailable offence or if security proceedings are initiated against him/her under the Code of Criminal Procedure, 1973 he/she can as a matter of right ask to be released on bail.

(ii) It is the duty of the arresting police office or the duty of the Magistrate to inform the person of the offence with which he/she is being charged and also whether it is a bailable or not.[45]

(iii) If it is bailable, then the police officer or the Magistrate is duty bound to release the person then and there if he/she is prepared to give bail.[46]

Before granting the bail to an accused the Court should take into account following factors concerning the accused:

(i) the length of his residence in the community;
(ii) his employment status, history and his financial condition;
(iii) his family ties and relationships;
(iv) his reputation, character and monetary condition;
(v) his prior criminal record including any record or prior release on recognizance or on bail;
(vi) the identity of responsible members of the community who would vouch for his reliability;
(vii) the nature of the offence charged and the apparent probability of conviction and the likely sentence insofar as these factors are relevant to the risk of non-appearance; and
(viii) Any other factor indicating the ties of the accused to the community or bearing on the risk of wilful failure to appear.[47]

The arresting police officer would be guilty of the offence of wrongful confinement, if he/she does not inform the asserted person about his/her right to bail in bailable offences, or fixes too high a sum as the bail amount and thereby refuses to release on bail and detains the person.[48]

(iv) Even in case of a non-bailable offence, Court can direct that any person under the age of sixteen years or any woman or any sick or infirm person accused of such an offence be released on bail.[49] If this Section is made fully operational, then there will be no custodial deaths of sick and infirm under trials.
(v) If the case of an undertrial prisoner accused of a non bailable offence is pending before a Magistrate and more than 60 days have elapsed after the first date of the recording of evidence was fixed then he/she has the right to be released on bail subject to the satisfaction of the Magistrate. The Magistrate has to record reasons for not doing so.[50]
(vi) Neither the police officer nor the Magistrate can fix the bail amount as too high without due regard to the facts and circumstances of the case.[51]
(vii) If the bail amount has no reasonable relation to the nature of offence alleged against a prisoner then he/she can firstly point out the prohibition contained in Section 440(1) and

secondly he can appeal to the Sessions Court or to the High Court for the reduction of the bail amount. In *Babu Singh* v. *State of U.P.*,[52] the Apex Court speaking through Krishna Iyer, J. stated that 'personal liberty' is deprived when bail is refused. It is 'too precious a value of our constitutional system recognised under Article 21', because of which the power to negate it must be exercised not casually, but judicially, with lively concern for the cost to the individual and the community.

12. Right to speedy trial

It is the fundamental right of every undertrial prisoner and those who have appealed the conviction to any higher Court be it the Sessions Court, High Court and the Supreme Court that their case be heard and disposed of quickly, fairly and justly. The Courts are duty bound to ensure this to all prisoners.

(i) Under the Jail Manual, it is the duty of the superintendent to inform the concerned Court and official visitors at the time of their visit to the jail of all cases of undertrial prisoners pending for more than one month. For those pending for more than three months, notice has to be given to the District Magistrate and the District and Session Judge. Where cases are pending for more than six months a special notice has to be given to the inspector general.

(ii) If the prison official deliberately do not send the prisoner to the Court on the appointed day and his/her case gets further adjourned, then they are guilty of violating this right.

(iii) If the escorting police personnel do not actually produce the prisoner before the Magistrate and simply sends the warrant to be signed by the Magistrate for the extension of the prisoner's remand, then the escort is equally responsible for the violation of this right.

(iv) If the Magistrate adjourns the case of the prisoner irresponsibily or signs the remand warrant in the prisoner's absence or without due consideration, then the Magistrate is guilty of violating this right.

(v) If the prosecution and the investigating police team do not submit the charge sheet or produce all the witnesses on the appointed days, then they are also responsible in their failure to ensure the right to speedy trial of the prisoner. The superintendent is duty bound to inform the prisoner concerned about the period of limitation under the Limitation Act of 1963 to appeal or apply for revision against an order of conviction and provide him/her with the facility to appeal or apply expeditiously.

(vi) If the officials in the Registrar's office at the concerned Court do not assign the appropriate case number to the appeal or revision application filed by the prisoner and thus his/her case gets delayed then they are also responsible for violating this right.

(vii) When a copy of the order or sentence is dispatched from the Appellate or Revisional Court, the same has to be personally delivered to the prisoner and an acknowledgement has to be obtained from him/her. This would ensure that it reached the prisoner on time and does not get misplaced in the transit.[53]

On one side of the coin, the accused persons are subjected to harassment due to delay in trial of Criminal cases and on the other side of the coin, many hardened criminals buy off immunity due to mainly the inertia on the part of the person incharge of administration of criminal justice. Almost global concept in criminal jurisprudence is the problem arising out of delay which is very prone to defeat justice. In many cases, the criminals became discharged from their cases and find some time and extra energy to commit further crimes but there can hardly be one-way traffic. Side by side it is clear that many undertrial prisoners are forced to languish in jail custody from year to year. As per the settled principle of criminal jurisprudence, a man, however grave his commission of the alleged offence may be, should be presumed to be innocent unless his guilt is established by cogent evidence in a Court of competent jurisdiction, may even in the Apex Court. Accordingly, the accused persons can demand speedy disposal of cases as guaranteed under Article 21 of the Constitution.[54]

Causes of delay in disposal of cases

The obvious causes of delay in disposal of the criminal cases are not very far to seek. The cases are:

1. Frequent adjournment petitions;

2. Lengthy cross-examinations without an useful purpose;
3. Lengthy arguments which on many occasions sound much like an empty vessel without much substance;
4. The inadequacy of staff;
5. The non-cooperation of the police;
6. The absence of judges;
7. The absence of competent judges. Poor suffer due to technicality and procedure while the rich is able to buy the legal time by illegal tactics.[55]

The Calcutta High Court in *M.K. Ghosh* v. *State of West Bengal*,[56] observed that the sword of Damocles should not hang over the head of accused persons for an indefinite period and that fifteen years elapsed from the date of occurrence. The said case did not end in finally and accordingly the Hon'ble High Court of Calcutta though it fit to quash the proceeding in view of the constitutional right of the accused under Article 21 of the Constitution for speedy trial. In the famous case of *Nimeon Sangma* v. *Home Secretary, Government of Meghalaya*,[57] *Hussainara Khatoon (I to VI)* v. *Home Secretary, State of Bihar*,[58] and *Mantoo Mazumdar* v. *State of Bihar*,[59] the Supreme Court declared that considerable delay in investigation of criminal cases, prolonged detention of under trials awaiting trial and judicial custody of an undertrial beyond the period of the maximum imprisonment possible on conviction for the offence, violate the personal liberty of undertrial prisoners under Article 21. In *Anil Rai* v. *State of Bihar*,[60] the Court observed that unexplained long interval between conclusion of arguments and delivery of judgment shakes the confidence of the people in the judicial system and affects rights of the parties under Article 21. In *Akhtari Bi* v. *State of M.P.*, the Apex Court held that to have speedy justice is a fundamental right which flows from Article 21 of the Constitution. Prolonged delay in disposal of the trials and thereafter appeals in criminal cases, for no fault of the accused, confers a right upon him to apply for bail.[61] In *Koluttumottil Razak* v. *State of Kerala*,[62] the Supreme Court while rejecting the request on behalf of the appellant to adjourn the matter on account of strike of the advocate observed that delay in disposing of the matter, wherein the appellant is in jail, would be a violation of Article 21 of the Constitution and accordingly the Apex Court proceeded with the hearing of the appeal after appointing an advocate as an *amicus curiae* to argue for the appellant.

13. Right to visits and access by family members of prisoners

The Supreme Court of India has ruled in *Sunil Batra (II)* v. *Delhi Administration*,[63] that:

(a) A sullen, forlorn prisoner is a dangerous criminal in the making and the prison is the factory;

(b) Visits to prisoners by family and friends are a solace in isolation; and only a dehumanised system can derive vicarious delight in depriving prison inmates of this humane amenity.

(c) The whole habilitative purpose of sentencing is to soften, not to harden the latent elements of criminal mind and this will be promoted by more such meetings.

  (i) Therefore, prison authorities are under a duty to make due provisions for the admission of such persons, with whom prisoners may desire to communicate.

  (ii) Such allowances shall be subject to consideration of security and discipline of the prison for which, the visitors shall disclose their true identity and address to the jailer and they can be searched for any prohibited articles.[64]

14. Right to write letters to family and friends and to receive letters, magazines, etc.

(I) the prisoner has the right to meet members of his/her family and friend and write letters to them. He/she is also allowed to get copies of papers and magazines, etc. at their own cost.

15. Right to evoke the writ of habeas corpus against prison authorities for excesses

(i) When every attempt to seek redress for one's genuine complaint fails, the prisoner can straightaway appeal to the High Court for the issuance of a writ of a *Habeas corpus*. This right would be available to any prisoner against any action of the jail authorities which is not commensurate with the sentence passed by the Court or other actions expected of the prison authorities.

(ii) If this action fails to bring in the required change, the prisoner can move petition to the Supreme Court for the protection of his fundamental rights. This is a guaranteed fundamental right of every citizen under the Constitution.[65]

16. Right to reformative programmes

The treatment of persons sentenced to imprisonment has to aim at establishing in them the will to lead law abiding and self supporting lives after their release and to enable them to do so. The treatment of prisoners through reformative programmes has to be such as will encourage their self respect and develop in them the sense of responsibility :

(i) Under this umbrella, prisoner have the rights to education, counselling, learning of meaningful skills, vocational training, mediation etc.[66]

Theoretically, the difficulties of a prisoner are over after his release since not only is his personal freedom recovered but his prison training makes him a fit person to start a new life on a clean slate. This is evident in view of the stigma, loss of job, loss of family ties and alienation from friends with may directly flow from the imprisonment.

17. Right to be compensated for violation of human rights

(i) When the criminal justice system fails to protect the fundamental rights of the prisoners, in such cases, the Supreme Court has recognised the principle of compensation to an accused for the violation of human rights. In *Rudul Singh* v. *State of Bihar*,[67] one of the pioneering decisions awarding monetary compensation for violation of fundamental rights, the Supreme Court held that the illegal detention of a person after his acquittal in trial, for 14 long years violated his fundamental right under Article 21. The Court had awarded a monetary compensation of Rs. 30000.

(ii) Even the National Human Rights Commission has recommended the award of compensation in cases where it has found that human rights of prisoner have been violated.

18. Rights in the context of employment of prisoners and prison wages

The Supreme Court has stated that punishment of rigorous imprisonment obliges the inmates to do hard labour not harsh labour. A vindictive officer victimising a prisoner, by forcing on him/her particularly harsh and degrading jobs, violates law's mandate.

(i) Civil prisoners have the right to carry on their trade and profession inside the jail after obtaining permission from the superintendent.[68]

(ii) Such civil prisoners have the right to keep their entire earning if they use their own implements. If the implements are supplied from the jail, then the Superintendent can deduct the cost and maintenance charges of such implements.[69] But such deductions cannot be too high and unreasonable.

(iii) A criminal prisoner who has been sentenced to rigorous imprisonment or who has offered to work voluntarily has the right not to be employed for more than nine hours at a stretch on any working day except in cases of an emergency and that too only on the written sanction of the superintendent.[70]

(iv) No prisoner shall be required to perform beggar and other similar forms of forced labour which are prohibited as exploitation under Article 23 of the Constitution of India.

(v) No prisoner shall be put to domestic work with any official in the prison administration.

(vi) Prisoners sentenced to rigorous imprisonment are entitled to receive remuneration from the proceeds of their work. But it is subject to certain deductions prescribed by the State Government for the maintenance of prisoners and prison buildings and for paying compensation to victims.[71] The Supreme Court has ruled that prison wages in any case cannot be less than minimum wages.

19. Right to information about prison rules

(i) Copies of jail rules should be exhibited both in English and in the local language in some place to which all persons in the prison have access.[72] If necessary these rules should be explained orally at the time of admission.

(ii) The Supreme Court of India rules that the State Governments should take steps to prepare in hindi and other regional languages a prisoner's handbook of rights and circulate copies to be kept in prisons to bring legal awareness to the inmates.

The information to be given should concern the disciplinary requirements of the prison; authorised methods of seeking information and making complaints and such other matters as are necessary to enable prisoners to understand both their rights and obligations and to adopt themselves to the life of a prison.

20. Right against arbitrary prison punishment

(i) Every prisoner has the right to have information as to the precise provision of the Prison Act and rules that he/she is alleged to have violated. He/she has the right to be heard in defence of disciplinary proceedings and to appeal as provided in rules made under the Act.

(ii) A prisoner can be awarded only such punishment by the superintendent which will not affect his/her health.

(iii) Upon being convicted of a prison offence, the prisoner has the right to be examined by the jail doctor to determine the extent to which such punishment will affect his/her health and the doctor has to certify the extent of punishment which the prisoners can undergo without injury to health.

(iv) No punishment in the form of reduced diet or of change of labour shall be executed until the prisoner has been examined by the medical officer who if he/she considers the prisoner fit to undergo the punishment, shall certify accordingly.[73]

21. Right not to be punished with solitary confinement for a prison offence

Keeping a person in solitary confinement for prolonged periods of time can result in irreparable psychological harm to the prisoner. When such a person is released, the society is at a greater risk of being harmed by him/her. Society is best protected when prisoners leave prisons as better human beings rather than less able to act as responsible citizens. Prison thus becomes antithetical to their traditionally professed role of protecting the society.

(i) The Supreme Court in *Sunil Batra (I)* v. *Delhi Administration*[74] has time and again ruled that no prisoner can be put away in solitary confinement as a matter of routine.

(ii) Solitary confinement is by itself a substantive punishment, which can be imposed only by a Court of law. Prison authorities cannot inflict this punishment according to their own whims and caprices without the express order of the Court.

(iii) Though the Prison Act authorises to impose solitary confinement on a prisoner under sentence of death, the Supreme Court has ruled that this expression should mean only that prisoner whose sentence of death has become final, conclusive, and indefeasible and which cannot be annulled or voided by any judicial or constitutional procedure.[75]

In number of cases the Supreme Court stated that solitary confinement has to be resorted to only in the rarest of rare cases for security reasons.

22. Right to air grievances and to effective remedy

(i) Every prisoner has the right to make a compliant regarding his or her treatments in the jail unless the complaint is evidently frivolous. For this right to be effective, the complaint must be dealt with promptly and confidentially if necessary.

(ii) If necessary, the complaint may be lodged on behalf of the prisoner by his or her immediate family members, friends or lawyer.

(iii) The Supreme Court has ruled that Grievance Deposit Boxes shall be maintained by or under the orders of District Magistrate and the Session judge which will be opened as frequently as is deemed fit and suitable action taken on complaints made by prisoners. It also ruled that access to such boxes should be afforded to all prisoners.[76]

(iv) District Magistrates and Session Judges are duty bound to personally visit prisons in their jurisdiction and afford effective opportunities for prisoners to express legal grievances.

(v) A prisoner can complain to members or special Rapporteurs of the State and National Human Rights Commission when they come to visit the prison or through post.

(vi) All such complaints should contain the exact and truthful details of the incident, the names of the people involved, the list of witnesses who were present during the incident, etc.

23. Right to be released on Parole, Furlough and Probation

(i) Parole

Parole is a legal sanction that lets a prisoner leave the prison for a short duration, on the condition that he/she behaves appropriately after release and report back to the prison on termination of the parole period. In other words the conditional release of a person convicted of a crime prior to the expiration of that person's term of imprisonment, subject to both the supervision of the correctional authorities during the remainder of the term and a resumption of the imprisonment upon violation of the condition imposed. It is usually regulated by Statutes and these provisions vary from state to state.

The Object of Parole: The object of Parole is to prepare the prisoner for adjustment to normal social life outside the prison and it, therefore, the transitory phase from imprisonment to normal freedom. Parole is a penal device which seeks to humanize prison justice. The main objectives of parole technique as stated in the Model Prison Manual prepared by the Government of India are-

(a) To enable the inmate to maintain continuity with his family life and deal with family matters;
(b) To save the inmate from the evil effects of continuous prison life;
(c) To enable the inmate to retain self confidence and active interest in life.

Parole is taken as an act of grace and not as a matter of right.

Eligibility for parole: Not every prisoner is eligible for release on parole. Different states may have different eligibility criteria. The following conditions must have been fulfilled before releasing a convict on parole:

(a) A prisoner is eligible for parole only after completion of one year of imprisonment and after earning first good conducts annual report.
(b) The prisoner should be convicted for more than four years of imprisonment.
(c) No parole can be granted to convicts sentenced to death penalty.

(ii) Furlough

The Jail Reforms Committee (1983) recommended that besides

the system of parole, there should also be the system of release of prisoners on furlough under which well behaved prisoners of certain categories should, as a matter of right, have a spell of freedom occasionally after they undergo a specified period of imprisonment so that they may maintain contact with their near relatives and friends and may not feel uprooted from society. The furlough period should count towards the prisoner's sentence.

A prisoner is eligible for release on furlough if he/she fulfils the following conditions:

(a) Imprisonment should be more than four years;
(b) Prisoner should have spent three years in jail;
(c) Prisoner should have earned three good conduct annual reports;
(d) Prisoner should not have committed any jail offence entailing punishment except warning.

State Government may restrict furlough to certain offenders whose release may have adverse impact on the security of the state or standards of morality of the society. Releases of prisoners on parole or furlough have been generally favoured by the courts in India as a rehabilitation and reformative measure.

(iii) Probation

Generally speaking, probation is a method of treatment of offenders who are considered fit to respond favourably to the rehabilitative processes within the society itself, without the necessity of being sent to institutional prisons. It is a custodial suspension of sentence of an offender who is not likely to resume a criminal career if kept under careful supervision, guidance and control. In other words, the release of offenders on probation is a treatment device prescribed by the Court for persons convicted of offences against the law, during which the probationer lives in the community and regulates his own life under conditions imposed by the Court of other constituted authority, and is subject to supervision by a probation officer. The term 'probation' is derived from the Latin word 'probare' which means 'to test' or 'to prove' It aims at rehabilitation of offenders by allowing them to live in society under supervision and surveillance rather than subjecting them to socially unhealthy atmosphere of the prison life. The release of an offender on probation enables him a free life in the community and reform himself as a normal human being in his own natural surroundings.

According to Homer S. Gunnings, probation is a matter of discipline and treatment. If probationers are carefully chosen and supervision work is performed with care and caution, it can work as a miracles in the field of rehabilitation of offenders.

The general conditions of allowing the benefit of release of an offender on probation may be summarised as follows:

1. No sentence be imposed initially, or if imposed its execution be suspended.
2. The offender should be given definite period to redeem himself.
3. During the probation period, the delinquent should be placed under the supervision of a probation officer.
4. The probation officer should keep the Court informed about the progress of the offender as regards to his rehabilitation.
5. If the delinquent responds favourably, his initial offence is deemed to have been scrapped, but if he fails to do so, or violates any condition of probation or indulges in law breaking, he may be brought before the Court and sentenced for the original offence as also for any other offence which he might have committed.

Thus, it would be seen that the original offence of the delinquent remains punishable throughout the period of probation and the offender is liable to be sentenced in case he violates the conditions of probation order. Again, probation is not a compulsive measure as it rests on voluntary acceptance of conditions by the probationer.[77]

Section 3[78] power of Court to release certain offenders after admonition

When any person is found guilty of having committed an offence punishable under Section 379 or Section 380 or Section 404 or Section 420 of the Indian Penal Code (45 of 1860), or any offence punishable with imprisonment for not more than two years, or with fine, or with both, under the Indian Penal Code or any other law, and no previous conviction is proved against him and the Court by which the person is found guilty is of opinion that, having regard to the circumstances of the case including the nature of the offence and the character of the offender, it is expedient so to do, then, notwithstanding anything contained in any other law for the time being in force the Court may, instead of sentencing him to any punishment, order releasing him on probation of good conduct under Section 4 release him after due admonition. In *Sunna* v. *State*,[79] the accused aged twenty years was found guilty of an offence under Section 380, Indian Penal Code for committing theft of a bicycle and some clothes. The Court ordered his release after admonition under Section 3 of the Probation of Offenders Act, 1958 because there was no previous conviction of the accused and the theft was committed due to sudden temptation without any premeditation. In case of *Sanchu Roy* v. *State of Assam*,[80] where the accused was about 19/20 years of age and had no previous criminal antecedents was sentenced to one year R.I. keeping in view the fact that the accused was of a tender age and the offence was committed ten years ago, the Supreme Court directed him to be released on probation of good conduct with a bond of Rs. 1000 with one surety of like amount.

As per Section 4 of the Act, the Court has power to release certain offenders on probation of good conduct. This Section permits release on probation of even the adult offenders who are not recidivists and slow potentiality for re adjustment to normal life in society. The Court may order release of such offender on entering a bond on probation of good conduct with or without surety. The benefit of probation cannot be extended to offenders whose offences are punishable with death or imprisonment for life. This Section further provides that the Court may call for the pre sentence report of the probation officer before making an order for release of offender on probation. The probationer may be ordered to be placed under supervision for a period of not less than one year with or without conditions as the Court deems fit and proper. The offender who has committed an offence which was heinous, grave and against the public security may be denied the benefit of probation by the Court. Thus, the Courts have generally declined to grant the benefit of release on probation to persons who are convicted for offences involving sex perversity, lust loaded criminality, corruption, adulteration, against public welfare, anti-social acts, etc.[81]

SOME ESSENTIAL REQUIREMENTS THAT MUST BE GIVEN TO PRISONERS IN JAIL TO ENSURE HUMAN DIGNITY

(i) Personal Hygiene

In order to enable the prisoners to keep their persons clean they should be provide with water and with such toilet articles as necessary for health and cleanliness.

(ii) Clothing and Bedding

(a) Every prisoner should be provided with an outfit of clothing, which is clean and kept in proper condition, for the climate and adequate to keep in good health and such clothing should not be in any manner degrading or humiliating.

(b) Every prisoner should be provided in accordance with local standards, a separate bed, which should be kept in good order and changed often enough to ensure its cleanliness.

(iii) Food

Every prisoner should be provided at the usual hours with food of nutritional value adequate for health and strength, of wholesome quality and well prepared and served. Drinking water should be available to every prisoner whenever he needs it.

In this connection the observation of Kuldip Nayar, who got first hand information of prison life during his incarceration during the Emergency in 1975 are quite revealing:[82]

> "The dal (lentils) was watery and the chapattis half baked . . . . I could see a few flies floating on the surface . . . . After some days I became so accustomed to finding flies in food that I would simply fish them out and start eating without a qualm . . ."

The present policy, at least in theory, is to provide standard diet sufficient enough to preserve health and strength. But how much of the prescribed food and of what quality eventually reaches the prisoner is a matter of speculation for it is common knowledge that corruption is rampant in jail administration. On the violations regarding food, Kuldip Nayar has the following observations to make:[83]

> "The wheat and rice given to prisoners were adulterated. There would be dust, stones and other elements mixed with them to increase weight. The wood given to us for the fuel was soaked in water for the same purpose. And the weighing machine was also tampered with . . . . Once, when we complained to the

warden that milk was more watery than usual, he laughingly said that everyone from the superintendent downwards shared the milk . . ."

The Jail Committee of 1980-83 has endorsed the above description regarding the hygienic, sanitary and dietary conditions prevailing in the country's prisons. The committee noticed dirt and stink in most of the prisons visited and a great paucity of latrines and toilets everywhere. The extremely unsatisfactory conditions regarding the food supplied to prisoners and its being the root cause of some of the troubles arising in jails are described thus:

> "Monotony of prison diet has ever been an additional ingredient of punishment. Half baked or over baked rotis, maggots and warms in cooked food, bad quality of vegetables and lesser issue of diet than that prescribed in rules are the common complaints about prisoners' diet . . . prisoners take resort to hunger strikes and demonstrations to protest against the quality and quantity of food issued to them".

Besides the quality and quantity of food, the arrangements regarding, preparation of food, management of kitchens, distribution of food and eating places were all found to be not at all satisfactory.[84]

(iv) Exercise and sport

Every prisoner, not employed in outdoor work should have at least one hour of exercise in the open air, if weather permits. Young prisoners and others of suitable age and physique should receive physical and recreational training during the period of exercise and for this purpose space, installations and equipment should be provided.

(v) Medical Services

The medical officer should regularly inspect and advice the concerned authorities:

(a) The quantity, quality, preparation and service of food;
(b) The hygiene and cleanliness of the institution and the prisoners;
(c) The sanitation, heating, lighting and ventilation, of the institution;
(d) The suitability and cleanliness of the prisoner's clothing and bedding; and

(e) The observance of the rules concerning physical education and sports, in cases where there are no technical personnel in charge of these activities.

Every institution should have the services of at least one qualified medical officer, having some knowledge of psychiatry and services of a qualified dental officer should be available to every prisoner.

(vi) Instruments of restraint

Instruments of restraint, such as handcuffs, chains, irons and straight jacket should never be applied as punishment. Furthermore, chains or irons should not be used as restraints and the other instruments of restraints should be used only in exceptional circumstances of security or on the medical grounds by the direction of medical officer.

(vii) Books

Every prison should have a library for the use of all categories of prisoners and they should be encouraged to make full use of it.

(viii) Education and re-creation

Provision should be made for the further education of all prisoners capable of profiting, thereby, including religious instruction in the countries where this is possible. The education of illiterates and young prisoners should be compulsory and special attention should be paid to it by the administration.

(ix) Insane and mentally abnormal prisoners

Persons who are found to be insane should not be detained in prisons and arrangements should be made to remove them to mental institutions as soon as possible, and treated in specialised institutions under medical management.[85]

Thus, it is crystal clear that every accused (prisoner) has got certain rights, while even remaining in jail, but those rights cannot be extended to such an extent that they interfere or clash with the rights of other prisoners. Commenting on pending cases under the Narcotics Drug and Psychotropic Substances Act, the Supreme Court last month came out with a pithy comment on the plight of the undertrial prisoners languishing in Indian jails: 'the laxity with which we throw citizens into prison reflects our lack of appreciation for the tribulation of incarceration; the callousness with which we leave them there reflects our lack of deference for humanity". According to the latest National Crime Records Bureau figures, the percentage of under trials in Indian jails was 64.7 in 2011. In states like Andhra Pradesh, Bihar and Meghalaya, the percentage exceeds to 80. Most of them suffer prolonged incarceration even in petty criminal matters merely for the reason that they are not in a position, even in bailable offences, to furnish bail bonds and get released.

Apart from the Prisoners Act, 1984 there is a Model Prison Manual in place and the various judicial pronouncements have made it clear that prisoners are entitled to human rights, the most important of which is presumption of innocence till proven guilty. As per the Supreme Court, when the undertrial prisoners are detained in jail custody for an indefinite period. Article 21 of the Constitution is violated. Yet, a vast majority are denied these rights because of lack of implementation. Most of the sufferor are poor, indigent, illiterate or semi literate. They do not know that they can be released on personal bond, entitled to free legal aid. This has been confirmed by a recent advisory issued by the home ministry to the states. It noted that only the poor and indigent are unable to put up bail and thus continue to be in jail for long periods. It also acknowledged that the lack of adequate legal aid and a general lack of awareness about rights of arrestees are principal reasons for the continued detention of individuals accused of bailable offences, where bail is a matter of right. It would be a miracle to expect that the judicial system can be reformed adequately to shorten the long list of pending cases. Yet some concrete steps can be taken immediately to mitigate their suffering. For a starter, it should be made mandatory for the jail authorities to educate them about their rights and provide them legal aid. The plight of the wrongfully confined prisoners is compounded when jail authorities refuses to release information about them in public domain. Recently, the Maharashtra Information Commission had to intervene to ensure that the 43 prisons in the State put information in the public domain about the number of under trials in their prisons who have already served half the maximum sentence for the crime for which they have been charged. As a result, a handful of detainees were released. It is imperative that State governments and union territories being the process of identifying the under trials entitled for release and start working toward their release. It is very much clear that all those waiting for justice from Courts have miserable life to undergo till they receive justice.[86]

Under trials languishing in jails for long years because of their inability to secure bail may soon be released following the centre directive to all states and union territories to review such cases. Saying only the poor and indigent continued to be in jails for long periods and that too for minor offences, the centre has asked states to release all such under trials who have completed half the maximum sentence they might have got if convicted of the offence committed. They are to be freed on personal bond without seeking any surety. The case against them however will continue in the Courts. In 2005, the case of Machang Lalung, a tribal from Central Assam shocked the nation's conscience. Lalung was arrested on the charge of physical assault (Section 326) of Indian Penal Code at the age of 23 and was released 54 years later at the age of 77 without ever going to trial. He died two years later in 2007. Keeping this in mind the government has also asked jail superintendents to conduct a survey of all cases where undertrial prisoners have completed more than one fourth of the maximum sentence and send the list to the District Legal Service Authority. It has also asked prison authorities to educate under trials on their right to bail and provide them legal aid through empanelled lawyers of District Legal Service Authority. In an advisory sent to all states and Union Territories, the home ministry said that under Section 436A of Criminal Procedure Code, an undertrial prisoner completing half the maximum period of imprisonment should be released by the Court on his personal bond with or without sureties, with the exception of those involved in heinous crimes.[87] An undertrial or a pre trial detainee denotes an unconvicted prisoner i.e. one who has been detained in prison during the period of investigation, inquiry or trial for the offence.

Notes and References

1. Kush Kalra, *Prisoners Right*, 14 (2013).
2. (1877) 94 US 113.
3. *A convict prisoner in the Central Prison, Thiruvananthapuram* v. *State of Kerala*, 1993 Cri LJ 3242.
4. *Balraj Singh* v. *Delhi Administration*, 29 (1986) DLT 106.
5. *Phul Singh* v. *State of Haryana*, AIR 1980 SC 249.
6. R. Sreekumar, *Handbook for Prison Visitors*, 5-14.
7. AIR 1981 SC 1767.
8. Section 27(3), Prisoners Act, 1894.
9. Section 24(3), Prisoners Act, 1894.
10. National Expert Committee Report on Women Prisoners (1980-83), 345.
11. Ahmad Siddique, *Criminology and Penology*, 210 (2011).

12. 2006 AIR SCW 2274.
13. Section 13, Prisons Act, 1894.
14. Section 24(2), Prisons Act, 1894.
15. Section 26(3), Prisons Act, 1894.
16. Section 26(2), Prisons Act, 1894.
17. Section 29, Prisons Act, 1894.
18. Section 35(2), Prisons Act, 1894.
19. Section 35(3), Prisons Act, 1894.
20. Section 39A, Prisons Act, 1894.
21. Section 40, Prisons Act, 1894.
22. AIR 1982 SC 6.
23. AIR 1981 SC 746.
24. AIR 1983 SC 378.
25. *Sunil Batra (II)* v. *Delhi Administration*, AIR 1980 SC 1579.
26. *Miss Veena Sethi* v. *State of Bihar*, AIR 1983 SC 339.
27. AIR 1987 SC 1333.
28. AIR 1982 SC 1470.
29. 1980 SCC (Cri) 23.
30. AIR 1995 SC 1795.
31. AIR 1983 SC 1086.
32. *Munna* v. *State of U.P.*, AIR 1982 SC 806.
33. AIR 1978 SC 1548.
34. AIR 1981 SC 1641.
35. AIR 1981 SC 928.
36. (1981) 1 SCC 635.
37. AIR 1982 SC 1167.
38. *Prem Shankar Shukla* v. *Delhi Administration,* AIR 1980 SC 1535.
39. *Ibid.*
40. *Citizen for Democracy* v. *State of Assam*, AIR 1996 SC 2193.
41. *Sunil Batra* v. *Delhi Administration*, AIR 1978 SC 1675.
42. *Francis Coralie Mullin* v. *Administrator, Union Territory of Delhi*, AIR 1981 SC 746.
43. AIR 1993 SC 1960.
44. AIR 1997 SC 610.
45. Section 50, Criminal Procedure Code.
46. Section 436(1), Criminal Procedure Code.
47. *Hussainara Khatoon* v. *Home Secretary, State of Bihar*, AIR 1979 SC 1360.
48. *Dharmu* v. *Rabindranath*, 1978 Cri LJ 864 (Ori).
49. First proviso to Section 437(1), Criminal Procedure Code.
50. Section 437(6), Criminal Procedure Code.
51. Section 440(1), Criminal Procedure Code.
52. AIR 1978 SC 527.
53. Dr. Ashutosh, *Rights of Accused*, 107, 108 (2013).
54. Prabhat Kumar Basumallik, "Speedy Trial", 1993 *Cri LJ* 63.
55. World Bank, *World Development Report, 2000-2001—Attacking Poverty*, 103 (2001).
56. 1990 Cri LJ 26.
57. AIR 1979 SC 1518.

58. AIR 1979 SC 1360.
59. AIR 1980 SC 847.
60. AIR 2001 SC 3173: 2001 Cri LJ 3969.
61. AIR 2001 SC 1528.
62. (2000) 4 SCC 465.
63. AIR 1980 SC 1579.
64. Section 41(2), Prisons Act, 1894.
65. *Sunil Batra II* v. *Delhi Administration*, (1990) 3 SCC 488.
66. *Ibid.*
67. AIR 1983 SC 1086.
68. Section 34(1), Prisons Act, 1894.
69. Section 34(2), Prisons Act, 1894.
70. Section 35(1), Prisons Act, 1894.
71. *State of Gujarat* v. *H.C. of Gujarat*, (1998) 7 SCC 392.
72. Section 61, Prisons Act, 1894.
73. Section 50, Prisons Act, 1894.
74. AIR 1978 SC 1675.
75. Section 30(2), Prisons Act, 1894.
76. *Sunil Batra (II)* v. *Delhi Administration*, AIR 1980 SC 1579.
77. *Supra* note 40 at 704-05.
78. The Probation of Offenders Act, 1958.
79. AIR 1967 Orissa 4.
80. (1987) Cri LJ 1378.
81. The Probation of Offenders Act, 1958.
82. In Jail (1979), 29.
83. *Ibid.*, 32-33.
84. *Supra* note 458 at 203, 204.
85. Dr. Ashutosh, *Rights of Accused*, 121-22 (2013).
86. Yogesh Vajpeyi, "Undertrials in jails: The idea of Injustice", the *New Indian Express*, April 28, 2013, available at www.newindianexpress.com/home/opinion.
87. Deeptiman Tiwary, "Undertrials in Jail for Long may be Freed", *The Times of India*, February 11, 2013.

6

Conclusion and Suggestions

Every civilised society maintains a system of criminal justice administration in order to punish the guilty and make the life of common man safe. There was no criminal law in uncivilised society. Every man was liable to be attacked on his person or property at any time by any one. The person attacked either succumbed or overpowered his opponent. A tooth for a tooth, an eye for an eye, a life for a life was the forerunner of criminal justice. As time advanced the injured person agreed to accept compensation, instead of killing his adversary. Subsequently, a sliding scale of satisfying ordinary offences came into existence. Such a system gave birth to the archoic criminal law. India has adversarial criminal justice system. The well recognised fundamental principles of criminal jurisprudence are "presumption of innocence and right to silence of the accused, burden of proof on the prosecution, and the right to fair trial. The criminal jurisprudence has given a wider area to the accused. The burden of proving the guilt of the accused is always on the prosecution and in case of any doubt; the accused would get the benefit of acquittal. The accused has several rights guaranteed to him under the Constitution and relevant laws. They have been liberally extended by the decisions of the Hon'ble Courts. The accused has the right to know about all the rights he has, how to enforce them and whom to approach when there is a denial of those rights. Fairness to accused has become a fundamental assumption in our criminal justice system. "The poor, illiterate and weaker sections in our society suffer day in and day out in their struggle for survival and look to those who have promised them equality, social, political and economic... a very large number of under trial prisoners suffer prolonged incarceration even in petty criminal matters merely for the reason that they are not in a position, even in bailable offences, to furnish bail bonds and get released on bail". The principles of rule of law and equality are imperative to have a "fair trial" in criminal proceedings in India, because, "when there is a goose on the trial side there ought not to be a fox on the jury". Fair trial in criminal proceedings seems to be a highly intellectual, comprehensive system of thought conveying that the affected person need not carry the impression that he ought to be satisfied with an unjust trial and unfair appeal. Thus, fairness of justice in theory as well as practice is the core of fair trial in criminal justice process inasmuch as that "it is the nature and the gravity of the crime but not the criminal, which are germane for consideration of appropriate punishment in a criminal trial. The Court will be failing in its duty if appropriate punishment is not awarded for a crime which has been committed not only against the individual victim but also against the society to which the criminal and the victim belong . . . and it should respond to the society's cry for justice against the criminal. "Equality, justice and liberty" is the trinity of fair trial recognised in the administration of justice of India where the affluent and the "lowly and lost" have the equality of access to justice in the administration of justice in general and the criminal justice system in particular. The Constitution of India lays down a social policy concerning equal justice and free legal aid "by suitable legislation or schemes or in any other way, to ensure that opportunities securing justice are not denied to any citizen by reason of economic or other disabilities. This social policy aims at: indigence should never be a ground for denying fair trial or equal justice particular attention should be paid to appoint competent advocates, equal to handling complex case, not patronising gestures to raw entrants at the Bar. The activist role of the judiciary has not only expanded the horizons of the criminal justice system but also infused a new leaf of life as well as confidence in the judicial system."

Judicial activism is gaining prominence in the present day. In the form of public interest litigation, individuals are getting access to justice. The area of judicial intervention has been steadily expanding through the device of public interest litigation. The judiciary has shed its pro status quo approach and taken upon itself the duty to enforce the basic rights of the poor and vulnerable sections of society, by progressive interpretation and positive action. It is very clear that, a right without a remedy does not have much substance. Truly, the Supreme Court has been called upon to safeguard the right of the accused, thus commonly play with the role of "guardian of the social revolution. It is essential that greatest care should be taken to see that no person accused of an offence or brought before a magistrate is unnecessarily put in custody and no such person is subjected to undue influence or physical or mental torture.

Every civilised nation must have one thing common in their criminal justice administration system that is minimum fair trial rights to every accused person irrespective of his or her status. It is settled in common law and also adopted by other countries too that criminal prosecution starts with 'presumption of innocence' and the guilt must be proved beyond reasonable doubt. The right to a fair trial is a norm of international human rights law and also adopted by many countries in their procedural law. It is designed to protect individuals from the unlawful and arbitrary curtailment or deprivation of their basic rights and freedoms, the most prominent of which are the right to life and liberty of the person. The concept of fair trial and rights of the accused is based on the basic principles of natural justice. Fair trial and the rights of the accused are secured by providing speedy justice. Speedy trial is necessary to gain the confidence of the public in judiciary. Delayed trial defeats the objective of the re socialisation of the offenders too. Delayed justice leads to unnecessary harassment. The right to speedy trial begins with actual restraint imposed by arrest and consequent incarceration, and continues at all stages so that any possible prejudice that may result from impressible and avoidable delay from the time of commission of offence till its final disposal can be prevented. It is declared that speedy trial is an essential ingredient of reasonable, just and fair procedure guaranteed by Article 21 and it is the constitutional obligation of the State to set up such a procedure as would ensure speedy trial to the accused. The State cannot avoid its constitutional obligation by pleading financial or administrative inadequacy. Aid of counsel to an accused person also insures fair trial. The requirement of fair trial involves two things, firstly an opportunity to the accused to secure a counsel of his own choice, and secondly, the duty of the State to provide a counsel to the accused in certain cases. The right to counsel is recognised as fundamental right of an arrested person under Article 22(1) which provides inter alia, no person shall be denied the right to consult, and to be defended by, a legal practitioner of his choice. Sections 303 and 304 of the Criminal Procedure Code are manifestation of this constitutional mandates.

Regarding the right to counsel and legal aid to the accused, the Constitution provides that no person who is arrested shall be detained in custody without being informed, as soon as may be, of the grounds for such arrest nor shall he be denied the right to consult and to defended by a legal practitioner of his choice. But the right to engage a counsel is meaningful only if the accused has no means to engage the same. A person too poor to afford a lawyer to defend himself is much handicapped during his trial. It is in this context, therefore, that the importance of legal aid to the indigent is to be appreciated in a developing country like India.

Let it not be forgotten that if law is not only to speak justice so require but also deliver justice, legal aid is an absolute imperative. If free legal services are not provided to such an accused suffering from poverty or indigence, the trial itself may run the risk of being vitiated as contravening Article 21. Criminal law and its process cannot be appreciated without some understanding of the rights and protections given to the accused person not only during his trial but also before and after the trial. These rights and protections aim at providing a fair trial to an accused person so as to eliminate any possible abuse of process resulting in miscarriage of justice. This has to be so since criminal law is expected to maintain certain values in a civilised society and the means to obtain conviction of a guilty person are no less important than getting the conviction itself.

Right to be produced before a Magistrate; This right simply states that the police cannot keep a person under arrest for a longer time than is necessary without producing him before a Magistrate. There are provisions in the Constitution and the Criminal Procedure Code according to which the police to produce an accused person before a Magistrate. These provisions go a long way in guarding the personal liberty of the individual. *Right to bail*; a person is guilty of an offence only after being found to be so by a competent criminal Court. Since the processing of a case by the police and the subsequent trial in the Court may take a fairly long time, it is desirable that wherever it is expedient to do so, the accused person must be released on bail since his guilt is yet to be established. As per the policy laid down in the various judicial decisions in India, releasing a person on bail should be the normal practice and refusal to do so an exception. Besides accepting the basic principle that there is no justification for depriving a person of his liberty unless his guilt is proved, such a policy has the advantage that overcrowding in jails, to some extent, can be avoided by making a liberal but judicious use of the bail technique. As regards the amount of bond, the Court provides that the amount of every bond executed shall be fixed with due regard to the circumstances of the case and shall not be excessive. This is absolutely necessary otherwise an accused person of limited means may be unable to execute the bond and may not, therefore, get the benefit of bail just because of his poverty. *Protection against self incrimination*; a cardinal principle of the English system of criminal jurisprudence is that an accused cannot be compelled to give evidence against himself. The principle has been recognised in the Indian legal system. The constitutional guarantee of the right in India is that no person accused of any offence shall be compelled to be a witness against himself. The principle is to eliminate the possibility of third degree methods being used against the accused person to extort confession or any other information from him. Some of the provisions in the Evidence Act and the Criminal Procedure Code also seek to achieve a similar objective like Sections 24 to 26 of Evidence Act and Section 316 of Code of Criminal Procedure. Section 316 of Criminal Procedure Code simply provides that no influence by means of any promise, threat or otherwise shall be used against an accused person to induce him to disclose or withhold any matter within his knowledge. *Protection against double jeopardy*; it is a well established principle that no man shall be twice punished if it appears to the Court that it is for one and the same cause. The principle has been incorporated in the Indian Constitution thus: no person shall be prosecuted and punished for the same offence more than once. While the constitutional guarantee recognises only autrefos convict (previous conviction) as a bar to the subsequent prosecution for the same offence, the provision in the Criminal Procedure Code incorporates autrefois acquit (previous acquittal) as well to bar another trial for the same offence. The main principle laid down is that a person who had once been tried by a Court of competent jurisdiction for an offence and convicted or acquitted of such offence shall, while such conviction or acquittal remains in force, not be liable to be tried again for the same offence. *Right to speedy trial*; "justice delayed is justice denied" is the well known maxim highlighting the importance of quick justice. In the context of the administration of criminal justice, it has a dual significance. Viewed from the angle of the accused person, it is in his interest that there should be a speedy trial so that there may be an early end to the proceeding against him resulting in acquittal or conviction.

The accused may have to spend long periods full of uncertainty and mental anxiety possibly in jail or in police lock up if the proceedings against him are not expedited. Speedy trial also limits the possibility of long delay impairing the ability of an accused person to defend himself effectively or handicapping the prosecution in the trial. Either of the two sides may suffer because witnesses may die, their memories may fade and testing may become more vulnerable to cross examination.

Besides the interest of the accused, it is also in the community's interest that the criminal proceedings come to a reasonably quick end since promptness of criminal sanctions is one of the requisites of the deterrent aspects of punishment; the other requisite being the certainty of the application of penal sanctions. The legal basis of the right was provided by the Magna Carta (1215) which proclaimed that justice or right will neither be sold nor denied or deferred to any man.

This right has been given extended scope to operate against long delay in the disposal of a mercy petition against the death sentence by the President of India. The problem of delayed criminal justice is endemic in the Indian judicial system though it has reached alarming proportions during the last two decades or so. *Right to know the identity of the police personnel making the arrest;* the accused as a person being arrested has the right to know the identity of the police personnel. *Right of person arrested to be informed of grounds of arrest and of the right to bail;* this is a precious right of the arrested person as it enables him to move the proper Court for bail or to make expeditious arrangements for his defence. This right impose an obligation on the police officer making arrest to communicate reasons of arrest to the arrested person 'immediately'.

Right to be medically examined; there are provisions of medical examination of an accused at the request of police officer, and of the examination of a person accused of an offence of rape. Code also provided for the examination of arrested person by medical practitioner at the request of the arrested person. It is an essential right which will afford the evidence to disprove the commission of any offence by the accused or which will prove the physical torture or maltreatment in police custody. *Right against handcuffing;* an accused person even if arrested has right not to be handcuffed. Handcuffing of an undertrial is unfair and not permissible under

Article 21 of the Constitution. Handcuffing can be resorted to in case of clear and present danger of escape only overthrowing the police control. Handcuffing must be justified and for it there must be sufficient material. It should be resorted to only in extreme cases. *Right of information of arrest to the relative of the accused;* the person arrested must be made aware of this right that he can informed to his friend or relative about his arrest or detention as soon as he is put under arrest or is detained. It is mandatory for the police officer making arrest of a person to inform the friend/relative or any other person to whom the arrestee wants to be informed about his arrest. *Penal laws not to be retrospective in operation;* it is a general principle of law that a person should be guilty of an act only if the act is an offence at the time of the act is done by him. If the act is not an offence at the time of its being done, it cannot be declared an offence by a subsequent law.

In other words, to give retrospective operation to a penal statute is highly unjust. Article 20(1) of the Constitution provides, no person shall be convicted of any offence except for violation of a law in force at the time of the commission of the act charged as offences, nor he subjected to a penalty greater than that which might have been inflicted under the law in force at the time of the commission of the offence.

The Article has two parts. The first part puts a restriction on making an act criminal by a subsequent law. The second part prohibits the imposition of a penalty greater than that to which the offender was liable at the time of committing the act.

Prohibition against self incrimination; Article 20(3) of the Constitution prohibits self incrimination. Such a protection is available in England and America also. In order to claim the protection of this right, it must be necessary that a person should be accused of an offence. This right provides that no person accused of an offence shall be compelled to give evidence against oneself. The right against self incrimination is available to an accused even at a stage prior to the actual trial or even at the stage when an F.I.R. is lodged and investigation is ordered by the Magistrate. Article 20(3) prohibits compulsion against self incrimination but there is no prohibition against a voluntary confession made without any inducement or threat. *Right against confession;* no confession made to a police officer is valid as evidence. All confession must be made to a Magistrate not below the rank of judicial Magistrate. The Magistrate taking the confession must give the accused due time out of the custody of the police, and make an effort to ensure that the accused was not coerced or intimidated in anyway, before receiving the confession. At the bottom of the confession the Magistrate must write out that he has informed the accused that this confession may be used against him and he is not obligated, in any way to incriminate himself. Thus, it is rightly said that a confession should be free and voluntary.

Article 21 of the Constitution known as the heart of the Constitutional Fundamental Rights. It is rightly stated that the convicts are not by mere reason of their conviction deprived of the basic fundamental rights. Thus, Article 21 provides for the protection of certain rights to convicts in jails. Free and fair trial has been said to be the sine qua non of Article 21. A fair trial would really means that trial before an impartial judge, a fair prosecutor and appropriate judicial atmosphere. Article 21 of the Constitution guarantees the right of personal liberty and thereby prohibits any inhuman, cruel or degrading treatments to the accused person. Any violation of this right attracts the provisions of Article 14 of the Constitution which enshrines right to equality and equal protection of law. *Right against solitary confinement, bar fetters and protection from torture;* solitary confinement in a general sense means the separate confinement of a prisoner, with only occasional access of any other person, and that too only at the discretion of the jail authorities. In strict sense it means the complete isolation of a prisoner from all human society. Torture is regarded by the police/investigating agency as normal practice to check information regarding crime, the accomplice, extract confession. Police officers who are supposed to be the protector of the liberties of citizens themselves violate precious rights of citizens. Torture is a wound in the soul so painful that sometimes you can almost touch it but is also so intangible that there is no way to heel it.

Custodial torture is a naked violation of human dignity and degradation which destroys, to a very large extent, the individual personally. It is a calculated assault on human dignity and whenever human dignity is wounded, civilisation takes a step backward. Fundamental rights occupy a place of pride in the Indian Constitution. Article 21 provides no person shall be deprived of his life or personal liberty except according to procedure established by law. Personal liberty, thus, is a sacred and cherished right under the Constitution. The expression life or personal liberty has been held to include the right to live with human dignity and thus it would also include within itself a guarantee against torture and assault by the State or its functionaries.

Article 22 guarantees protection against arrest and detention in certain cases and declares that no person who is arrested shall be detained in custody without being informed of the grounds of such arrest and he shall not be denied the right to consult and defend himself by a legal practitioner of his choice. Prisoner's right have been recognised not only to protect them from physical discomfort or torture in prison but also to save them from mental torture. *Right to get the matter settled through plea bargaining;* plea bargaining refers to pre trial negotiations between the defendants, usually conducted by the prosecution, during which the defendant agrees to plead guilty in exchange for certain concessions by the prosecutor. *Right of the accused to have copies of statements and documents;* it is a statutory duty of the Magistrate to furnish to the accused free of cost with copies of statements of all person examined by the Magistrate, statements and confessions recorded, documents on which prosecution relies. This right enable the accused to get adequate information about the charge against him and to prepare for his defence. *Right of the accused to examine the witnesses in his presence;* this right simply provides that evidence for prosecution and defence should be taken in the presence of the accused. Right to open trial; it simply provides that trial of an accused shall be commenced in open Court, which simply means that the public should have access to the Court.

Reasonable opportunity to defend the case must be given to the accused i.e. right to representation. Accused person to be competent witness, where the accused voluntarily offers oneself to be examined as a defence witness, and the prosecution is entitled to examine him.

Procedure where accused does not understand proceedings; the provision regarding this is discussed under Section 318 of Criminal Procedure Code. The provision of this Section is not applicable to a person of unsound mind. The Section applies to a person who is unable to understand the proceedings due to deafness or dumbness or ignorance of the language. The provisions of this Section are mandatory in character. If such inquiry or trial results in conviction of the accused who does not understand the proceedings, the trial Court shall forward the proceedings to the High Court with a report of the circumstances of the case, and the High Court shall pass sentence or an order thereon as it deems proper. The object is that the High Court should be in a position to satisfy itself that the accused is ensured a fair trial. While dealing with the rights of prisoners it is very much clear that in the Constitution of India, there is no specific guarantee of prisoner's rights. But there are certain rights given under Part III of the Constitution, which are available to the prisoners too, because a prisoner remains a 'person' in the prison. A 'prisoner' is a person who is deprived of his personal liberty; due to the conviction of a crime, and imprisonment is the most common method of punishment provided by all the legal systems. Imprisonment makes the prisoner repent about his past conduct. The judiciary protects the right of prisoners and recognises their rights. They are protected from torture and solitary confinement.

It is interesting to note that judiciary has played a major role in ushering prison reforms in the country. With Justice Krishna Iyer's Judgment in *Sunil Batra's* case came the era of judicial activism which brought forth major changes in the way prisons are run and the importance given to reformation process in prisons and the need for humanitarian outlook towards prisoners. Judicial pronouncements related to prison administration have been mainly related to the need of keeping the human dignity of the persons in mind and dealing with whole array of issues such as need for speedy justice for under trials, free legal aid to prisoners, right to communication, protection against torture and ill treatment, wages to prisoners and rights of children accompanying women prisoners, etc. Article 21 of the Constitution of India has indeed been broadly interpreted by the Supreme Court while deciding on rights behind bars. The Supreme Court of India has given a number of judgments on conditions of prisons and prison inmates in India. Release of prisoners on parole/ furlough is an important rehabilitation tool. It is a legal right of every prisoner. In our country, the prisons were in very bad state regarding the conditions of criminals and under trials. Inhuman atmosphere, the brutish dealings of criminals, insanitation solitary confinement and third degree methods were in rampant operation in jails.

Prison administration in India has been facing many problems and the consequent criticism therefore. The prisoners are in an unhealthy atmosphere. The clubbing of young and hard core criminals gives rise to more criminal tendencies amongst the young offenders. It also gives rise to homosexuality due to sexual abuse of young offenders. The food served to the prisoners is not to the standard to which they expect which often leads to revolt amongst the prisoners. The problem of women prisoners and mentally retarded prisoners is also grave. The corrupt prison officials may exploit the prisoners and their families monetarily or otherwise in return of providing facilities to the prisoners. The brutal assaults on the prisoners by the jail officials and wardens are sometimes reported. They are mercilessly beaten up and subjected to other forms of inhuman treatment. There is campaign to eradicate these things from the prison system. The Jail Reforms Committee 1980-1983 has also made recommendations regarding prisoners' rights and the committee appears to have been inspired and influenced by judicial pronouncements on various issues. The committee has recommended the incorporation of certain rights like right to human dignity, rights to minimum needs, right to communication, right to access to law, right of meaningful and gainful employment, right to be released on due date, for the betterment of the prisoners. Despite the rights, there are also certain provisions in the Act with regard to discipline with the prison and as such in addition to the special protection granted to prisoners in the form of rights, also have responsibilities like to obey all lawful orders and instructions issued by the competent prison authorities, to abide by all prison rules and regulations, to maintain the prescribed standards of cleanliness and hygiene, to use Government property with care and not to damage or destroy the same negligently or wilfully. Thus, from the above discussion it is very much rightly said a prisoner, be he a convict a under trial or a detenu, does not cease to be a human being. They also have all the rights which a free man has but under some restrictions. Just being in prison does not deprive them from their fundamental rights. The importance of affirmed rights of every human being needs no emphasis and, therefore, to deter breaches thereof becomes a sacred duty of the Court, as the custodian and protector of the fundamental and the basic human rights of the citizens. The Supreme Court has gone a long way fighting for their rights. However, the fact remains that it is the police and the prison authorities who need to be trained and oriented so that they take the rights of accused and prisoner's seriously.

SUGGESTIONS

1. The Criminal Justice Administration should be changed

The unsatisfactory state of Criminal Justice system in India has nothing to do with the adversarial system. The reason for that unsatisfactory situation lies elsewhere. India's social structure and attitudes are very much conditioned by entrenched habits of discrimination. There are various forms of discrimination, among which one may mention caste discrimination, discrimination of indigenous people and minorities. Discrimination weighs heavily on the justice system. They have created severe obstacles for development of India's justice system in general and the criminal justice system in particular. The investigative machinery regarding crimes is terribly underdeveloped both in terms of attitudes as well as facilities. Further, the justice that one may get is also associated with poverty. The level of poverty in India is so appalling that the result is that the poor cannot afford justice. Beside these the sphere of the criminal justice system is backward, inefficient and obsolete.

The following are some of the problems of our trial procedure which pose as hurdles to speedy dispensation of cases:

Firstly, investigation though is the foundation of the criminal justice system but is unfortunate that it is not trusted by the laws and the Courts themselves the same can be explained by a perusal of Sections 161 and 162 of the Criminal Procedure Code which provides that the statements of the witnesses examined during investigation are not admissible and that they can only be used by the defence to contradict the maker of the statement, the confession made by accused is also not admissible in evidence. It is common knowledge that police often use third degree methods during investigation and there are also allegations that in some cases they try to suppress truth and put forward falsehood before Court for reasons such as corruption or extraneous influences political or otherwise. Unless the basic problem of strengthening the foundation is solved the guilty continue to escape conviction and sometimes even innocent persons may get implicated and punished. Thus, this is one of the sphere which needs a change in order to secure justice, this is the desirability of time to bring some changes in police investigation functioning.

Secondly, the police officers face excessive workload due to lack of manpower and the public at large is non co-operative because of the public image of police officers and there is lack of coordination with other sub system of the criminal justice system in crime prevention to add to the agony there is a lot of misuse of bail and anticipatory bail provisions, more over it is difficult for the police officers to work independently due to political and executive interference. It has been observed that investigation is mostly handled by lower level officers, namely, Head Constable and ASI etc. The senior officers of the police stations particularly the SHOs generally do not conduct any investigations themselves. This results in deterioration of quality of investigation. It is therefore necessary to address ourselves to the problems and strengthen the investigation agency.

Thirdly, the investigation of a criminal case however good and painstaking it may be, will be rendered fruitless, if the prosecution machinery is indifferent or inefficient. One of the well known causes for the failure of a large number of prosecutions is the poor performance of the prosecution. They engaged in corrupt practices.

Fourthly, the most notorious problem in the functioning of the Courts, particularly in the trial Courts is the granting of frequent adjournments on most flimsy grounds. This malady has considerably eroded the confidence of the people in the judiciary. Adjournments contribute to delays in the disposal of cases. They also contribute to hardship, inconvenience and expense to the parties and the witnesses. The witness has no stake in the case and comes to assist the Court to dispense justice. He scarifies his time and convenience for this. If the case is adjourned he is required to go to the Court repeatedly. He is bound to feel unhappy and frustrated. This also gives an opportunity to the opposite party to threaten or induce him not to speak the truth therefore the right to speedy trial is thwarted by repeated adjournments.

Fifthly, one of the major causes for delay even in the commencement of trial of a criminal case is service of summons on the accused. A lot of time has been wasted in this process.

Lastly, our country suffers from low judge population ratio because of which the pendency of work increases therefore the judges take a long time in delivering judgments this again add to enlargement of the time frame of a case to be decided from its institution point because of which the litigants feel that litigation is a time consuming and lengthy procedure the two areas which need special attention for improving the quality of justice are prescribing required qualifications for the judges and the quality of training being imparted in the judicial academics.

As a result of the study it is quite clear that the evolution of the criminal justice administration shows that it has not been able to keep crime under control, piles of pending criminal cases in Courts are causing inordinate delay in their disposal. Thus, there is imminent need to bring changes in criminal justice administration so that the State should recognise that its primary duty is not to punish, but to socialise and reform the wrongdoer. It is also most important that the laws should ensure that human rights are respected by seeing that the law is strictly adhered to. The principles of liberty and legality, which are results of historical development of present day society, should be considered inviolable.

2. More Courts for the speedy disposals of pending cases should be establish

An independent and efficient judicial system is one of the basic structures of our Constitution. If sufficient number of Courts or judges are not appointed then the justice would not be available to the people, thereby undermining the basic structure. It is well known that justice delayed is justice denied. Time and again the inadequacy in the number of Courts or judges has adversely been commented upon. Not only have the law commission and the standing committee of the parliament made observations in this regard, but even the head of judiciary has had more occasions than once to make observations in regard there to Mr. Justice Balakrishnan said that of the more than 15000 Courts in the country only 13600 were functioning and over 1600 non functional owing to vacant positions of judicial officers. The governments are under an obligation to provide an adequate machinery for justice, to appoint more judges and to give them better emoluments and facilities, to build more Court houses, to enact better laws, to devise better dispute resolution procedures, and to administer more effectively and equitably, rather than to blame lawyers and judges for the increase and proliferation of litigation.

Some points which need more concentration are:

(i) *Modernisation and advancement of Courts:* more attention should be paid towards the advancement of the Courts like computerisation of Courts, judicial officers have been provided with laptop with net connectivity.

(ii) *The vacancies in the post of judges should be fulfilled*: the judicial delays are blamed primarily on the vacancies in the post of judges and the antiquity of laws. To provide the speedy disposal of cases it is essential to create more Courts and appoint more qualified judges to speed up the justice deliver system.

(iii) *Mobile Courts should be established:* there is a new way to reach citizens in need of speedy and inexpensive justice in remote areas with the help of mobile Court. Mobile Court will be a milestone towards provision of easy and inexpensive justice to the people of remote areas. This is a large vehicle with a small courtroom, judge's chamber, driver's cabin and litigants waiting section. Thus, in order to provide speedy justice it is essential to setup more rural and mobile Courts to the common man. "Gram Nayalaya" (rural Court) must also be established.

(iv) *More investigation agencies should be established:* it is rightly said that it is necessary in order to maintain pace with the rapid change that it is the time to increase the number of Central Bureau of Investigation Courts and other investigation agencies. In the last 10 years, the cases investigated by the CBI were pending disposal and there was need for more Courts to handle them.

(v) *Fast track Courts should be established:* the nationwide outrage over the gang rape and murder of a 23 year old woman in Delhi has led to a call for speedy trial of grievous criminal cases responding to the public outcry, the government recently announced that it would set up 1800 fast track Courts to deal with heinous crimes, especially those committed against women. But the question being asked is how effective these Courts are. It is truc that our country plagued by a huge shortage of judges and lack of adequate judicial infrastructure, fast tracks Courts will not necessarily translate into speedy justice, in India there are 11 judges per million people as against the ideal ratio of 60 judges. The government should first appoint more judges before setting up fast track Courts. In a span of 10 years fast track Courts disposed off 28 lakh cases out of the 35 lakh cases that were transferred to them. People have lost faith in the judiciary system because of long delays in trials. Fast track Courts give people the hope that there is light on the other side of the tunnel. Thus, to create separate fast track Court may plays a vital role to provide quick justice to the needy people.

3. Indian Major criminal laws should be changed

While keeping in mind the various components of the present criminal justice system, it is desirable that the system needs changes. Most of the major criminal law such as the Indian Penal Code of 1860, the Police Act, 1861 and the Indian Evidence Act, 1872, Prisons Act, 1894 are still in force with only peripheral amendments. The structure of the police and its working style has not changed much.

The indelible legacy of the British era sustains. Most of the criminal laws, procedures, institutions and principles evolved during the British period still even govern the functioning of various components of the criminal justice system. It is the reality that our country needs new laws and not just amendments. To make some restraint on the crimes and to meet with the rapid change in the society, it is essential to frame new and more effective criminal laws.

4. Education system especially legal education system should be changed

The legal profession is expected to play a dynamic role in the administration of justice. Law schools being the secruiting grounds for the legal profession, there is a need to inject new spirit into the content of legal education to make lawyers and legal professionals socially relevant and professionally competent to secure the constitutional mandate of access to justice.

(i) Introduction of legal aid a compulsory practical subject: Legal aid to the poor got a new lease of life. Even though more than a decade has passed since the formal introduction of legal aid in law school curriculum in India, there is no comprehensive study examining the functioning of law school based legal aid in India. It is found that number of colleges have designated faculty to conduct legal aid activity. But only a miniscule of them provides the facility of academic credit to the faculty in terms of workload/lecture hours and for the students in terms of grades or marks. This has considerably reduced the enthusiasm in the conductance of legal aid activity and many often consider them burdensome or additional work in the process the cause of legal aid is substantially dampened. It is also found that the law colleges have spread very little effort in informing the community about their existence and availability of services. This wide gap has indeed substantially reduced the impact of free legal service by the law colleges. Education shall be directed to the full development of human personality and to the strengthening of respect for human rights and fundamental freedoms. It shall promote understanding, tolerance and friendship among all people, racial or religious groups. Due to lack of proper awareness and lack of proper education, we have to tolerate crimes against human rights.

Some other aspects regarding education which need more emphasis:

- Some of the legal subjects should be introduced as a

compulsory subject to the lower classes at school and as well as to the higher classes which helps the students to became more familiar with basic laws and rights.

- In legal education system more focus should be paid to practical training.

5. More legal awareness at grassroots level should be spread

It is the demand of the time to work at the grassroots to understand the problems of the marginalised communities and extend legal services for their interests. To ensure that legal literacy programmes are taken, there is a need for college or universities to have legal aid cells in each district so that students would be able to provide legal services. "As of now most institutes have the clinics on their premises but the purpose may not be served completely because nobody takes it seriously. There is need to bring in some sort of accountability so that colleges move beyond legal camps and start extending legal aid. The aim of the scheme is to provide inexpensive local machinery for rendering legal services of basic nature like legal advice, drafting of petitions, notice, replies, applications and other documents of legal importance and also for resolving the disputes of the local people and thereby preventing the disputes reaching Courts.

- *Legal aid clinics to be set up in every village to reduce litigation:* by setting up of legal aid clinics in every village, it is expected that it will definitely reduce litigations. It will function from panchayats offices. But one of the most important points which need more concentration is that merely setting up of legal aid clinics does not serve the proposed purpose without taking effective steps for its functioning.

6. Prison administration in India should be improved

The prison administration is one area which is the most neglected one by the State authorities. Keeping in view the prison population, this is one field which requires immediate care and treatment. Despite number of committees and commissions having been formed to look into this area no heed has been paid to their recommendations, which have been made time and again for effective prison administration.

Some of the areas which need improvements are:

(i) Reducing prisons overcrowding

Prisons in most of the states are overcrowded and the inmates are living in deplorable conditions. They are denied even the basic amenities. Reducing the number of undertrial prisoners was one of the most important agenda which needs more attention. As per the statistics published by the National Crime Record Bureau, 3.91 lakh prisoners are confined in jails in 2010 against authorised capacity of 2.90 lakh all over the country. All the prisoners are not convicts, more than two third of them are under trials whose cases are pending either with the police or in the Courts. The under trials are a part of the floating population of the prison and their number never gets reduced since bailed out prisoners are immediately replaced by fresh arrestees. Overcrowding is a central and critical issue for prison administration in the country.

Is building more prisons going to be the solution to the problem of overcrowding?: Not really, as experience around the world has shown that no matter how much capacity you add to prisons soon get filled up. There is a need for finding the long term solution to the problem of overcrowding.

It can be reduced by using correctional measures like premature release, release young, old, infirm, women and first time convicts on probation in petty offences, release on bail. Alternative methods of correctional like fine, community service and probation, etc. are becoming popular throughout the world. Unfortunately, the jurisprudence of non-custodial correctional measures has not yet taken roots in the justice delivery system in India.

(ii) Modernisation schemes for improving physical infrastructure

Another aspect related to prison system which needs improvement is the physical infrastructure leading in terms of increasing the capacity of prisons, building more prisons and modernisation of prisons by way of improved technology and security systems, improved kitchens, better water supply and sanitation and better medical facilities. No doubt, this is needed, and better infrastructure can come with more finance and focus. Development of prison staff and correctional and training programmes for prison inmates are the important in the scheme of prison reforms.

(iii) Health and Sanitation

Imprisonment is a trauma. It is not easy for every prisoner to come out of the mental agony attached with incarceration. Community living in overcrowded barracks becomes cause of so many skin and hygiene related diseases. In adequacy of proper diet, toilet facilities and to the health and sanitation related problems. A prisoner is in need of more health facilities than a normal person. It is imperative to design and make available proper and adequate material facilities in prisons. Improvement of health and sanitation facilities should be an important agenda of prison reform.

(iv) Women Prisoners

Jails were not designed for women. 5 percent of total prisoners are women. They suffer in the prisons because of non-availability of women related facilities in the jails. There is an urgent need to take up a study to pin-point the facilities which every jail must create for the women prisoners. Sometimes, dependent infants also land up in prisons with their mothers or female care takers. Facilities required for development of such infants should be an important reform agenda.

(v) More legal aid clinics in prisons should be established

To provide speedy justice to under trials and to protect the prisoners from inhuman treatment it is necessary that the State legal services authorities to set up more legal aid clinics in prisons. More legal aid clinics would help the prisoners who were languishing in the prisons without trial, to get justice.

(vi) Correctional approach should be adopted

Jails are no more torture cells. They are reformation and rehabilitation centres. Thus, the following points need thinking and change in the existing practices:

- Probation, parole and furlough should be used liberally. There is need to make amendments regarding relevant laws suitably if needed.
- Education programmes offered by IGNOU, NIOS and other educational institutions should be introduced.
- More and more open jails and open camps should be established.
- Opportunities to have contact with outside world by the prisoners should be increased.
- Meaningful work facilities must be given to all the convicts who have been sentenced to rigorous imprisonment.

Transparency demands that wherever possible, prison management system should be computerised. This will leads to ensure justice, equity, objectivity and fair play, it is desirable that discretion of jail officials in allotting accommodation, work and other day to day working should be minimised. It will remove large number of grievances of prison inmates.

Bibliography

BOOKS

Agarwal, Dr. H.O., International Law and Human Rights, (Central Law Agency, 15th Edition).

Bakshi, P.M., The Constitution of India, (Universal Law Publishing Co., 11th Edition, 2012).

Bhargava, M.L., Rights of Accused (Protection for Arrested Person Pre-trial and Post-Trial), (Kamal Publications, 2013).

Chakrabarty, R., Criminal Jurisprudence, (Kamal Publications, 2008).

Dr. Ashutosh, Rights of Accused, (Universal Law Publishing Co., 2nd Edition, 2013).

Hyder, Dr. B., Rights of Accused in Criminal Trial, (Gogia Law Agency, 2003).

Jain, Prof. M.P., Indian Constitutional Law, (Lexis Nexis Butterworths, Nagpur, 6th Edition, 2011).

Jain, M.P., Outlines of Indian Legal History, (N.M. Tripathi, 1981).

Joshi, Dr. K.C., The Constitutional Law of India, (Central Law Publication, 1st Edition, 2011).

Juneja, Dr. P.C., Equal Access to Justice, (The Bright Law House, 1993).

Kalra, Kush, Prisoners' Right, (Shree Ram Law House Publication, 1st Edition, 2013).

Kumar, Prof. Narender, Constitutional Law of India, (Allahabad Law Agency, 2012).

Lal, Batuk, The Law of Evidence, (Central Law Agency, 19th Edition, 2011).

Malik, Shailender, The Code of Criminal Procedure, (Allahabad Law Agency, 18th Edition, 2011).

Mallick, M.R., Bail Law and Practice, (Eastern Law House, 2nd Edition).

Mishra, S.N., Quating from Manusmariti, Indian Penal Code, (Allahabad Law Agency, 1983).

Monir, M., The Law of Evidence, (Universal Publishing Co., 7th Edition, 2008).

Pandey, Dr. J.N., The Constitutional Law of India, (Central Law Agency, 49th Edition, 2012).

Pillai, Dr. K.N. Chandrasekharan, R.V. Kelkar's Criminal Procedure, (Eastern Book Company, 5th Edition, 2011).

Pillai, K.N. Chandrasekharan, R.V. Kelkar's Lectures on Criminal Procedure including Probation and Juvenile Justice, (Eastern Book Company, 4th Edition, 2011).

Pranjape, Dr. N.V., The Code of Criminal Procedure, (Central Law Agency, 2012).

Pranjape, Prof. N.V., Criminology and Penology, (Central Law Publications, 14th Edition, 2010).

Puri, S.K., Indian Legal and Constitutional History, (1st Edition).

Qadri, Dr. S.M.A., Ahmad Siddique's Criminology and Penology, (Eastern Book Company, 6th Edition, 2011).

Ratanlal and Dhirajlal, The Code of Criminal Procedure, (Lexis Nexis—Butterworths Wadhwa, Nagpur, 20th Edition, 2012).

Singh, Dr. Avtar, Principles of the Law of Evidence, (Central Law Publications, 19th Edition, 2011).

Singh, Dr. Deipa, & Singh, Dr. K.P., Criminology, Penology and Victimology, (1st Edition, 2013).

Srivastava, Dr. S.S., Criminology and Criminal Administration, (Central Law Agency, 3rd Edition, 2007).

ARTICLES

"Admissibility of DNA Technology in the Indian legal system", available at www.legallyindia.com/esayblog/admis. . .

"Article 20—Constitution of India—Lawzonline.com", available at www.lawzonline.com/bareacts/indian.

"Article 20(3) of Constitution of India and Narco Analysis", available at www.legalservice.com/article/.

"Article on Bail, Judicial Reforms", available at www.legalhelplineindia.com/crimial . . . .

"Bureau of Justice Statistics", available at www.bjs.gov/../WFBCJIND.txt.

"Confession", available at http://en.wikipedia.org/wiki/ confession_ (law).

"Criminal Justice System under Hindu Period", available at www.assignmentpoint.com/hindu/arts/law.

"Fair Trial in Criminal Proceedings in India", available at www.wfrt.org/humanrts/fairtrial/wrft_kb.htm.

"Fairness to the Accused with respect to the Indian Evidence Act, 1872", available at www.mightylaws.in/458/fairness_accused.

"Fundamental Constitutional Rights as a Criminally Accused Person", available at www.lawinfaboulder.com/criminal_Cou.

"Is the Indian Criminal Justice System more inclined towards the accused?", available at www.manupatrafart.com/articles/Po.

"Legal Aid in India—expert lawyer, India, available at www.expertlawyer.in/legalaid_in_india.

"Legal Protection available to the Accused during a criminal trial", available at www.legalservices.co.in/blogs/entry/leg. . . .

"Manusmriti . . . the Criminal Justice Tenets in the Ancient Indian Hindu Code", available at www.erces.com/.../ v03_05.htm.

"Plea Bargaining—A New Development in the Criminal Justice System", available www.neerajaarora.com/ plea-bargaining. . . .

"Power to Pardon—An Analysis", available at www.lawteacher.net/ lawteacher/..../essays

"Rights of Accused Persons—Indian Kanoon", available at www.indiankanoon.org/search/%3F from Inpu . . . .

"Rights of Accused: undertrial prisoners and convicts—Indian Kanoon", available at www.indiankanoon.org/ doc/1276759/.

"Rights of an accused under Indian Laws", available at indianlaws.blogspot.com/2012/09/rights. . .

"Rights of the accused and exceptional Circumstances, available at wiki.ibj.org/index.php/India...

Aiswarya, "Rights of Prisoners—A Myth or Reality?

Anand, Justice A.S., "Third Degree Methods, Criminal Act", *The Tribune*, (December 11, 2000).

Bhatia, Dr. K.L., "Fair Trial in Criminal Proceedings in India", available at www.wfrt.org/humanrts. . . . htm

Gautam, C.S., "Rights of an Arrested Person, Criminal Procedure Code, 1973", available at www.csgautma.org/2012/03/10/ Criminal-Pr. . . .

Jain, Viveak, "Rights of Accused", available at www.mightylaws.in/ 511/rights_accused.

Khare, Harshit, "Self-incrimination : A Study—Lawyersclubindia".

Kumar, Arvind, "Essay on Protection against Arrest and detention as per Indian Constitution", available at www.preservearticles.com/201111. . . .

Maheshwari, Vidhan, "Right to Bail as a Constitutional Right".

Sourasubha, "Plea Bargaining —an Analysis of the concept", available at www.legalserviceindia.com/articles/. . . .

Tiwary, Deeptiman, "Undertrials in Jail for Long may be freed", *The Times of India,* (February 11, 2013).

Vajpeyi, Yogesh, "Undertrials in Jails: The idea of injustice", *The New Indian Express,* (April 28, 2013), available at www.newindianexpress.com/ home/opinion.

Verma, Sonakshi, "The Concept of Narcoanalysis in view of Constitutional Law and Human Rights".

Vivekanandan, Vijoy, "The Conceptual Analysis of the Principle of Double Jeopardy", available at www.lawcollegedehradun.com/lawreview . . . .

NEWSPAPERS

The Hindu

The New Indian Express

The Times of India

The Tribune

STATUTES

Criminal Procedure Code, 1973

The Constitution of India

The Indian Evidence Act, 1872

The Prison Act, 1894

The Probation of Offenders Act, 1958

Indian Penal Code, 1860

REPORTS OF COMMISSION

Law Commission of India, 14th Report on Reforms of Judicial Administration.

Law Commission of India, 118th Report on Article 20(3) of the Constitution of India and the Right to Silence.

The National Human Rights Commission "Guidelines for the Administration of Polygraph Test (Lie Detector Test) on an accused" in 2000.

National Expert Committee Report on Women Prisoners, (1980-83).

JOURNALS

Criminal Law Journal
All India Reporter

WEBSITES

http://en.wikipedia.org/wiki/ confession_(law).
indianlaws.blogspot.com/2012/09/rights
wiki.ibj.org/index.php/India
www.assignmentpoint.com/hindu/arts/law.
www.bjs.gov/../ WFBCJIND.txt.
www.csgautma.org/2012/03/10/Criminal-Pr
www.erces.com/.../ v03_05.htm.
www.expertlawyer.in/legalaid_in_india
www.indiankanoon.org/ doc/1276759/
www.indiankanoon.org/search/%3F
www.lawcollegedehradun.com/lawreview
www.lawinfaboulder.com/criminal_Cou
www.lawteacher.net/lawteacher/..../essays
www.lawzonline.com/bareacts/indian.
www.legalhelplineindia.com/crimial . . . .
www.legallyindia.com/esayblog/admis.
www.legalserviceindia.com/articles/
www.legalservices.co.in/blogs/entry/leg
www.manupatrafart.com/articles/Po
www.mightylaws.in/458/fairness_accused
www.mightylaws.in/511/rights_accused
www.neerajaarora.com/plea_bargaining
www.newindianexpress.com/home/opinion
www.preservearticles.com/201111
www.wfrt.org/humanrts/fairtrial/wrft_kb.htm.

Index